WE ARE KINGS

We Are Kings

Political Theology and the Making of a Modern Individual

Spencer Jackson

University of Virginia Press
Charlottesville and London

University of Virginia Press
© 2020 by the Rector and Visitors of the University of Virginia
All rights reserved
Printed in the United States of America on acid-free paper

First published 2020

1 3 5 7 9 8 6 4 2

ISBN 978-0-8139-4471-5 (hardcover)
ISBN 978-0-8139-4472-2 (paper)
ISBN 978-0-8139-4473-9 (ebook)

Library of Congress Cataloging-in-Publication Data is available for this title.

CONTENTS

Acknowledgments — vii

Introduction: Secularism Is an Imperial Theology with a Socialist Secret — 1

1 Dryden's Political Theology and the Making of a Modern Subject — 27

2 The Domestic Novel's First Heroine: Alexander Pope and the Construction of a National Theological Subject — 69

3 "Beyond What the Crown Itself Can Confer": Clarissa and the Antinomian Heart of the Modern British Subject — 107

4 The Other Side of Discipline: Marriage, Slavery, and the Ambivalent Politics of Maria Edgeworth's Domestic Subject — 140

Epilogue: An Immanent Language of Change — 179

Notes — 183

Bibliography — 195

Index — 209

ACKNOWLEDGMENTS

SEEING THIS book in print fills me with an immense sense of gratitude. To work on it I received the support of two postdoctoral fellowships, one for a year at the UCLA Clark Memorial Library and another for three years at the University of Queensland node of the Australian Research Council Centre for Excellence in the History of Emotions (Europe 1100–1800). I also have had the great fortune of excellent teachers in my life whose traces are to be found everywhere in *We Are Kings*, beginning with my high school English teacher, Nicole Furlonge, who first taught me to take literature seriously as a means of grappling with the world and indeed changing it. Furlonge's *Race Sounds: The Art of Listening in African-American Literature* (2018) is a testament to these lessons. At Occidental College, I was lucky enough to study under Warren Montag, with whom I took numerous courses and spent countless office hours discussing the intersection of literature, philosophy, and politics. From Warren, I learned that academic study, at its best, is a calculated political act. While working with him from 2001 to 2004, I was immersed in antiwar organizing, much of which as a member of the International Socialist Organization (ISO), an experience that cemented my conviction that art and ideas are inevitably interwoven with politics and that any honest study of them should begin with this fact.

This book is also a product of the UCLA Comparative Literature Department, where I did my graduate work from 2006 to 2012. Under the influence of my early mentors at UCLA, Stathis Gourgouris, Aamir Mufti, and Eleanor Kaufman, I learned not about any profession, but ideas, a world of ideas, with which I was encouraged to grapple and believe in with a fervor that cannot be quantified. Eleanor Kaufman was an unfailing supporter who taught me to think with theoretical rigor and, more fundamentally, to see the abstraction of theory as a potential good in itself—that is, as an alternative, and preferable, mode of being. Stathis brought me into graduate school and modeled an intellectual nimbleness and ambition that remain pivotal to my thinking today. As I progressed in my graduate studies at UCLA, I found a second home in the English Department, where I received generous supervision and encouragement from Saree Makdisi, Anne Mellor, Debora Shugar, Sarah Kareem, and Helen Deutsch. To the latter, I owe a profound debt. Helen exemplifies an intellectual range and attention to literary form that have remained essential touchstones in my work, but more than anything, Helen practices a form of mentorship—learned, open, and intensely enthusiastic—that I've come to see as the hallmark of a great teacher. She read many different and often contradictory iterations of *We Are Kings*, many well after I had graduated from UCLA, and she consistently encouraged me to follow my instincts and experiment with whatever moved me in the moment. In the process, Helen allowed me to develop a voice of my own. Helen's generosity is without parallel, and I will be forever grateful for what she has given me: an ability to think for myself.

I finished *We Are Kings* at the University of Queensland, and I owe a sincere thanks to my colleagues there, including Peter Holbrook, Simon During, Xanthe Ashburner, Kenneth Chong, Brandon Chua, Paolo Magagnoli, Daniel Midena, Karin Sellberg, and Lisa O'Connell. Simon During has been a generous supporter of *We Are Kings*, and Lisa O'Connell offered incisive feedback on the history of English marriage at a key moment in the project. My supervisor, Peter Holbrook, meanwhile, had a profound impact on revisions of *We Are Kings*. Peter's clarity and commitment to tackling big ideas were inspiring. He models a kind of public humanities that other academics would do well to follow. Peter also introduced me to fellow travelers Ewen Fernie and Simon Palfrey, whose ambition and sincerity of purpose were a breath of fresh air. Simon, in particular, was an ardent supporter of this book, and his insights on it, as well as the critical method it practices, were essential. Simon's capacity for perception, to truly and creatively understand the art and indeed people around him, is breathtaking. I am grateful to have crossed paths with him.

And, finally, I owe a sincere thanks to Angie Hogan for believing in this project and for engaging with it so generously. I also would like to thank the rest of the marketing and editorial team at the University of Virginia Press, and Emily Shelton for her thoughtful editing of the final manuscript. And, by way of conclusion, I would like to thank a few of the friends and family who made the writing of this book possible: my comrade in graduate studies Sina Rahmani, my colleague at the Clark Zirwat Chowdhury, my dear friends Nathan Rayman and George Olesky, my brother and eternal confidante Scott Jackson, and my partner and love Jacqueline Meyer, who has taught me so very much. I am also grateful to my parents, David Jackson and Barbara Spencer, for their steadfast support, especially my mother, who kindly read and commented upon various sections of this book. I wrote much of *We Are Kings* while unemployed or working as an adjunct, periods when I had no colleagues or offices, only a desk and loved ones willing to give their time and critical prowess. I would like then to dedicate this book to all those who nurtured this endeavor, but especially Helen Deutsch and Barbara Spencer, two women who have navigated male-dominated professions and grappled along the way with harassment, sexism, and systemic underappreciation, but, through it all, persisting to build lives of dignity and self-respect. To them, I give my deepest thanks.

WE ARE KINGS

INTRODUCTION

Secularism Is an Imperial Theology with a Socialist Secret

Eighteenth-Century Literature and the Making of Britain's Imperial Faith

When Donald Trump asserted during his inaugural address on January 20, 2017, "From this moment on, it's going to be America first," media pundits around the globe declared that a scandal was upon us. A dramatic shift in American foreign affairs and in the Western project more broadly was occurring. The same scandal heralded by Brexit and the rise of nationalist parties throughout much of Continental Europe had taken control of the West's preeminent power, but what exactly had changed? In the same speech Trump stated, "We all salute the same great American flag," and if it is united around this fact, then "America is unstoppable," for "we are protected by God." Trump assured his global audience that "we will not seek to impose our way of life on anyone, but rather to let it shine as an example for everyone to follow." In all of this, the message is clear: America is special. It has been set apart by God, and its constituents are ennobled by this fact. This is not anti-Western rhetoric; rather, it is, as this book will help demonstrate, the very substance of the West itself.

We Are Kings returns to the literature written during the ascent of America's imperial predecessor because it is in the literature of eighteenth-century Britain that one can see what we are now accustomed to ignoring—namely, that the idea of the modern West is the product of the politicization of Christian Scripture. Over the course of what has been called the "long eighteenth century," from roughly 1660 to 1832, the British Empire became the world's preeminent imperial power, a position it would hold until the early twentieth century at which point the United States would steadily succeed it. During this period, literature played a crucial political role as authors working in both poetry and prose wove together a new understanding of the British nation and subject as God's chosen agents for the world's salvation, an ideological framework that would help shape the self-presentation of the British and American empires as well as the larger configuration of "the West" to which they both lay claim.

We Are Kings focuses on Tory Augustan verse and domestic fiction, two of the most canonical and seemingly least similar forms of writing from the British eighteenth century. The embittered, antimodern poetry of John Dryden, Jonathan Swift, and Alexander Pope—to name a few of the conservative misfits who made up the Tory Augustan movement—seems hardly a fit for the virtuous romances of early novelists such as Samuel Richardson, Maria Edgeworth, and Jane Austen. And yet these camps belong together insofar as they offer two of the strongest articulations of Britain's new national faith and, in particular, of the modern individual who stands at the very center of it. Drawing from the contemporary theoretical movement of "political theology," *We Are Kings* shows how poets and novelists, men and women, conservatives and progressives alike, came together in the eighteenth century to cast Britain as God's new Israel and its constituents as consequently individuated, nationalized, and sovereign. *We Are Kings* pays particular attention to the figure of this new constituent, the modern individual, because this individual persists within the Anglo-American world from the eighteenth century to today as an essential beacon of both subjection and of hope, a fundamental ambivalence that has been lost by a scholarly community too taken with despair.

By the mid-twentieth century, a consensus had developed in literary criticism: eighteenth-century British literature—first and foremost, the novel—was said to have marshaled a new secular world into being. From Ian Watt to Georg Lukács, scholars of this period hailed the emergence of the novel as a harbinger of a decisively new culture, one that saw reality as the product not of inherited stories or God, but, rather, in the words of Watt, "particular individuals having particular experiences at particular times and at particular places" (31). The novel shines for such critics as modernity's exemplary genre—or, as Lukács famously states, "the epic of a world that has been abandoned by God" (88). Over the past half century, a range of scholars, most prominently among them J. Paul Hunter, Nancy Armstrong, and Michael McKeon, have challenged this mid-twentieth-century consensus by drawing attention to the various forms of writing (e.g., spiritual autobiographies, conduct manuals, and romances) that anticipated and prefigured the novel, suggesting that it emerged as the product of earlier literary forms rather than simply as the effect of a naïve and unprecedented turn to the particularity of reality itself.[1] Writing within and alongside this revisionist current, scholars such as Hunter, G. A. Starr, Leo Damrosch, and, more recently, Simon During have taken particular issue with the supposed secularism of the novel by demonstrating the theological narratives, problems, and modes of thinking that persist within it, a reinterpretation that again underlines the fact that the novel has a form; it is not pure mimesis.[2]

We Are Kings draws a new line of continuity between an important subgenre of the novel, the domestic, and a key literary precursor, Tory Augustan verse, in order both to develop this long-standing effort to demystify the novel's origins and, at the same time, to take this demystification in a different direction. Whether canonical or revisionist, theorists of the novel have generally agreed that whatever the early novel was, the neoclassical British Tory Augustans were not a part of it. Reacting against the modernization of Britain in the first half of the eighteenth century, the poets, politicians, and intellectuals who constituted this movement were, in the words of Hunter, the "final cry of a dying world," devotees, as Damrosch concludes, of "the old *nomos*" (126, 265).[3] Revisionist scholars of the Tory Augustans—most influentially, Helen Deutsch and Catherine Ingrassia—have questioned such assessments by reframing the relationship between this movement and early modernity as, in the words of the latter, a "mutually informing dialectic" (9). Building on these efforts but going further, this book argues that Tory Augustan poets and domestic novelists were in a sense not opposed at all, since they each worked to construct the truly unifying faith of the British long eighteenth century: nationalism.

While sharing some of the skepticism of earlier revisionist critics regarding both the absolute novelty and secularism of the novel and of eighteenth-century Britain more broadly, *We Are Kings* is ultimately about the flourishing of a new political faith rather than the persistence of an old religious one. It is *not*, as in Hunter, Starr, Damrosch, and During, a matter of demonstrating that eighteenth-century Britain was more religious than once thought and thus pushing the dawn of modernity forward to the nineteenth century; instead, this book is an argument that secular modernity itself, the very culture celebrated by Watt and Lukács, is the product of reformulated religion. At times canonical and at others revisionist, *We Are Kings* interprets the world of eighteenth-century British literature as both new and not secular. By reading this literature through the prism of political theology, this book offers something needed not only by literary studies, but by critical theory as well. Although theorists of political theology have succeeded in unmasking the major political and economic institutions of Western modernity as secularized theological formations, they have failed to answer the essential question of how one should respond to the ensuing remystification of modern life. Thinkers including Jacques Derrida, Gil Anidjar, Giorgio Agamben, and Talal Asad have neglected to say what comes after critique, and this is what *We Are Kings* uses literature to answer. The imaginative arts are a source of ambivalence and critique as well as wonder and creation, and *We Are Kings* turns to literature to recover the nuance and sense of political hope that has been lost in the many theoretical critiques of modernity formulated over the past fifty years.[4]

Although we have not entered a postcritical age, as Rita Felski claims in *The Limits of Critique* (2015), the diagnosis at the heart of her important book is very much correct: scholars must abandon the purity of the either/or and embrace the complicity of real engagement. What has come to pass as "critique" in the academy—abyssal renunciations of a present depicted always as hopelessly fallen—is a problem, and Felski makes a much-needed plea for cultural critics "to embrace a wider range of affective styles and modes of argument" and to refrain from insisting that art always has to be approached suspiciously, as if it were invariably a manifestation of some nefarious "already established scheme" (3, 171). In this book, I answer Felski's challenge in the language of a revised Marxism.

The place of Karl Marx in this discussion should hardly be surprising, since it was Marx, after all, who anticipated political theology and many other recent critiques of secularism with his insistence that "the perfected Christian State is ... the *atheistic* state, the democratic state, the state that relegates religion to a place among the other elements of civil society" ("On the Jewish Question" 36). Far from abandoning Christianity, secular modernity, according to Marx, perfects it by rearticulating the Christian opposition between a fallen humanity and its heavenly fulfillment as the secular dichotomy of a fallen civil society and the redeemed political community of the state. The equality proclaimed by modern democratic states is, for Marx, nothing more than a new spiritual promise of redemption proffered to a society that continues to know no such justice. From a Marxist perspective, the very existence of a distinct political sphere is a marker of modern humanity's neo-Christian alienation, and the individualism that emerges within and alongside this sphere only further signifies the degradation of life under modernity. Marx unmasks all the lofty panegyrics to individual liberty, so central to the Anglo-American political tradition, as merely celebrations of subjection, affirmations of what is in truth the disempowering "separation of man from man" (42).

While Marxist in terms of its critique, this study stands apart from Marx first and foremost by taking the modern individual and the literature that helped create it as causal agents in their own right rather than merely mimetic reflections of an underlying economic order. This is an interpretative shift with political consequences. Though the past twenty years have seen many important efforts to correct the simplistic image of Marx as a vulgar economist, the fact remains that one cannot read Marx's work without acknowledging that, among its arguments, it articulates an undeniably economist argument, a conviction that economics determines reality in a modern capitalist age.[5] And what also must be admitted is that Marx's economism—his conviction that a traditional definition of economics forms the base, while culture and politics belong to a secondary domain termed the superstructure—is directly tied to the messianic universalism that persists within Marx's work, from his philosophical writings of the early 1840s to the later volumes of *Capital* (1867–83). Marx's narrow and deterministic definition of the economy is what allows him to posit the uniformity of capitalist society in all times and all places, an assumption that in turn authorizes an eschatological faith in the inevitability of a global proletarian revolution.[6]

The problem, however, with this Marxist schematic is that capitalism has always also been cultural: its economy at work in parliaments, homes, schools, and novels, as well as on factory floors.[7] To acknowledge this expansiveness is to admit both that capitalism exists in cultural vernaculars and that any struggle against it must therefore be formulated within the specificity of particular geographic, cultural, and national contexts. Rather than limiting the political relevance of Marxism, recognizing the diversity of capital and the cultural specificity of capitalism is an opportunity, firstly, to responsibly extend Marx's critique to non-European parts of the world; and, secondly, to apply Marx's own dialectical approach to the culture and politics of capitalist modernity as well. Capitalism is not only the most destructive economic system ever to be invented—it is also, according to Marx, the most productive, and it is high time for scholars to approach the culture of capitalism in the same nuanced, dialectical fashion.

Such a reorientation means leaving behind not only Marx's economism, but also the abyssal skepticism of many twentieth-century neo-Marxists who have advanced a model of critique perhaps best exemplified by Max Horkheimer and Theodor Adorno's *Dialectic of Enlightenment* (1947), a work that importantly expands on Marx's critique of secularism, while offering even less in terms of a way out. *Dialectic of Enlightenment* perfectly illustrates what Felski describes as "the one-eye gaze of critique," which assumes "a melancholy estrangement from ordinary life" as "the price to be paid for sharpened perception" (18, 41). Writing against the backdrop of World War II in exile in a Los Angeles, California, that was experiencing a Hollywood Golden Age, Horkheimer and Adorno skewered the culture of modern capitalist society as a contradiction in terms. For them, "authentic" art comes only from rejecting "social coercion" in favor of expressing something "more than what already is" (13, 103). Art under capitalism, on the other hand, is merely ideological: it takes over from "objective religion" as the means by which society's rulers impose order from above (94). With capitalism, culture becomes an industry (*Kulturindustrie*), a system, fabricated upon the basis of already-made forms designed not to shepherd the miracle of the new into being, but, rather, merely to generate profits and slavish imitation. Art imitates earlier art, which the public imitates in turn, forming a feedback loop that renders the most intimate gestures of human life scripted, while personality itself—the idea that there is "anything peculiar about us"—becomes "hardly more than dazzling white teeth and freedom from body odor and emotions" (136).

While Horkheimer and Adorno are right to valorize the world-altering power of art, they are wrong to assume that art withers before commerce, and that those who write about art can themselves remain abstracted from the commercial world with which art has almost always been intertwined. Rediscovered by student radicals in the 1960s and 1970s, after two decades of relative obscurity, *Dialectic of Enlightenment* helped inspire a generation of scholars to formulate rejections of modernity so hyperbolically "radical," so pure, that they are for all intents and purposes apolitical: they have no easily understood bearing on contemporary struggles.[8] And it is especially ironic that such arguments have enjoyed a particular popularity with critics of art and literature, given that aesthetic criticism by necessity begins with an experience of engrossment that is in essence a form of corruption. To evaluate a work of art is to become enveloped by it and the world it reflects; it is to become complicit.

Cultural critics are specialists of worldly objects of transformation, of an aesthetic labor that engages the world while also metamorphosizing it. To say this is in a sense merely to extend Marx's own miraculous, resurrectional conception of labor to art: "Living labor must seize on these things [machines, yarn, books, paper, pen etc.], awaken them from the dead, change [*verwandeln*] them from merely possible into real and effective use-values" (*Capital: Vol. 1* 289). Whether commodified or not, art is labor performed upon the objects of the past, and through it one creates new thoughts, meaning, and actions, which is to say that one quite literally changes the world. To interpret such work, to perform one's own labor upon it as a scholar and a critic, is thus always to make a decision reflective of the object itself: how did this work remake its time and how ought we to remake our own.

Derived from the Greek verb *krinein*, meaning to distinguish, to separate, and to judge, critique is not the entirety of the aesthetic experience, but it is an inescapable part of it. As Stathis Gourgouris makes movingly clear in *Lessons in Secular Criticism* (2013), art and writing about art are intrinsically critical because they are at their foundation poetic—that is, they are driven by the "force" of *poiésis*, the Greek root for "poetry," signifying a "making" that is always a matter of "bringing otherness to bear on the world," a "forming" that is always also "an altering" (7–8). Art is transformative action performed within and upon a social body. To acknowledge this is to see art and the aesthetic as at once constitutive in their own right and irremediably reflective of a broader social universe of politics and economics at the same time. Art is a special kind of labor, but it is nevertheless still labor. It has never ceased to exist under the pressures of commercialization, and its popularization in the early stages of British modernity signals the rise of a society that democratizes art and culture to truly ambivalent political effects.

My aim then in returning to the writing of eighteenth-century Britain is to become complicit in the art and thought of this period, and to ask from the interiority of its secularized theological nationalism both what a sacred model of the nation and subject means and what it makes possible. After some three centuries of oscillating between dis- and re-enchantments, it is time to move past the secular heroism that animates works such as *Dialectic of Enlightenment*. The vital question today is not whether we can finally reach the promised land of a world liberated from religion and myth; instead, it is why have these entities persisted despite all the critiques, and, most important, what their persistence enables. Marx was wrong to depict the struggle against capitalism as necessarily a struggle against religion, and, ironically, his error proceeded from his own theological conception of politics as the metaphysical work of history rather than people. For Marx, a universal subject has arisen, one promising "*a total redemption of humanity*," and before such a subject, pregnant with the inevitability of the world's emancipation, all other religions inevitably must give way ("Contribution to the Critique of Hegel's *Philosophy of Right*" 64–65). Capitalism will end when people have the power to make themselves *both* economically and politically equal, and the truth is religion is as likely to contribute to as obstruct this process.

By articulating a new literary history of the modern individual, showing the theological nationalism that grounds it, *We Are Kings* aims to recover the potential within this individual for subjection as well as wholesale emancipation. Opening with Dryden's Restoration panegyrics on the divinity of Charles II and ending with Edgeworth's Romantic-era tales of African slaves and Irish peasants, this book recasts the individual that is said to be one of the great secular innovations of eighteenth-century British literature as a fundamentally theological entity modeled by both poets and novelists after the medieval figure of the divine king.[9] Dryden's post–Civil War portrait of Charles II as a mortal body endowed with the immortal identity of the nation is an at once medieval and modern formulation. In a book crucial to this study, Ernst Kantorowicz's *The King's Two Bodies* (1957), Kantorowicz shows how jurists and monarchs throughout medieval and early modern Europe worked to infuse secular politics with the divine sovereignty once reserved for the Catholic Church alone. Though broad in scope, Kantorowicz's study begins in the rather narrower context of late sixteenth- and early seventeenth-century England because it was in this time and place that the exceptionalism inherent in both Protestant theology and royalist mysticism came together to make England an exemplary object in the history of political religion. The Elizabethan conception of the English monarch as a sacred being, head of God's chosen nation as well as his national Church, asserts a universality that eighteenth-century authors extended to the entirety of a potentially global British body politic. The divine king's rightful claim to rule the world becomes the global promise of the British Empire, and his sovereign individuated mode of being becomes the right of its every subject.

While historians ranging from Linda Colley to J. C. D. Clark have emphasized the importance of religion to national identity in eighteenth-century Britain, they have missed the truly ascendant faith of this period, which was neither the ecumenical Protestantism of Britain (Colley) nor the orthodox Anglicanism of England (Clark), but the profane political theology of Empire.[10] One can find the same oversight in recent philosophical accounts of the supposed twilight of religious meaning in Western modernity as a whole. Thinkers in this vein, such as Charles Taylor and Thomas Pfau, depict the Reformation and the contemporaneous dissemination of Christianity into everyday life as the beginning of religion's decline.[11] What such narratives miss is the Christianity that everywhere surrounds us in the rituals and rhetoric of present-day Western nationalism. When medieval and early modern jurists began to depict England as God's chosen vehicle for global salvation and the king as its privileged representative, they helped initiate a tradition of politicizing the Christian faith that runs from the Middle Ages to the present as the essential backbone of the modern Western nation and subject.[12]

The great innovation of eighteenth-century British literature was to turn the king's two bodies, mortal and immortal, into a popular mode of being and in the process solve a central-medieval-through-early-modern political dilemma: how to ensure the unity of the monarch's divine sovereignty with the mortal body politic he or she represented. Each of the four chapters in this book focuses on characters—such as the patriot in Dryden's late work "To My Honour'd Kinsman" (1700), the poet in Pope's "Windsor Forest" (1713), the domestic heroine of Richardson's *Clarissa* (1747–48), and the heroes of Edgeworth's "The Grateful Negro" (1804) and *The Absentee* (1812)—who become modern individuals only by inhabiting a once-exclusively royal mode of being.

Best remembered for satirizing their contemporaries as, in the words of Pope, a "Tribe of ... Pimps, Poets, [and] Wits," the British Tory Augustans rebelled against a society witnessing the interrelated rise of finance, the expansion of the state, and the steady centralization of agricultural production, to name only a few of the developments that made this an era of profound social transformation ("Sober Advice from Horace"

1–2). The two key historical works for my assessment of this period are Steven Pincus's *1688: The First Modern Revolution* (2009) and A. G. Hopkins and P. J. Cain's *British Imperialism: 1688–2000* (2000). The first book emphasizes the political changes that led to the formation of a "new kind of modern state" in this era, while the second demonstrates how the nonindustrial aspects of capitalism, enduring and frequently neglected, first emerged in 1690s Britain in the areas of global trade, agriculture, and, most important, financial and commercial services (3).[13] Authors such as Dryden, Pope, Swift, and Lord Bolingbroke were the avowed enemies of these political and economic transformations, yet, in a paradox that is crucial for this book, it is through this resistance that they came to make an invaluable contribution to the very modern culture they despised.

Although they conceived of themselves as stalwarts of a timeless tradition, the British Tory Augustans were in fact innovators, particularly in poetry, where they formulated new ideas of the nation and the individual that would become hallmarks of Britain's post-1688 social order. As Dryden writes in "To My Honour'd Kinsman," the patriot individual, "charg'd with Common Care," is "Blessed" because he embodies the sovereignty and freedom of a "bless'd Abode," that is, a blessed nation (1, 178). Tory Augustan authors cultivated an embattled, individuated, and nationalized mode of being to resist modernity, and, in so doing, they became ironic participants in it. There is a lesson here for those who attempt to find alternatives to twenty-first-century capitalist modernity in the history of those conservative reactions against it. The strategy of opposing a culture of novelty in the name of tradition—which is pursued by a range of later authors from Austen and Samuel Coleridge to Ezra Pound and Michael Oakeshot—in many ways begins with the British Tory Augustans, and what must be remembered is that this foundation is not so much opposed to modernity as integral to it. Capitalism and nationalism arise together in long eighteenth-century Britain as the competing yet mutually reinforcing poles of a new modern age; the first of these poles foments the social conditions that the second claims to solve. The modern individual thus emerges in part from an antimodern cultural movement because this movement offered the democratized nobility of national belonging as compensation for the indignity of modern commerce and commodification, those processes that reduce all things, human and otherwise, to substitutable bearers of economic value.

When Alexander Pope declares his allegiance "TO VIRTUE ONLY and HER FRIENDS," he does so in opposition to a society he depicts as given over to commercial vice, where "the thronging millions to the pagod run, / And offer country, parent, wife, or son" ("First Satire of the Second Book of Horace" 121). The similarly embattled heroine of Richardson's *Clarissa*, on the other hand, demonstrates "her LOVE OF VIRTUE" in opposition to a world where brothers, fathers, mothers, sisters, and suitors treat young women as objects, commodities to be traded in pursuit of profit and social advancement or, alternatively, playthings to be used for sadistic delight (657). However different Tory Augustan verse and domestic fiction might appear on the surface, the same fundamental drama underlies each. Whether it is Pope's Horatian Satires or Richardson's novel, Tory Augustan poetry and domestic fiction center on the saga of individuals heroically defending the transcendent virtue they bear from a commercial society threatening to degrade it.

This book focuses on poetry written by politically alienated Catholics and fictional prose featuring characters isolated from formal political power because it was figures such as the disenfranchised Catholic poet, the persecuted young woman, the enslaved African, and the Irish peasant who best exemplified the expansiveness of a subjectivity that has never adequately been defined by the halls of Parliament or the pages of legal declarations. Well before the 1832 Reform Act expanded the voting franchise to nearly one-fifth of adult males while for the first time explicitly excluding women, literature was already democratizing Britain's national identity on the level of the self.[14] While a particular form of subjectivity might appear inconsequential in comparison to the rights of a fully enfranchised subject, it is worth recalling Michel Foucault's argument in *Discipline and Punish* (1975) that the modern European subject is a product principally not of formal democratic politics, but rather of a "a micro-physics of power ... that cannot be localized in a particular type of institution or state apparatus" (26). This is not to dismiss the importance of electoral politics, but, rather, to say that it should not blind us to the politics occurring elsewhere in the seemingly apolitical spaces of workshops, plantations, schools, novels, factories, and homes. Drawing from the work of Foucault as well as one of his key interpreters, Nancy Armstrong, *We Are Kings* reiterates Armstrong's seminal contention that domestic fiction played an important role in developing the modern subject that Foucault traces in a series of historical studies from the early to mid-1970s. With this said, however, *We Are Kings* departs from both

Armstrong and Foucault in making the crucial additional point that the modern British subject, crafted in part by domestic fiction, is made from theology, and that it is therefore never wholly owned by the political powers that claim it.

The individuality that domestic novels cultivate is not novel; it is the expansion of a centuries-long political theological project that reaches a kind of culmination with England's 1530s break from Rome. In *The King's Two Bodies*, Kantorowicz makes a persuasive argument for understanding the English Reformation as the product not simply of the Reformation and its leaders—most notably, Martin Luther, John Calvin, and Henry VIII—but also of a much longer and more widespread tendency throughout medieval Europe to treat the Christian Church in secular political terms. When the last Catholic Archbishop of Canterbury, Reginald Pole, reprimands Henry VIII by stating, "Your whole reasoning comes to the conclusion that you consider the Church a *corpus politicum*," he attempts, in the words of Kantorowicz, "to restore the supra-political character of the Church and to undo the process of secularization which the *corpus Ecclesiae mysticum* had succumbed to ever since the thirteenth century" (229–30).

Pole's protest went unheard, and its failure is confirmed both by the increasing acceptance of the monarch's quasi-theological status in post-Reformation England and by the contemporaneous sacralization of the body politic he or she represented. At the same time that the king's role as "the chief power" over all "the Estates of this Realm, whether they be Ecclesiastical or Civil" is enshrined into the Church of England's *Thirty-Nine Articles* (1562), authors of opposing denominations and political affiliations were working together to depict England not as one nation among many, but as the nation set apart by God as his chosen vehicle for global salvation (13). Partisans on all sides of early modern English politics, from royalists like Edmund Plowden to Puritans like Phineas Fletcher, were united by the shared conviction that, in the words of Fletcher, the "world's sole Pilot . . . hast embark't [his] light . . . in this poor Isle" ("Locusts" 1–3).

However anachronistic such images of the nation and subject might appear to twenty-first-century readers, the truth is that they shouldn't. Founded upon the interrelated ideas of individual liberty and manifest destiny, the sovereign king and the godly nation, the national theology of early modern England establishes the ideological framework for the later British and American empires as well as the broader configuration of the

West.¹⁵ In a 2013 speech defending the extrajudicial American drone war, president Barack Obama spoke of the same flag as Trump, promising that "long after the current messengers of hate have faded from the world's memory, alongside the brutal despots, and deranged madmen, and ruthless demagogues who litter history—the flag of the United States will still wave from small-town cemeteries to national monuments, to distant outposts abroad. And that flag will still stand for freedom." The United States conceives of itself as God's chosen subject within a global economy of salvation. Whatever violence it inflicts—when it kills a wedding party in Afghanistan, for example—it does so in the midst of fulfilling the dream of a modern-day Revelation.¹⁶

"Secularism" is the word we have for the deeply theological conviction that Western nations' claims to act on behalf of "freedom" are rational, and thus in some sense beyond religion and embedded within the truth of nature itself, and that all those who reject this act of politico-theological presumption, "the East," are mad. In the midst of the contemporary war on terror, British and American political leaders including George Bush, Tony Blair, Hillary Clinton, and Theresa May have repeatedly depicted their enemies as opposed not just to a specific set of values, but to the progressive movement of history itself, to the supposed rational teleological truth that lies buried within history as the world's inherent purpose. The United Kingdom and the United States fight then not for their particular interests as individual nations, but, instead, as Hillary Clinton states, for "democracy, freedom, open markets and other values that ... elevate the people of the world even as they protect our people here at home."¹⁷ In the words of Tony Blair, "Ours are not Western values, they are the universal values of the human spirit."¹⁸

Behind such formulations, ringing in the echo chamber of history, is the literary nationalism that accompanied Britain's eighteenth-century rise to imperial prominence, prophecies such as Pope's declaration in "Windsor Forest" that "the time shall come, when free as Seas or Wind / Unbounded Thames shall flow for all Mankind" (395–96). The difference between contemporary Western political discourse and that of "Windsor Forest" is that Pope cannot draw upon centuries of secular tradition; instead, he must consciously create it by reformulating Scripture in newly national and popular terms. Pope's prophecy is a knowing reiteration of the book of Isaiah's apocalyptic vision, "In the last days ... the LORD's house shall be established in the top of the mountains ... and all nations shall flow unto it" (2:2). By returning to literature in which such allusions remain overt, *We Are Kings* aims not only to correct the historical record by showing the role that Christian theology played in the making of Western secularism, but also to delineate the new political possibilities that are engendered by a nonsecular understanding of Western modernity. It is not enough to criticize our world; we must also change it, and it is in the spirit of this humanist conviction that this book undertakes a literary historical exploration in order to make a present-day political intervention.

Political Theology and the Promise of Sovereignty

The past twenty years have seen a flurry of critiques of Western secularism, and *We Are Kings* draws from and pushes forward the particular discourse of political theology, which has played an especially important role in efforts to reconsider the meaning of secularism today. Political theology is a theoretical movement beginning in early twentieth-century Europe and gathering momentum in the past half-century under the global influences of liberation theology and poststructuralist theory. The German legal theorist and later Nazi party intellectual Carl Schmitt coined the phrase "political theology" in a 1922 essay in which Schmitt intervened in the constitutional unrest of the Weimar republic by making, among other claims, the now-seminal argument that "all significant concepts of the modern theory of the state are secularized theological concepts" (36). Despite this troubling point of origin, political theology has become an important discourse on the European, American, and Latin American left, having been promoted by left-wing theologians from the 1960s to the present as well as by neo-Marxist continental philosophers and cultural critics from the 1990s onward.[19] Encompassing theologians, anthropologists, philosophers, and literary critics, scholars of contemporary political theology is bound together by an overarching commitment to tracing the dissemination of Christianity within the major political, economic, and cultural institutions of Western modernity.

Although other literary critics—principally Victoria Kahn, Graham Hammill, and Julia Reinhard Lupton—have brought political theology to the attention of British literary studies, they have tended to do so while rejecting its chief premise—namely, that secularization is not secular.[20] *We Are Kings* is the first book to interpret eighteenth-century British literature from the perspective of political theology, and it does so with the goal both of affirming this movement's central thesis and of taking it past the point of mere criticism. No thinker has done more in recent history to elucidate Western political theology than the contemporary Italian philosopher Giorgio Agamben, yet none also better exemplifies the political shortcomings of critique in the left-wing humanities today. Agamben's great merit for this project is that he places Foucault's study of the modern Western subject within an explicitly political theological context by demonstrating how this subject is born of the internalization of a sovereignty that is theological in nature. Agamben, in other words, shows the compatibility of Foucault's analysis with the line of continuity that this book draws from Dryden's image of the divine king in the mid-seventeenth century to Edgeworth's domestic protagonists in the early nineteenth.

In *Discipline and Punish* and *History of Sexuality*, volume 1 (1976), as well as in his contemporaneous lectures at the Collège de France, Foucault narrates the birth of European modernity in terms of a transition from a premodern "sovereign" mode of power to a properly modern both "disciplinary" and "biopolitical" one. Power in the first mode, as Foucault writes, "was essentially a right of seizure: of things, time, bodies, and ultimately life itself," while in the second "power [is] bent on generating forces, making them grow, and ordering them" (*History of Sexuality* 135). In the nine volumes that make up his twenty-year *Homo Sacer* series (1995–2015), Agamben demonstrates the fundamental interpenetration of Foucault's two major historical periods. For Agamben, sovereignty first and foremost seizes life, and biopolitics—or the transformation of life into the essential object of politics—is thus synonymous not with modernity, as Foucault contends, but with the entirety of the Western political tradition. Sovereignty and biopolitics together form, according to Agamben, the "originary structure" of Western political power from the Ancient Greeks and Romans to the twenty-first-century Anglo-European West.[21]

The historical breadth and level of abstraction in Agamben's analysis causes him to overlook the centrality of nationalism and race to the development of the modern West, oversights I discuss in chapters 2 and 4 of this book. There is, however, another issue with Agamben's work that relates not to the scope of its narrative, but to the Manichean conception of modernity that structures it. Agamben demonstrates a pervasive tendency among contemporary critical theorists in treating the history of Western modernity as an unambiguous descent into further oppression. The "exemplary space" of the modern West is, as Agamben infamously states in the first volume of *Homo Sacer* (1995), the "concentration camp," and the secularized theology driving its political and economic order nothing more than the perfection of domination (4). Like so many theorists today, Agamben pairs a wholesale, undialectical rejection of Western modernity with the related assertion that emancipatory politics can begin only in a space entirely beyond our present, as well as the history that has made it. When speaking of a political alternative, Agamben proposes a particular "form-of-life" possible only after the political, theological, and economic structures of power stretching from the ancients to the moderns have been rendered "inoperative" (*Use of Bodies* 225). Agamben portrays his alternative as one without government, without labor, and even without relations—that is to say, for those operating within the reality of twenty-first-century politics, Agamben offers no alternative at all.[22]

Refusing to view politics in this all-or-nothing manner, this book begins with the dialectical assumption that every new form of subjection is simultaneously a potential tool for liberation. Drawing from Georges Bataille's seminal study of sovereignty in *The Accursed Share*, volume 3 (1949), *We Are Kings* finds political hope in the very biopolitical internalization of sovereignty that would appear to indelibly bind modern life to power. The constitution of the modern subject is a mark of domination, a means of better binding that subject to the sovereignty of the nation, yet it is at the same time a potential elevation, an endowment of the British subject with an authority once reserved for monarchs alone. Like the kings before them, modern subjects bear the sovereignty of a political whole. They stand forever capable of making a claim upon the state that claims them, and the fact that they haven't, that the United Kingdom, the United States, and the West more broadly persist in an oligarchic condition in which the sovereign power to shape one's life is exercised by a few and deprived from the many, is a sign not that modernity must be abandoned, but, rather, that it finally must be accomplished.

Writing in the aftermath of World War II and the near-apocalyptic failure of modernity that it represented, Bataille makes precisely this gambit, arguing that the tragedy of modernity is not that it has happened, but that its subjects have refused to affirm the emancipatory promise that it embodies. In the third volume of *The Accursed Share*, Bataille represents the regicide of the English king Charles I in 1649 and the French king Louis XVI in 1793 as the bloody, emancipatory origin of a culture whose democratizing promise has remained unfulfilled. Bataille's portrait of Western modernity's primal, regicidal scene offers a sense of hope that critical theory has since lost:

> The rebel... liquidated that royal subjectivity that imposed itself upon him and deprived him of his own subjectivity, but he was not able to regain for his own part that of which the king's glory had deprived him. As far as monarchic society is concerned, he was only an object, but nothing was changed in republican society, except that in front of him there was no longer a *subject* whose sovereign character seemed to be the sole cause of his limitation. In a society that has done away with institutional sovereignty, personal sovereignty is not given, for all that. Even the man who fought to abolish that which oppressed him, which reduced him to the level of things, must still by some stroke or other recapture that of which oppression had deprived him. What is more, he has lost what the monarchic society at least had, a rather complete representation of the human being, such that this being could not allow himself to be confused with things, reduced to objectivity. (254–55)

The "glory" that Agamben calls for "rendering inoperative" is precisely what Bataille encourages the West's postregicidal modern subjects "by some stroke or other [to] recapture" (*Kingdom and Glory* xiii).

The strength of Bataille's analysis is that it sketches a philosophical path to liberation that makes use of modernity rather than dreams of a future entirely beyond it. The problem, however, is that Bataille writes as if the promise of modernity were evenly distributed, as if the category of the subject were not from the beginning stratified by a series of hierarchal divisions based on gender, race, nation, sexuality, and class. While Bataille may be correct that all subjects, poor and rich alike, have forgotten the promise of sovereignty, the possibility of regaining it is not equally available to all, and, by ignoring this fact, Bataille turns his theory of sovereignty into a potential apologia for the very modern culture he criticizes. Bataille presumes equality where there is none, arguing that modern subjects can inhabit the position of "the sovereign individual [who] consumes but doesn't labor" by indulging in "nonproductive consumption," which is accessible, according to Bataille, through activities such as art, sadomasochism, and religion, to name a few of his favorite examples (198, 422). The essence of sovereignty for Bataille is in the end a consumer experience; it is the feeling of existing "beyond utility," of momentarily looking upon a utilitarian world of things through the transcendent eyes of a king (197, 199). Despite the lofty rhetoric, Bataille actually downplays the significance of sovereignty by treating it as an individual's "*inner* experience" rather than a foundational legal principle that authorizes the rise of an imperial Western culture while at the same time embedding within that culture the possibility of its wholesale transformation (241).

Far beyond any particular individual's experience, sovereignty is first and foremost a divinely grounded right to govern, a definition that runs from John of Salisbury's writings in the twelfth century and Edmund Burke's in the eighteenth to the discourse of Western leaders today. In the words of Salisbury, "His [the king's] will should never be found opposed to justice" because the monarch embodies the law itself, and this cannot be wrong, "for all Power is from the Lord God" (28). While Burke five centuries later will vacillate on the question of what ultimately authorizes political power, at times identifying common sense and at others custom, his answer in the end always returns to the same Pauline conviction invoked by Salisbury. "I may assume," Burke explains in *An Appeal from the New to Old Whigs* (1791), "that the awful Author of our being is the Author of our place in the order of existence; and that having disposed and marshalled us by a divine tactick, not according to our will, but according to his, then he has, in and by that disposition, virtually subjected us to act the part which belongs to the place assigned us" (99). Such explains the glory of the sovereign for Burke: rulers derive their power from God, and their subjects thus owe them an obedience that is simultaneously political and theological in nature.

A crucial problem, however, emerges with the democratization of sovereignty beginning in the eighteenth century and continuing into the present. Even if this democratization occurs only in principle—that is, if it is only articulated in legal statutes, stories, and political speeches, while being systematically violated in practice—the fact nonetheless remains that the dissemination of sovereignty forms an essential fault line within the West's postregicidal political order. The idea that nonmonarchical individuals have a share in governance, that they too bear "the Common Cause" of the nation, as Dryden puts it in "To My Honour'd Kinsman," establishes a persistent basis for rebellion in two major senses (190). In the first, modern subjects may speak in the language of rights and resist established power in the name of the privileges it has granted them. While certainly effective in particular circumstances, such resistance is ultimately a form of loyalism that reinforces the system it questions. The second mode of agitation, on the other hand, is at once a heightened form of loyalism and an even more decisive act of revolt. It is similar to the first mode insofar as it is a kind of internal critique, but it differs from it in that it is an internal critique that calls the authority of the entire system into question. In this second mode, one unearths the theological foundation of the state's authority in order to be able to oppose that state in the name of a sovereignty that is no longer its own. This is a form of rebellion that divides the state from itself by exploiting the godly crack that runs through the foundation of modern Western power as the ur-principle of both its constitution and its dissolution.

In the two novels *Clarissa* and *The Absentee*, Richardson and Edgeworth put this second mode of revolt into narrative form, and, in chapters 3 and 4, I outline the lessons to be drawn from their efforts. *Clarissa* and *The Absentee* are essential works for my argument because they each illuminate the nonsecular nature of British modernity while also articulating the strategy for liberation that it unwittingly empowers. Like all domestic novels, both works use the process of preparing for marriage to cultivate modern national subjects, yet in each case it is these very subjects who use the sovereignty they have internalized to resist rather than obey. The eponymous heroine of Richardson's novel and the final Irish Catholic narrator of Edgeworth's stand as ideal novelistic subjects who dramatize the possibility of detaching sovereignty from the imperial nation that claims it. The heroine who opposes patriarchal British authorities by drawing upon the "God within her" and the colonized Irish Catholic carriage driver who organizes a "great bonfire" anticipating the dawn of an anticolonial Revelation stand as key figurations for the kind of political theological resistance that British modernity involuntarily makes possible (853, 200). Richardson and Edgeworth illustrate something present but latent in the embattled individualism of Dryden's patriot and Pope's poet, and that is that the modern British individual is subjected but potentially free.

From the Renaissance conception of the monarch as a person "utterly void of Infancy, and old Age" and the formation of the Church of England as the guardian of "true religion" to present-day representations of the United Kingdom as the embodiment of "the universal values of the human spirit," the history of Britain's national theology testifies to something that its imperial managers have long sought to forget: that sovereignty is mobile (Plowden 212a–13; *Book of Common Prayer* 238;

Blair). It rests on a foundation that is not here and that is therefore never entirely in the possession of any secular power that claims to exclusively hold it. *Clarissa* and *The Absentee* thus highlight a tension at the heart of Britain's larger imperial project: it depends on a form of authority whose very transcendence renders it forever vulnerable to democratizing acts of usurpation.

Clarissa and *The Absentee* exemplify a mode of resistance that reverberates throughout the history of the British and American Empires as an enduring basis for revolt: retheologize the secularized political authority you carry as a national subject and then oppose that now distinctly religious sovereignty against the nation that claims it. One need not look far for contemporary examples testifying to the continuing relevance of this strategy. In June 2015, the African American activist and filmmaker Bree Newsome climbed a flagpole in front of the South Carolina State House in order to remove the Confederate flag that South Carolina still displayed along with ten other American states. When Newsome ascended the thirty-foot pole, she drew the attention of police officers who yelled for her to descend, to which she responded, "You come against me with hatred and oppression and violence. I come against you in the name of God. This flag comes down today!" After successfully removing the flag, Newsome descended while reciting the Lord's Prayer and Psalm 27.

By claiming "to come against" the forces of American political power "in the name of God" and reciting Scripture as she did so, Newsome might seem to oppose America's political order from the external position of religion. What should be clear by now is that the very opposite is the case. Newsome's invocation of a divine right that supersedes secular law challenges the authority of South Carolina and the United States more broadly at their very foundation, at the point where they claim to have inherited the mantle of their colonial British predecessors as God's chosen vehicle for global salvation.

The United States, like the United Kingdom before it, conceives of itself as standing at the center of a global, secularized, Judeo-Christian economy of salvation. This is part of the backdrop for Newsome's action, and it explains why her strategy has such a perplexing effect. Like Richardson's heroine and Edgeworth's Irish Catholic carriage driver, Newsome is at once a national hero and the undoing of that very nation. Liberation theology is often thought of as a movement that opposes secular society from the outside, from the external position of religion. In *Clarissa* and *The Absentee*, Richardson and Edgeworth offer a different perspective. Movements for equality that invoke, in the words of Martin

Luther King Jr., "the law of God" are not simply confronting the state with another form of authority (93). They are challenging the state from within by rejecting one of its most central assumptions: that sovereignty can ever fully belong to human law.

The final message of Edgeworth's novel and of this book as a whole is that early imperial Britain brought divine sovereignty into the political life of Anglo-American modernity and, in doing so, guaranteed a history of never-ending conflict until that bright day when sovereignty is finally shared, and not merely in terms of formal abstract rights, but in the holistic political and economic sense of the power subjects have to shape their own lives. Far beyond either an individual's experience of excess, as Bataille suggests, or a bygone relic of an earlier age, as critics conventionally understand it, sovereignty is instead a foundational political principle that embeds within the modern West a single inexorable fact: a socialist society of the equally sovereign is its highest possibility for existence from which it may flee but never escape.

Why Not Just Reject the West and Begin Anew?

At this point it is essential to address what many readers might be wondering: Why look for alternative possibilities within the modern West, given the horror that it has wrought over three centuries of genocidal imperialism, racism, and gross inequity? Is it not finally time to give up on this thing called "the West"? After all the very hope that this book says it finds in the model of the modern Western subject seems to be exactly what Foucault long ago warned against when he writing in *Discipline and Punish* that "the man, whom we are invited to free, is already in himself the effect of a subjection much more profound than himself" (30). The problem with such pronouncements, however, it that they presume freedom to exist only in a space entirely beyond power. If complicity with power were an obstacle to emancipatory politics, then there would be no such politics at all. As Foucault himself acknowledges in his later work, the modern individual cannot be so easily dismissed if one would like to theorize the possibility of liberation as well as domination within the history of the modern West.[23] What Foucault in the late 1970s and early 1980s would recognize is that freedom is a condition one can create only with and through power.

In the tradition, then, of this late Foucault, *We Are Kings* is an exploration of the role canonical British literature has played in formulating a political theology of both domination and freedom. This book is a search for an immanent language of change. The lessons it draws are not meant to indicate a universal course for political action in all times and all places; rather, they pertain to the specific history of imperial Britain from its early stages in the seventeenth century to its legacy within global politics today. The counttercolonial strategies it articulates are relevant to those places where nation-states follow in the same secularized Christian footsteps as imperial Britain. In the twenty-first-century present, this country is first and foremost the United States. By returning to this canon and finding a basis for hope within it, *We Are Kings* makes, among other claims, the argument that the United States can be changed from within, that the same Western culture that structures its discourses and apparatuses of oppression also contains the basis for its wholesale socialist transformation. In saying this, I am aware that there are many reasons to remain skeptical. First among them is the immediate context for Newsome's action—namely, race.

The United States, the country that has most clearly inherited Britain's imperial mantle, is also the place where race and racism have most clearly been used to organize national subjects into a hierarchy of the chosen, the redeemable, and the damned. Although indebted to the work of Foucault and Agamben, this book also draws from Alexander Weheliye's important critique of them, in *Habeas Viscus* (2014), for failing to ever fully address the significance of race to the modern modes of power that they study. While Foucault and Agamben each touch upon race's centrality at various points in their careers, with Foucault describing the modern Western conception of history as a "race war" and Agamben identifying "racism as the apparatus through which sovereign power . . . is reinserted into biopower," Weheliye convincingly demonstrates how both thinkers fail ever to grapple with race in a sustained fashion because doing so would require them to situate Western modernity within particular historical, geographic, and national contexts (*Society Must Be Defended* 60; *The Kingdom and the Glory* 76). Foucault and Agamben instead presume an unstated yet always-present universality to their analyses, developing, in the words of Weheliye, a "bare life and biopolitical discourse that aspires to transcend racialization" by speaking in a conceptual language that purports to precede race and indeed every other form of historical particularity (4). Given all of this, it should not be a surprise that, when it comes to sketching political alternatives, Foucault, at least until his later years, and Agamben, throughout his work, offer only vague invocations of a world beyond this one.

Ironically, however, Weheliye himself falls into the same trap. Like Agamben and the early Foucault, Weheliye unequivocally rejects Western modernity as nothing more than the perfection of domination, and, as a result (and, again, like his interlocutors), Weheliye is compelled to look beyond history for political hope. With the idea of "habeas viscus," Weheliye aims to describe a space suffuse with emancipatory potential because it exists simultaneously within the history of a racist modernity and beyond it. As Weheliye explains, "Habeas viscus translates the hieroglyphics of the flesh"—that is, the corporeal history of modernity—"into a potentiality in any and all things, an originating leap in the imagining of future anterior freedoms and new genres of humanity" (137). Despite Weheliye's assertions to the contrary, habeas viscus turns the flesh into a messianic object, an immanent mark of difference whose alterity signifies the alternative future lying within the origins of our past (136–37). Weheliye's political metaphysics are compelling but ultimately of little practical use because they imply a model of politics where theories of being rather than people do the action.

In its own way, *We Are Kings* is a plea for academics to again think of politics as a matter of human actors operating within the particularity of specific times and specific places.[24] For the left-wing academy to again connect to concrete political action, it must forsake the siren call of new ontologies and the myth of political purity that they promise. Instead, the academy ought to embrace its complicity with history and with power and begin searching for the sources of political hope that nevertheless exist within them. The notion that one can act upon a principle entirely untouched by race is not something twenty-first-century activists can or should expect. The question is not how to find a space beyond race; it is to ask what within the history of a racist modernity will allow racism to be undone. In the West today, inequality in terms of economic and political power is synonymous with racism. In the United States, the median wealth of whites outnumbers that of blacks by ten to one.[25] Within this context, the struggle against racism is first and foremost a fight for human equality. By returning to the literature of America's imperial predecessor, this book uncovers an immanent basis upon which one might act in pursuit of this aim. The British literary canon helped bring sovereignty into the world, and, upon its basis, we can demand the only kind of society with which this dissemination makes sense.

The Structure of This Book

Chapter 1 begins by tracing the political subjectivity of the King in Dryden's Restoration panegyrics "Astraea Redux" (1660) and "To His Sacred Majesty" (1661) in order to show how Dryden's essentially medieval image of the divine king represents an early prefiguration of the modern individual. Marshaling Steven Zwicker's seminal account of Dryden's use of biblical typology, chapter 1 demonstrates how Dryden's sacralized image of Charles II in "Astraea Redux" and "To His Sacred Majesty" anticipates the more clearly modern figure of the patriot that Dryden develops in his late poem "To My Honour'd Kinsman." In a departure from a point of consensus among Dryden critics, including Zwicker, this chapter depicts Dryden's patriot as an expansion of rather than a break with his early royalist political philosophy. Dryden infuses the private biological life of the patriot with the collective and immortal identity of the nation and thereby inaugurates the novelistic tradition of democratizing a political subjectivity once reserved for monarchs alone.

Chapter 2, on Pope's "Windsor Forest," is a key turning point in my argument because it is Pope who translates the oppositional subjectivity of Dryden's patriot into the specifically domestic novelistic terms of an embattled protagonist heroically maintaining his or her virtue through writing. Published to commemorate the Treaty of Utrecht in 1713, "Windsor Forest" is a nationalized reformulation of the book of Isaiah that represents Britain as God's new Israel and Pope's own authorial persona as one of its exemplary constituents. Pope's poetic identity poses a fundamental challenge to J. G. A. Pocock's influential secular account of the neoclassical revival in early eighteenth-century Britain. From "Windsor Forest" to his Horatian satires of the 1730s, Pope develops a neoclassical model of self-possession that synthesizes republican humanism with an English literary tradition of national theology that encompasses works ranging from the arch-Calvinist to the high royalist.

The inevitable internal discord of any society that claims divine sovereignty yet attempts to hoard it among a privileged elite is the focus of chapter 3, on Richardson's *Clarissa*. Building on Nancy Armstrong and Leonard Tennenhouse's *The Imaginary Puritan* (1992), I interpret *Clarissa* as a captivity narrative in which a young heroine and self-identified slave uses her relationship with death and God to pursue a strategy of resistance that critics, including Armstrong and Tennenhouse, have almost uniformly dismissed as apolitical. Richardson's at once devout and unruly heroine represents a novelistic rejoinder to Max Weber's seminal thesis on the mutual dependence of the Reformation and the modern individual. Clarissa uses her internalized and largely discursive relationship with God not to become a gendered subject of capitalist modernity, but to achieve a withdrawn and emancipated life that threatens the very foundation of eighteenth-century social order. Drawing from the work of John Wesley, George Whitefield, and Lady Huntingdon, I depict *Clarissa* as Richardson's definitive articulation of his own popular Anglican philosophy, which combines an orthodox emphasis on sin with a Wesleyan notion of spiritual perfection.

From Dryden's King and Pope's poet to Richardson's heroine, slavery runs as a thread through my book, and, in my final chapter, I clarify the significance of the slave as an exemplary figure against which a modern British self is constructed. My chapter opens with a domestic short story set in Jamaica and written in the shadow of the Haitian Revolution, Edgeworth's "The Grateful Negro." In it, Edgeworth portrays her enslaved African prince protagonist as independent in his self-governance and yet submissive in his political will, a paradoxical combination expressing both the potential universalism of Enlightenment-era humanism as well as its hegemonic limits. The second half of the chapter turns to Edgeworth's Irish novel *The Absentee* because it explodes this central Enlightenment myth and in the process shows the consequences of slavery's role in the making of the modern self. Developed in opposition to slavery and the capitalist dispossession it heralded, the modern British self contains the germs of an emancipation we have yet to see.

1

Dryden's Political Theology and the Making of a Modern Subject

Why Dryden Is Modern

John Dryden is an odd place to start for a study of the modern individual. Dryden, after all, was a monarchist who is probably best remembered today for inaugurating the now well-worn Tory habit of opposing English modernity in the language of tradition. Following a brief period in which he worked in the secretary of state's office under Oliver Cromwell, Dryden spent the majority of his career writing poems and plays that sought to perfect the unity of king and country, which the mid-century execution of Charles had fundamentally shaken. In an era still reeling from regicide and civil war, Dryden pursued what was an essentially high medieval aim of using verse to depict Charles's two sons, the Restoration king Charles II and then his Catholic brother and brief successor James II, as men endowed with the immortal identity of the English nation as a whole. The ascent, however, of James's daughter Mary and her husband William to the throne in 1688 put an end to Dryden's days of political influence, depriving him of his positions as poet laureate and historiographer royal and, more abstractly, challenging his now seemingly outdated theory of divine right. The once-dominant Dryden, who previously had spoken on behalf of power to England's community of readers from the middle class upward, was compelled to withdraw from public life and to veil his politics in translations, fables, and odes. Ironically, it is this late, relatively powerless Dryden who, in the end, has had the greater cultural impact as a result of his nostalgic self-proclaimed successors, such as Alexander Pope, Henry St. John Bolingbroke, and John Gay, who took to celebrating the displaced Dryden of the 1690s as a tragic symbol of the loss of traditional England.

Until recently, Dryden scholars tended to agree with this eighteenth-century assessment. While some represented his late writings as the beginning of an antimodern political tradition stretching from the British Tory Augustans to Leo Strauss, others interpreted this same work as a retreat from politics altogether.[1] Over the past thirty years, however, there has been an effort led by Michael McKeon and Elliott Visconsi to challenge this consensus by recasting Dryden's politics as either protomodern in his later years, as McKeon argues, or as committed from the very beginning to "systematic public enlightenment," as Visconsi contends (74). For revisionist scholars, the overlooked modernity of Dryden's writing hinges on the idea that at some point Dryden took to subtly undermining a theological conception of politics, an incipient secularism that earlier critics missed.

While undoubtedly convincing in one major respect—Dryden was modern—these revisionist scholars have failed to recognize that Dryden's place within British modernity demands a reevaluation of exactly what British modernity means. These critics assume that if Dryden were modern, then he also must have been secular. In this chapter, I make no such assumption, and the result is a new interpretation of both Dryden and the imperial British culture he helped to shape. Beginning with two poems that typify Dryden's early politics, "Astraea Redux" and "To His Sacred Majesty," and then moving to an epistolary ode, "To My Honour'd Kinsman," that exemplifies Dryden's later writing, this chapter uncovers what has remained unsaid in scholarship on Dryden. In both his early and late writing, Dryden was a poet of political theology. From his early depictions of Charles II as a divine being to his later representations of private individuals as endowed with the same transcendent political value, Dryden devoted a lifetime of verse to disseminating the Christic subjectivity of the Catholic pope to mortal English bodies. Dryden participated in a process of modernization that entailed not the abandonment of Christian theology, but, rather, its politicizing democratization. The late Dryden was an aging poet who embraced the post-1688 transformation of England as an opportunity to expand and perfect the national faith that he had spent his career developing.

With the improvement of roads, the development of a postal service, the increasing importance of a London-based parliament, and the creation of the Bank of England, to name only a few examples, the 1690s was a decisive period for the unification, urbanization, and financialization of early modern English life.[2] While Dryden's "To My Honour'd Kinsman" clearly contains criticism of contemporary political events, particularly of King William's aggressive foreign policy on the Continent, its development of the figure of the patriot reflects the general tenor of a period that saw greater political unity achieved through the expansion of the English state into once relatively unregulated aspects of society. This point is further substantiated in the final section of this chapter in an exploration of the surprising continuity between "To My Honour'd Kinsman" and the very different but nevertheless analogous Societies for the Reformation of Manners (SRM), a contemporaneous evangelical movement that used a network of lay informants to encourage the enforcement of secular law in urban areas, principally against prostitution and other moral crimes from Sabbath-breaking to cursing. The SRM sought to show that, as one of their enthusiasts put it, "Divine Service is not Confined to Consecrated Places," because they operated under the very modern assumption that God's sovereignty remains indistinguishable from secular political authority (Woodhouse 50). While they certainly address different spectrums of the social body, one gentlemanly and the other popular, both Dryden and the SRM work to endow the behavior of nonroyal constituents, from the country gentleman to the London bawd, with a new degree of theological and political value.

Although Dryden was as much a playwright as a poet, this chapter focuses on the latter, because it is in his poetic works that Dryden constructs a cohesive and optimistic political theology centered at first on the king and later on the twin figures of the king and the patriot. As Laura Brown has noted, Dryden reserved his plays for his more pessimistic meditations on the potential failure of his political theology to subdue the body politic's tendency to violently separate the king's mortal body from the higher, mystical body of the nation ("Dryden and the Imperial Imagination" 73).[3] In this chapter, I am more interested in what Dryden builds than what he takes apart.

The monarchist Dryden rather than the republican John Milton serves as my starting point for reconsidering the emergence of a modern subject because this subject is radically different from what Western ideologues have long contended. Whereas Milton's revolutionary insistence on the separation of secular and spiritual authority prefigures the way twenty-first-century Western democratic states like to present themselves, it is Dryden's opposing affirmation of the spiritual basis of political authority that informs how these governments actually function. When Milton defends the right of Parliament to execute Charles I in his *The Tenure of Kings and Magistrates* (1650), he articulates a model of popular sovereignty that remains a far cry from the oligarchic politics of Anglo-America today: "Since the King or Magistrate holds his autoritie of the people, both originaly and naturally for their good in the first place, and not his own, then may the people as oft as they shall judge it for the best, either choose him or reject him, retaine him or depose him though no Tyrant, meerly by the liberty and right of free born Men, to be govern'd as seems to them best" (13). As Milton states elsewhere in the same work, "To say, as is usual, the King hath as good right to his Crown and dignitie, as any man to his inheritance, is to make the Subject no better than the Kings slave," which is a problem, since "all men naturally were borne free, being the image and resemblance of God himself" and thus have a theologically grounded right to self-governance (11, 8). To think otherwise, from Milton's perspective, is to commit a sin. In the words of the critic Nigel Smith, Milton, "monarchist in heaven, republican on earth," uses the absolutism of God's sovereignty in the hereafter as the irreducible guarantee of our popular right to freedom in the here and now, a paradoxical combination of submission and resistance that runs throughout *We Are Kings*, but, crucially, does so from within the very monarchical culture Milton opposed (263).[4]

My argument, then, in starting with Dryden rather than Milton is not that seventeenth-century English radicalism disappears from the pages of history—in fact, just the opposite. At the heart of this book is the contention that England's Civil War–era radicalism persists within the conservative reaction that would appear to mark its irrevocable decline. From Dryden's insistence that Charles II stands as a mortal being endowed with a "more sacred Head," to Richardson's image of Clarissa as a "WOMAN in her charming person" but an "ANGEL . . . in her mind," to present-day activists like Bree Newsome, there is a single thread (1.46, 1299). It is the conviction, soaked in the legacy of the English Civil War, that we mortals may become something more, that we can speak "in the name of God," to quote Newsome herself echoing Cromwell's declaration that his soldiers act as the "instruments of Providence" (4.719). Within all of this, the same presumption persists: mortals can become the hand of God, and the common subject a king.

Dryden's Biopolitics and the Myth of the Uniquely Modern

By insisting on the continuity of Dryden's oeuvre, from his king- to his patriot-centered writing, I part from the still-pervasive scholarly tendency to isolate early English modernity from the premodern world that gave rise to it. While my reading of the politicization of life in "To My Honour'd Kinsman" is particularly indebted to Foucault's idea of biopolitics, I reject Foucault's suggestion that this concept belongs to a distinct historical period with its own unique epistemology. Foucault first articulates his idea of biopolitics in the final chapter of *The History of Sexuality*, volume 1, in which he depicts it as a kind of completion of the early modern shift from a sovereign form of power that functioned through a process of "deduction" to one that was "generative" and that sought to "administer, optimize, and multiply" the life of its subjects (136, 137). According to this narrative, biopolitics begins with the seventeenth-century emergence of disciplinary techniques and institutions, which treated every "body as a machine" capable of "optimization" (139). In doing so, such disciplinary strategies demonstrated the potential for political control to be applied in detail and en masse, rendering every member of a body politic a potential subject of political calculation (139). Upon this foundation, biopolitics develops in the eighteenth through nineteenth centuries as a form of governance that takes the life of these disciplined individuals as the primary object of politics. While Foucault presents disciplinary and biopolitical modes of power as operating in tandem, he clearly identifies biopolitics as the ascendant mode of political rule.

Although many late seventeenth-century English developments—most notably, the growing popularity in the 1690s of political arithmetic and demographic studies—indicate that biopolitics indeed rises to prominence as a strategy at the turn of the century in England, I would like to follow Agamben's lead in understanding biopolitics as an intensification of the primordial "inclusion of bare life in the political realm," which structures every regime of sovereignty from the ancient to the modern (*Homo Sacer* 6).[5] Foucault himself in the first of his 1978 lectures at the Collège de France cautions those that take his successive modes of power as distinct historical periods: "There is not a series of successive elements, the appearance of the new causing the earlier ones to disappear," but rather "what ... changes is the dominant characteristic, or more exactly, the system of correlation between juridico-legal mechanisms, disciplinary mechanisms, and mechanisms of security [the biopolitical mode]" (*Security, Territory, Population* 8). The irony in this warning is that Foucault reaffirms the very "stagist" model that he criticizes by continuing to associate in this same lecture each of these three modes of governance with a specific stage or period in the development of modernity.

To appreciate the premodern theological basis of the modern biopolitical subject that Dryden formulates in "To My Honour'd Kinsman," one must abandon the effort to map the emergence of the modern subject according to a series of distinct historical periods each with its own corresponding episteme.[6] While magisterial in its clarity and scope, historian Dror Wahrman's *The Making of the Modern Self* (2004) exemplifies the pitfalls of organizing the early stages of modern English history with a series of epistemological breaks. Wahrman, like Foucault, constructs a tripartite system to trace the successive stages of selfhood from the seventeenth through nineteenth centuries. According to this model, the constitution of the properly autonomous subject of modernity in the late eighteenth and nineteenth centuries is preceded by both the mutable, "other-oriented," and "socially turned" conscience of the early eighteenth century, and the "solipsistic" and "God-driven Protestant" conscience of the seventeenth century (308–9).

Wahrman most clearly demonstrates the inadequacy of this approach to understanding the emergence of the modern subject when he contrasts the American Revolution, which produced an "unnatural confusion of fundamental identity categories," to the English Civil War, in which "God's will ... endowed them [each side] with a self-explanatory axiomatic identity distinct from that of their adversaries" (223, 231). The fiction of the epistemological break, and the myth of the secular age that it authorizes, prevent Wahrman from recognizing the way God functioned in the Interregnum as a site for fundamental debates over the meaning of the self rather than as a source for stable, predetermined categories of existence. When Dryden writes in the antiexclusionist tract "Absalom and Achitophel" (1681), "Religion and redress of grievances, / Two names that always cheat and always please," he underlines the danger of those opposing James's ascension by associating them with the destabilizing political theologies of the Civil War era such as the constitutionalism of the Levellers, the agrarian communism of the Diggers, and the antihumanist pantheism of the Ranters (747–48). The disruptive function of God reached an apotheosis in the latter group's philosophical system, in which the presumed return of Christ acts as a kind of universal dissolvent that reduces every category of existence to a single plane of being everywhere animated by the all-encompassing force of the divine.⁷

Beginning with the premise that history cannot be organized by a series of epistemological breaks, I hope to open up the possibility of viewing the surprisingly modern subject that Dryden envisions at the turn of the eighteenth century as a new step in the long-standing struggle to make secular English power godly. Dryden's "To My Honour'd Kinsman" at once signifies and helps to enact a modern transformation in biopolitics because it extends the biopolitical control that had previously been reserved for kings and high church officials to a nonroyal individual. This individual emerges as a kind of delayed effect of the late medieval transition from ecclesiastical coronation to dynastic succession, which Kantorowicz sketches in *The King's Two Bodies*. By shifting the seat of the Holy Spirit from the rituals of anointment and the voting of electors to the "royal blood itself," legal theorists from the twelfth to the sixteenth centuries developed a "royal species of man" that rooted the king's second, supernatural body within life itself (331). No longer dependent upon the sacred rituals of coronation, the dynastic king finds the justification for his rule in the intrinsic and immediate bond that exists between his species body and the transcendent authority of the divine. The immortal aura of sovereignty separates from Church rituals as it becomes invested in the biology of an innately sacred royal line.

From the perspective of Kantorowicz's study, Agamben's argument that a state of legal exception exists at the very heart of modern democratic power appears simply to reflect the provenance of modern governance—that is, biopolitics—in the dynastic king of the later Middle Ages, who, in the words of Kantorowicz, is "the very Idea of Justice which itself is bound to Law and yet above the Law because it is the end of all Law" (96). With the wane of the Church's influence over the contours of kingly authority, jurisprudence "felt invited to create its own secular spirituality" that transformed the king into a *typus Christi* (97). The fully empowered, biopolitical king comes quite literally to embody not only the doubleness of Christ, but also the paradox of royal authority itself—namely, that the king derives his sovereignty over the law from the fact that he stands as an exception to it.

By drawing a line of continuity from Dryden's king to his patriot, this chapter builds from Agamben's work on the structural link between the formation of a modern individual and the king's sovereign right to exception. In an extension of Carl Schmitt's thesis in *Political Theology*

(1922) that "sovereign is he who decides on the exception," a point that Schmitt undoubtedly inherits from medieval jurisprudence, Agamben argues that "sovereignty . . . is the originary structure in which law refers to life and includes it in itself by suspending it" (*Political Theology* 5; *Homo Sacer* 27). The exception that binds the body natural of a given heir to the collective, immortal body of the nation forms a template for the constitution of a subject who becomes properly biopolitical once his or her excepted body natural is privileged as the "new subject of politics" (*Homo Sacer* 124).

The Cosmopolitan King and the Political Theology of Young Dryden

Steven Zwicker's contention, in *Dryden's Political Poetry* (1972), that "Dryden's career as political poet can be read as a series of attempts to forge a sacred history of the English nation" represents an essential starting point for my effort to uncover the ultimately cohesive political theology that animates Dryden's verse (5). Zwicker's insight, however, will also provide the basis for a critique of his own division of Dryden's poetry into three distinct phases. According to Zwicker, in Dryden's first phase, immediately following the 1660 restoration of the Stuarts to the throne, he writes panegyrics that employ the biblical method of typological exegesis in order to depict Charles's struggle to reconcile a divided people as a correlate to God's effort to redeem the wavering and long-suffering nation of Israel. The bitterness in later fiercely partisan works, such as the political satires "Absalom and Achitophel" and "The Medall" (1682), characterizes the declining optimism of Dryden's second phase, in which the elect people of England come to resemble the Israelites through their stubborn refusal of God's grace. After losing hope in the redemptive potential of the political sphere altogether and converting to Catholicism in 1685, Dryden, according to Zwicker, enters his final phase, in which he focuses his attention on the inscrutable power of the Catholic Church in works such as *The Hind and the Panther* (1685) and the corresponding "possibility of individual grace" in poems such as his "Ode to Anne Killigrew" (1686) and the elegy "Eleonora" (1692) (120). While Zwicker's model captures Dryden's escalating frustration with the continual deferral of "political redemption," it obscures the way Dryden's later fascination with "individual grace" extends rather than opposes his early monarchism (120).

Dryden develops his vision of the English king as the planet's sole divine mediator and the English people as God's elect in triumphant Restoration panegyrics such as "Astraea Redux" and "To His Sacred Majesty." In these two works, Dryden exemplifies his commitment to completing the medieval transition from ecclesiastical- to dynastic-based succession in strictly national terms. Since Dryden composes "Astraea Redux" in celebration of the return of an unanointed heir and "To His Sacred Majesty" in commemoration of this heir's official coronation ceremony, the King's equally divine image in both poems underlines Dryden's allegiance to a dynastic model of sovereignty that is ostensibly independent of the Church. Dryden represents the King in these panegyrics as the typological correlate or the antitype of a multiplicity of characters—God, Christ, Noah, Moses, Aeneas—in the hopes of giving a transcendental basis to the bond between Charles's body natural and the collective body of England. Dryden begins "Astraea Redux" with an epigraph that enshrouds the work in an anxious sense of expectation for the perfection of this union. Taken from Virgil's *Eclogues* (6.6), the epigraph, "*Iam Redit et Virgo, Redeunt Saturnia Regna*" or "Now returns the Virgin, Saturn's reign returns," announces the arrival of Astraea, the Roman goddess of justice, who fled Earth during the Iron Age and was to return only with the start of a new, golden one. The deferral of this idyllic present through the first section of Dryden's poem, which narrates the chaos and violence of England's Civil War and Interregnum, builds anticipation for the resolution that Dryden announces in the poem's final two stanzas. With the movement from the isolation of England's inward chaos, when the country was a "world divided from the rest," to the triumphant globalism of the poem's final line ("the world a monarch, and that monarch you"), Dryden articulates the potential unity of a planet subjected to the transcendent authority of a single divinely sanctioned king (2, 323).

Written just weeks after his return from exile, "Astraea Redux" portrays Charles's restoration as a sign that the divine redemption promised in the poem's Virgilian epigraph has reached a point of simultaneously political and Christic fruition. Dryden's prophetic imagery reaches its height near the end of the poem with the exclamation:

> How Shall I speak of that triumphant Day
> When you renew'd the expiring pomp of *May!*
> (A month that owns an Interest in your Name:
> You and the Flow'rs are its peculiar Claim.)

> That Star at your birth shone out so bright
> It stain'd the duller Suns Meridian light,
> Did once again its potent Fires renew
> Guiding our eyes to find and worship you. (284–91)

The metrically discordant "You" that punctuates this passage in the fourth line draws attention to the singularity of a king who stands apart from both author and audience just like the Christ figure with whom he is typologically related in the ensuing depiction of his birth. Given that a contemporary historian of the court reported that "it is observed, that at [Charles II's] Nativity at London, [there] was seen a Star about Noontime," it seems that Dryden's allusion to the star of Bethlehem represents something more than a mere allegorical gesture (quoted in Hooker and Swedenburg 232). Dryden's association of the King with Christ instead exemplifies his tendency to profane the biblical method of typology by putting it to political use.

Unlike allegory, where one term acts as an illuminating symbol for a privileged term, biblical typology, as Zwicker explains, establishes a relationship between two terms in which both are not only "literal," but also "historically true" (24–25). Dryden's explicit equation of Charles with Christ in his retelling of the King's nativity tale so disturbed Samuel Johnson that he would not quote it alongside other examples of Dryden's "ambition for forced conceits" in his *Lives of the English Poets* (1779–81), leaving readers with only an oblique reference to a moment when Dryden "mentions one of the most awful passages of Sacred History" (1.263). In a half-hearted attempt to save Dryden from the charge of blasphemy, Edward Hooker and H. T. Swedenburg argue that his nativity tale "indulg[es] in hyperbolical flattery and toy[s] with sacrilege" only as a means of expressing his "exuberant joy" and "breathless excitement" at the King's return (219). Rather than merely "toying with sacrilege," Dryden pursues a calculated campaign of sacrilege in which he uses a specifically biblical rhetorical method to equate the son of God with the unanointed ruler of a single nation. Dryden effectively redeploys the authority and rhetorical devices of one religion to create another: that of the king's second body.

To make matters worse for the faint of heart, Dryden's reinterpretation of Matthew's star of Bethlehem equates the innocent babe of a virgin mother with the object of mass sexual attraction that was the libertine-leaning Charles following his exile in such erotically charged locales as the French court. The image of Charles's nativity star reawakening the love of his subjects represents the culmination of Dryden's effort in "Astraea Redux" to translate Christian and pagan resurrection narratives into the language of politics. Dryden establishes the romantic conceit of Christ/Charles as an absent lover whose prophesized return is eagerly awaited by his followers early in the poem when he depicts the English body politic as jealous of the recently betrothed Infanta Maria Theresa:

> While our cross stars denied us Charles's bed,
> Whom our first flames and virgin love did wed.
> For his long absence church and state did groan;
> Madness the pulpit, faction seized the throne. (19–22)

With the repetition of the first-person plural "our" in the opening couplet, Dryden interpellates his reader as a part of a collective, which he equates in the following two lines with both the Church and the state.

By personifying these institutions as Charles's heartsick bride, Dryden employs a well-established strategy of secularizing the marriage of bishops to the *corpus mysticum* of the Church in an effort to bind the carefully constructed corporate body signaled by the pronoun "our" with the natural body of the king. Kantorowicz locates the idea of the Church incarnating the mystical body of Christ within the twelfth century when the transubstantiation debates of the eleventh century prompted canonists to shift the idea of *corpus mysticum* from the Eucharist to the Church and the concept of Christ's physical body, *corpus Christi*, from the Church to the Eucharist (196). As the bearer of Christ's mystical as opposed to literal body, the Church became capable of entering into figurative marriages with its mortal representatives, a rhetorical maneuver that allowed the Church to continue to represent itself as synonymous with a divine realm that it no longer literally embodied. The Church discovered a means of maintaining its sacred identity following the relocation of Christ's body to the ritual of the Eucharist, but in doing so it developed a rhetorical strategy that later artisans of profanity would use to sacralize the political union of king and nation. In Dryden's redeployment of this motif in the seventeenth century, the national collective rather than the Church bears Christ's mystical body, and it is the king as opposed to a bishop whom this mystical entity comes to figuratively wed.

Through his figurative marriage to the body politic, the king becomes endowed with a both secularized and nationalized version of Christ's *corpus mysticum*. This, however, is merely the start of Dryden's sacrilege. His typological equation of Christ and Charles in "Astraea Redux" ultimately works to infuse the literal body of Christ into the dynastic bloodline of a now innately sacralized monarch. Dryden's narration of the King's nativity scene culminates with Charles being posited as an object whose beauty inspires the kind of transcendental worship that brings disparate bodies into a single sacred whole: "Did once again its potent Fires renew / Guiding our eyes to find and worship you" (290–91).[8] By isolating the second-person pronoun "you" at the end of this couplet and stanza, Dryden dramatizes his departure from the third-person pronoun "him," used both earlier in the poem and in Matthew's nativity tale.[9]

The familiar "you" punctuates the poem because it narrows its addressee to a single man-God figure and aligns the corporate body, signified by the frequent use of the first-person plural pronoun "our," with the perspective of the author. While this configuration of a corporate body fixated on a single object of worship is in part merely a representation of the scene at Charles's landing at Dover at which an "infinite crowd" greeted the King with "shouting and joy," it is also—and more important—an attempt to constitute the English nation as the inseparable second body of the King (Hooker and Swedenburg 232). As James Winn and Elliott Visconsi have noted, Dryden followed William Davenant in conceiving of poets as "mythopoetic" actors who use the creative power of fiction to "cultivate the souls of a divided and traumatized nation" (Visconsi 37).[10] However, rather than poetically constituting an idea and feeling of national identity in the hopes of encouraging a more self-conscious and rational form of judgment in his readers, as Visconsi suggests, Dryden's Restoration poetics instead aim to better subject the English people to the immortal sovereignty inscribed within the very blood of their king.[11] Dryden, in other words, pursues a hegemonic strategy of enlightenment that endows the English body politic with the capacity to accept a king whose right to rule is given to him in advance. As the literal embodiment of Christ's persistence on earth, the king stands for Dryden as the predestined husband of the nation and the mystical body it bears.

Writing less than fifteen years after a king was killed in the name of saving the King, Dryden's effort to cultivate a national soul that is bound to the blood of the king clearly represents a response to the English people's recently demonstrated capacity to divide the corporate sovereignty of the king's higher, immortal body from his merely natural one. The 1649 execution of Charles I was indeed, as the historian Christopher

Hill asserts in *Century of Revolution* (1961), "the most important political event of the century," because it dramatized the potential dissolution of any marriage between the mystical body of the nation and the mortal frame of the king (224). Despite the providential portrayal of Charles II's return in "Astraea Redux," it was in fact the Convention Parliament of 1660 that summoned Charles from Holland in an effort to suppress the revival of the radical pamphlets, agitation, and general social disorder that followed the death of Oliver Cromwell in 1658.[12] The propertied Presbyterians who had struggled to maintain control of the Interregnum since crushing the Levellers and other army radicals at Burford in 1649 decided, as Hill writes, to "sacrifice religion to social order" in 1660 because they again faced a potential alliance between the army and the radicals who challenged, among other rights, hereditary privilege and private property (*Century of Revolution* 143). Dryden's own infamous shift from republicanism to royalism appears from a broader historical perspective to be simply another example of the widespread, cross-denominational panic that struck the English upper classes in the years following Cromwell's death. While Dryden indeed shared the fear of enthusiasm that this panic inspired, his writing was not intended to merely cultivate a more skeptical approach to one's political commitments. Dryden may have mocked the religious zealotry and precritical absolutism of many low-church radicals, but he did so only as a means of bolstering his own triumphantly enthusiastic claim that the English king stood as God's one true representative. Running from one form of absolutism while embracing another, Dryden wielded literature as a political weapon in the war against the "bloody Anabaptists" and "giddy, hot-headed, bloody multitude" that threatened to use the army to "pull down all worldly constitutions" (quoted in Hill, *The World Turned Upside Down* 280).[13]

Although ostensibly written to commemorate Charles's coronation in April 1661, in truth Dryden's "To His Sacred Majesty" works to undermine the significance of this very event, since it portrays the king's power as rooted in the divine biology of his dynastic line rather than in the borrowed majesty of the Church. In a similar movement to "Astraea Redux," Dryden's coronation panegyric begins in the dark ages of the Interregnum and ends with an all-encompassing vision of a globe unified by its subjection to a single king. "To His Sacred Majesty" expands this vision even further by ending with a depiction of Charles's future heirs, or the "souls of kings unborn," an image that only reinforces this coronation poem's discordant fixation with rooting sovereignty in life rather than ritual (120). After typologically representing Charles as a Noah figure who saved the elect nation from a "Deluge" of sin, Dryden effectively portrays the act of anointment as an empty ritual:

> Next, to the sacred Temple you are led,
> Where waites a Crown for your more sacred Head:
> How justly from the Church that Crown is due,
> Preserv'd from ruine and restored by you! (45–48)

With the isolated, emphatic interpellation of the King, Dryden again configures the poet as the mythopoetic representative of a nation addressing the King as the only legitimate *character angelicus*, or mediator, between the human and divine realms. Dryden's explicit subordination of the Church to the "more sacred Head" of the monarch signifies his effort to transfer the "set apart" and hence sacred realm of the divine to the physical body of the King (*OED* 3a). According to this dynastic model of kingship, the crown is indebted or "due" to Charles from the Church not as a justifiable reward for his actions, such as the restoration of the established Church in 1661, but because the crown as the embodiment of the English body politic is intertwined with his very existence.

Dryden's depiction of the crown as "due" to Charles touches upon the tension in the relationship of the crown and the dynastic monarch in suggesting that the former, despite being mystically intertwined with the blood of the dynastic line, can indeed be separated from it and lent out to competing institutions of authority. In an earlier reference to the crown in "Astraea Redux," Dryden portrays the dynastic heir as an antitype of Christ as well as Aeneas because all three had to manage the triangulated existence of being a mortal person distinguished from all others by both a divine fate and a related but still distinct responsibility for the collective body of the people (49–54). The symbol of an impersonal and corporate crown moves from church oaths and rituals to become in the high and late Middle Ages, as Kantorowicz explains, "the embodiment of all sovereign rights ... of the whole body politic" that despite "descend[ing] on the king by right hereditary" remained nevertheless superior to him as well as its other "individual members" (381). In depicting the King as either marrying the body politic or simply using his awe-inspiring eroticism to inspire its devotion, Dryden experiments with two different medieval rhetorical strategies for ameliorating the potentially explosive paradox of a king whose mortal body can become the victim of the very corporate entity it exemplifies.[14]

Once rooted within the problems and debates of medieval political theology that in many ways reached their height for England in the seventeenth century, Dryden's frequent allusions in "Astraea Redux" and "To His Sacred Majesty" to the King's forgiveness and extrajudicial mercy can be read not only as a political endorsement of enlightened benevolence, but also as an expression of the right to exception that constitutes monarchical sovereignty. While Dryden clearly supported Charles's policy of tolerance for crimes committed during the Civil War and Interregnum, his praise for the King's willingness to exceed the law should be understood first and foremost as an affirmation of monarchical exceptionalism. Whether his authority is grounded in the transcendent basis of Christ, justice, or God himself, the king exists throughout the medieval and early modern period as the exemplar of human life precisely because he exceeds it. The king exemplifies the body politic because he is the physical incarnation of its mystical foundation. In transgressing the laws of this body politic, he therefore merely affirms the estrangement that legitimates his right to rule.

The ontological doubleness of the king perhaps finds its clearest moment of expression in the prophetic writings of a twelfth-century pamphleteer now known as the "Norman Anonymous," who, in the words of Kantorowicz, "visualizes in his king two different forms of 'being': one natural or individual, and the other consecrated or (as the author calls it) deified and apotheosized" (59). In this royalist formulation, the king's being is privileged with sole access to the immutable and absolute Being of the divine. Dryden offers his own expression of the exceptional nature of the king's being in the following passage from "Astraea Redux":

> Not ty'd to rules of Policy, you find
> Revenge less sweet than a forgiving mind.
> Thus when the' Almighty would to *Moses* give
> A sight of all he could behold and live:
> A voice before his entry did proclaim
> *Long-Suff'ring, Goodness, Mercy* in his Name.
> Your Pow'r to Justice doth submit your Cause,
> Your Goodness only is above the Laws;
> Whose rigid letter while pronounc'd by you
> is softer made. (260–69)

The symmetry in the first half of the lines that make up one of the conceptually denser couplets of the poem, "Your Pow'r to Justice" and "Your Goodness only," works to subtly equate Charles's authority with a moral rather than a legal quality of virtue that, particularly in the seventeenth century, was ascribed to the divine.[15] Like the earlier reference to the medieval conception of the king as the "very Idea of Justice," the "Cause" or legitimacy of Charles's power derives from a transcendent notion of "Justice" that simultaneously grounds and exceeds the legal order it establishes (Kantorowicz 96). The metrical organization of this couplet—"Your Pow'r to Justice . . . doth submit your Cause / Your Goodness only . . . is above the Laws"—in effect opposes the divine jurisprudence in the first five syllables of each line to the legal framework articulated in the latter five. The tension that structures each line mirrors the more straightforward opposition between the message of legal conformity in the first line and of divine transgression in the second.

In both their form and content, Dryden's couplets express that capacity of the couplet form described by J. Paul Hunter in "Binarism and the Anglophone Couplet" (2000) as the power to "suspend opposing viewpoints . . . without choosing between them" (136). Rather than resolving the tension between divine and secular law, Dryden uses the formal power of the couplet to portray the lawlessness of the divine as the originary violence that allows the secular to exist as a stable system of order. As the figure for both, the king stands as a reminder that the law's highest form of expression is paradoxically its own transgression. Charles's preference for a policy of oblivion thus becomes a broader sign in Dryden's poem for the exceptional lawlessness that persists within the law as its contradictory yet nevertheless essential guarantee. In *Lines of Equity*, Visconsi highlights the disjunction between the merciful image of Charles in "To His Sacred Majesty" and his actual role in overseeing the period of "violent retribution" that followed the restoration of monarchy (19). Despite this apparent discordance between Charles's much-publicized mercy and his actual widespread use of extrajudicial violence, I would like to suggest that both of these actions conform to the same structural necessity that the king personify the law by exceeding it.

While placing characteristic emphasis on the union of king and nation in "To My Sacred Majesty," Dryden also represents these two as potentially divided with his image of the body politic as a savage multitude in need of the King's colonizing influence. The King's separation from the body politic assumes a racialized form in Dryden's depiction of his singular capacity for mercy:

> You for their Umpire and their Synod take,
> And their appeal alone to *Caesar* make.
> Kind Heav'n so rare a temper did provide
> That guilt repenting might in it confide.
> Among our crimes oblivion may be set,
> But 'tis our King's perfection to forget.
> Virtues unknown to these rough Northern climes
> From milder heav'ns you bring, without their crimes. (83–90)

With the third couplet's parallel first-person possessive formations—"our crimes" and "our King's"—Dryden establishes a familiar sense of political unity only to shatter it with the next couplet. In associating the King's heaven-endowed mercy with milder climates, which in the contemporary imagination meant imperial Rome, Dryden portrays the Restoration as a process of recolonization of a people who, according to a widely read contemporary book on climate theory, were "like Beasts, They are strong in their Passions, and Weak in those Faculties, that should controul, and keep them in."[16]

Rather than acting as a mere metaphor for the restoration of order, Dryden's typological correlation of the return of Charles to the throne with the Roman colonization of ancient Briton represents a pivotal step in portraying the divinely sanctioned English monarch as the planet's only legitimate source of authority. Dryden's correlation of Charles with Caesar in the lines quoted above marks an attempt to use the singularity of the king's exceptional status to establish an otherwise impossible line of descent from the consul of first-century BCE Rome to the monarch of seventeenth-century England.[17] In opposition to critics such as Laura Brown who read Dryden's invocations of Rome as a simple ideological effort to reinforce the legitimacy of a burgeoning British Empire, Paul Hammond argues in *Dryden and the Traces of Classical Rome* (1999) that the shift between present and past in Dryden is a movement of "deconstructive solicitation" that represents "a poetic rethinking of the language of the present by means of a turn towards those very foundations which contemporary culture had claimed for itself" (30). Although Dryden's career-long engagement with the image of Rome is indeed more complicated than a mere ideological confirmation of empire,

Hammond's attempt to distinguish the "reciprocal estranging" of modern and ancient in Dryden's work from the political significance of the name "Rome" in the dawning stages of the British Empire reflects a more fundamental problem with the way Derrida's central deconstructive notion of *différance* has been interpreted in the Anglophone world (30).

In imagining the "collocation" of ancient and modern in Dryden's work as somehow antithetical to the rhetoric of empire, Hammond mistakenly reads Derrida's critique of metaphysics as an inherently subversive political project, a reading Derrida and his followers encouraged. While Derrida, writing in the politically tumultuous moment of late 1960s France, indeed uses the language of revolt to introduce *différance*, his insistence on an originary state of difference in truth cannot be so easily applied to concrete political questions such as empire.[18] By simultaneously disrupting and deferring the metaphysical effort to locate a moment of full presence at the origin of being, Derrida challenges a "kingdom" of presence that has certainly inspired rhetoric on either side of the colonial question (60).[19] With his portrait of a king who is both within and beyond a society that is itself at once ancient and modern, Dryden demonstrates the possibility of putting the logic of difference to work on behalf of a colonial cause. Rather than deriving his authority from the metaphysical presumption of pure presence, the King in "To My Sacred Majesty" instead stands sovereign over the collective life of the English people precisely because he is *différance*.

By grounding the hopefulness of his early Restoration poems in a racialized disjunction between a sacred, Roman-derived King and the unruly natives whom he must colonize, Dryden not only employs a logic of difference, but also prepares the way for the depictions later in his career of the English body politic as an unredeemable force that can be contained only by the Hobbesian assertion of the sovereign's unconditional right to authority. Dryden's comparison, early in "Astraea Redux," of Civil War rebels to pre-Roman British tribes exemplifies how his effort to constitute a cohesive body politic with the king at its head begins with an assertion of the essential difference between these two entities:

> The Rabble now such Freedom did enjoy,
> As Winds at Sea that use it to destroy:
> Blind as the *Cyclops*, and as wild as he,
> They own'd a lawless savage Libertie,
> Like that our painted Ancestours so priz'd
> Ere Empires Arts their Breasts had Civiliz'd. (43–48)

By correlating the "rabble" of England's revolutionary period with the savage man of seventeenth-century state-of-nature theories, Dryden makes the English body politic the equivalent of the foreign populations confronted by Britain in its expanding colonial ventures. Given that Dryden frequently uses the sea as a metaphor for Britain's rise to a position of global dominance, most notably in "Annus Mirabilis" (1667), his metaphorical association of Civil War rebels' struggle for freedom with the "winds at Sea that use it [freedom] to destroy" reinforces the global scope of these domestic dissenters.[20] The sea becomes the basis for the global sovereignty that Dryden imagines in the final line of "Astraea Redux"—"the World a Monarch, and that Monarch *You*"—only through the transformation of this worldly rabble into indissociable elements of a global body politic anchored in the exceptional and divine status of England's king (323).

Dryden equates the English Civil War with contemporary revolts in the colonies, such as the Native American campaign against English settlers in 1675–76, and, in doing so, Dryden undermines the broad, now-familiar argument that a stable, premodern European self becomes unsettled only after its early modern confrontations with colonial others.[21] Dror Wahrman exemplifies this argument in affirming that "it was in the seventeenth- and eighteenth-century colonial context, as the shock effect of early encounters was superseded by sustained interaction and closer long-term familiarity" that the colonists lost confidence in the "identity categorizations that they had brought with them from the mother country" (213). Dryden's frequent depictions of the English rabble as primitive savages demonstrates the problem with this now-canonical mode of scholarship, which presupposes a stable English or European identity that precedes disorienting encounters with the colonized.[22] Rather than conceiving of the world in terms of the familiar metropole and the unfamiliar colonies, Dryden develops a cosmopolitan political theology that identifies anyone who opposes the divinely sanctioned mission of the one true authority as savage and thus in need of colonizing redemption.

Far from representing an anomaly, Dryden's primitivist depiction of the domestic rebels who "own'd a lawless savage Libertie" in England's revolutionary period reflects popular seventeenth-century opinion among the increasingly reform-minded English upper classes who began, in the words of one contemporary, to view the "commoners and cottagers" associated with the radicals of the Civil War as "generally Savage and Paganish" (Hoppit 352). Dryden's representations of the English rabble as foreign and premodern should, therefore, not be read as merely rhetorical flourishes, but, rather, as a sign that the English sense of self was plagued by the proximity of others from both within and without. This was a period, after all, that saw the widespread "othering" of native commoners and cottagers who resisted the colonization of the English countryside by refusing to relinquish their tradition-based claims to hold land in common. Viewed from the perspective of Dryden's political theology, the British colonial project represents an effort to constitute a pacified global body politic upon the basis of the English king's unique claim to a divinely sanctioned position of sovereignty. The English king stands for Dryden as a kind of world-less force that descends from a foreign, transcendental domain to redeem a country that remains as capable of premodern savagery as any of its colonies.

With its unsettled notion of English identity and emphasis on the sacred foundations of political power, Dryden's political theology may appear to twenty-first-century critics as simply a relic of premodern nationalist discourse. But to dismiss the contemporary relevance of Dryden's politics would be to miss the role they played in justifying not only England's early forays into colonization abroad, but also its domestic campaign to simultaneously colonize and modernize its own native savages. By helping to usher England into the age of modernity, Dryden's seemingly anachronistic political poetry demonstrates the inadequacy of the nineteenth-century narrative of modern development to the case of England itself. In the past forty years, critics, particularly those working on non-Western cultures, have challenged the idea that modernity necessarily entails embracing the triangulated forces of secularism, democracy, and capitalism.[23] What a close reading of Dryden adds to this conversation is the suggestion that an exemplary nation of European modernity, England, itself became modern through the force of God and king.

Writing with a fervor that is as messianic as it is modern, Dryden concludes the resurrection narrative of "Astraea Redux" by casting Charles as a figure as singular and totalizing as time itself:

> Abroad your Empire shall no Limits know,
> But like the Sea in boundless Circles flow.
> Your much lov'd Fleet shall with a wide Command
> Besiege the petty Monarchs of the Land:
> And as Old Time his Off-spring swallow'd down
> Our Ocean in its depths all Seas shall drown. (298–303)

The movement from the second-person possessive pronouns to the triumphant first-person plural possessive that begins the final line, "Our Ocean," provides a global image for the unification of the English body politic and king. In portraying this unified English body politic as the presumptive seat of global authority, Dryden establishes the contradiction that Laura Brown describes in her reading of "Annus Mirabilis" as the "image of a metropolis in which all the material desires of an expansionist culture are met *in situ*, without the need for travel or movement" (67). The typological association of "Our Ocean" with the Renaissance figure of Father Time, itself an amalgam of the Greek Gods Cronus and Chronos, explains this contradiction because it grounds the English claim to global sovereignty in its dynastic monarch's unique connection to the perpetuity of time itself. With the allusion to Cronus, a primeval Titan famous for swallowing his children, Dryden underlines the redemptive promise of his poem as a whole since Cronus was the precursor to the Romans' Saturn, whose return Dryden imagines in the messianic epigraph to his work. The reference to Chronos, the god of time, is even more important because it marks the extreme limit of the king's estrangement from the dynamics of collective life. Always doubled, the king moves through life as the expression of a space beyond it. He acts above all else as the representative of a sphere where continual change coheres into the totality of time. Dryden's portrait of an inert yet expansionist metropolis is thus something much more profound than a mere act of obfuscation, as Brown suggests. Instead, it is a fitting image for a nation whose totalizing claim over the movements of the world is rooted in its king's singular connection to the world-less immobility of eternity.

Democratizing the Divine and Making the Patriot

While Dryden's faith in the capacity of the unique status of the king to found a cohesive body politic certainly diminishes in the late 1670s and 1680s, his turn to the patriot in "To My Honour'd Kinsman" is less of a break from this earlier model as it is a new response to the same underlying problem: the mob. The fear that is already present in Dryden's depiction of the Civil War rabble in "Astraea Redux" becomes an insurmountable obstacle to Dryden's vision of the English elect embracing the paternal care of their sacred leader. William Dowling's assertion that the figure of the mob in "Absalom and Achitophel" is "a moral rather than a social category" demonstrates the tendency of critics to oversimplify Dryden's complicated mid-career shift in his political thinking (80).[24]

Although the portrait in "Absalom and Achitophel" of the English as "God's pampered people" indeed signals a real moral crisis, it also undeniably reflects the social and political upheavals of the "Exclusion Crisis" that shook England from 1678 to 1681, and Dryden—in a very personal way—in 1679 (47).

With Parliament attempting to interrupt the dynastic process of succession to ensure that Charles's Catholic brother James did not assume power, England in the late 1670s was on the brink of another civil war. In one of his more provocative political interventions, Dryden wrote a preface to Nahum Tate's play *The Loyal General* (1679) in which he compared exclusionist petitioners such as the Earl of Shaftsbury to the regicidal rebels of the 1640s. As retaliation, Dryden, according to the account provided by his biographer James Winn, was attacked by "three thugs with cudgels" who beat the "diminutive poet . . . senseless," leaving him with a "painful crippling of [the] limbs" that he was to suffer from for the rest of his life (325).[25] Dryden's autobiographical encounter with the violence of this period only underscores the need to read his shifting portraits of the mob as at least in part a reflection of social conditions.

In "Absalom and Achitophel," as well his other major Exclusion Crisis tract "The Medall," Dryden depicts the campaign to impose Charles's devoutly Protestant yet illegitimate son the Duke of Monmouth upon the throne as a sacrilegious struggle to use the brute force of the English mob to destroy the civilizing divinity of kingship. The movement to block the ascent of Charles's rightful heir becomes in Dryden's imagination the typological equivalent of Israel rejecting God's promise of a merciful new covenant. By pitting the savage power of the people against the redemptive force of dynastic continuity, exclusionist leaders were willfully obstructing an elect nation from achieving its prophesized salvation. In the following lines from "Absalom and Achitophel," Dryden envisions the triumph of the less than modern, undercolonized English mob as a rejection of God's gift of grace:

> What standard is there in a fickle rout,
> Which, flowing to the mark, runs faster out?
> Nor only crowds, but Sanhedrins may be
> Infected with this public lunacy
> And share the madness of rebellious times
> To murder monarchs for imagined crimes.
> If they may give and take whene'er they please,

> Not kings alone (the Godhead's images),
> But government itself at length must fall
> To nature's state, where all have right to all. (786-94)

Dryden names the anti-Papal crowds and Whiggish Parliament members who opposed the will of the King as modern-day Sanhedrins in order to represent the political refusal of the King's claim to incarnate the divine as a reenactment of this Jewish Council's decision to persecute rather than embrace the similar assertions of Christ. By using the language of scripture to privilege political fidelity over Protestants' religious concerns, Dryden underlines the centrality of the king to his own personal faith.

Given his long-standing commitment to the mythology of the English nation and king, Dryden's decision to convert to Catholicism following the ascent of a Catholic monarch in 1685 should hardly be surprising. Raised as a member of the Puritan gentry, Dryden began his political career by working for the Protectorate of Cromwell and wrote his first major poem, "Heroic Stanzas" (1659), as an elegy to the recently deceased rebel turned Lord Protector. In "Heroic Stanzas," Dryden celebrates Cromwell as one whose "grandeur deriv'd from Heav'n alone, / for he was great ere Fortune made him so" (21-22). One year later he would hail the return of England's dynastic king with even greater enthusiasm, and while the speed of this shift was an enduring source of embarrassment for Dryden, the idea that it indeed was a change is, in a certain sense, wrong. Dryden's faith in the power of sovereignty to unify the nation and sacralize the bodies of its mortal constituents remained constant. Dryden's religious affiliations—Puritan, Anglican, Catholic—shifted while the real underlying object of his faith stayed the same: it was the capacity for a heaven-derived sovereignty to redeem England and, through it, the world. As Dryden writes in "Heroic Stanzas," Cromwell, whose "count'nance did imprint an awe," moves through England, Scotland, Ireland, Europe, and South America bringing both conquest and peace for Cromwell fought "to civilize as [much as] to subdue" (73, 68).

The fear that Dryden expresses in "Absalom and Achitophel" is the same one that animates his "Heroic Stanzas." In "Absalom and Achitophel," Dryden warns of a "fickle rout" that will infect Parliament and "murder monarchs," just as he represents the crowd of the Interregnum in "Heroic Stanzas" as a threat to the salvation promised by Cromwell's burgeoning imperial order (785, 780).²⁶ Both spell despair because they challenge the exceptional, extrajudicial space of grace that gives the law its mystical foundation and the sovereign his second body. Dryden concludes his other major Exclusion Crisis work, "The Medall," with an image of the permanent state of unrest that would result from the evaporation of the law's paradoxically lawless foundation:

> Thus inborn broils the factions would engage,
> Or wars of exiled heirs, or foreign rage,
> Till halting vengeance overtook our age,
> And our wild labours, wearied into rest,
> Reclined us on a rightful monarch's breast. (318–22)

With the meaty phrase "inborn broils," Dryden describes the English body politic's descent into its native, "inborn" state of violence. Its redemption lies only in the inevitable embrace of a foreign yet somehow still native king. Dryden maintains his faith in the redemptive promise of this figure throughout his career; what he discovers in "To My Honour'd Kinsman" is simply the fruitfulness of democratizing it.

The tumult of the seventeenth century convinces the elder Dryden that the exceptional subjectivity of the king must become the shared burden of England's every constituent. In a shift that is in truth merely an extension of his early political theology, Dryden expands the collective second body of the king into the unruly sphere of the English body politic by constructing the novel figure of the patriot. As a new locus for the king's divine and corporate sovereignty, the patriot emerges both in reaction to the breakdown of dynastic succession in 1688 and, more broadly, as a means of finally perfecting the colonization of the mob that continually threatened to splinter the nation. With his much-needed revisionist claim that the often underappreciated Revolution of 1688 "was, like all other revolutions, violent, popular, and divisive," Steven Pincus has recovered the important role that the mob played in a revolution that had long been dismissed by historians as either, in Hoppit's words, a "Dutch invasion" or as, in Hill's, a largely bloodless "restoration of power to the traditional ruling class" (8, 3, 275). Instead of representing a mere "restoration" of traditional forms of order to a country wracked by the unrest of the Exclusion Crisis and the Duke of Monmouth's rebellion, the revolutionary movement against James II involved, as Pincus notes, "extensive mob violence," which "terrified local populations" and caused significant "damage to property and individuals" (223). Pincus's account sheds new light on Parliament's 1689 decision to offer the crown jointly to Charles's daughter Mary and her Dutch husband, William of Orange, while James remained in exile in France. Rather than simply marking a shift in its political calculations, this decision on the part of Parliament was in fact what Dryden feared: a capitulation to the supposedly "inborn" savagery of the English body politic.

Following the Revolution of 1688, Dryden loses the public posts of poet laureate and historiographer royal, faces double taxes as a Catholic, and is generally deprived of his once-prominent place in English society. Dynastic succession, the linchpin of Dryden's early political faith, also falls apart in this period with Parliament effectively controlling the process in 1689 and 1701. Dryden's decision, therefore, in the midst of all of this to modify his political theology and find a way to reconcile it with the modernization of England should be read as a remarkable testament to his faith in the possibility of a social redemption that was now as personal as it was political (435–36). In a certain sense, Dryden uses his own alienated position as a Catholic in the fiercely anti-Catholic climate of 1690s England as the basis for imagining the possibility of a patriot whose claim to sovereignty is rooted paradoxically in his withdrawal from the public domain of power.

Dryden's patriot emerges against the backdrop of a series of changes in the years following 1688, from the expansion of the state to improvements in river navigation, all of which unified England in a financial and material sense, enabling Dryden to conceive of a private rural individual holding sovereign political power. By reading the figure of the patriot that Dryden develops in this moment as a sign of the intensification rather than the diminution of the theologization of the political sphere, the rest of this chapter will challenge the canonical interpretation of the fate of political theology in this era, which Julian Hoppit nicely summarizes with the assertion that "the breaking of hereditary succession in 1689 and 1701 killed once and for all the belief that monarchs were descended transcendentally from God" (41). While such statements are in some sense true, they nevertheless obscure the way that the unconditional sovereignty that bound the king to the timeless sphere of the divine becomes the basis for the construction of the new biopolitical figure of the patriot. Rather than marking a break with political theology, the subsumption of the body politic by the mystical and corporate sovereignty of the nation, once reserved solely for the king, supports Pincus's assertion that "the issue in the later seventeenth century was not that religion came to mean less to English men and women but that it came to mean something different" (479).

Written as a commemoration of his cousin, Dryden's "To My Honour'd Kinsman, John Driden, of Chesterton in the County of Huntingdon, Esquire" represents the withdrawn life of this country gentleman, depicted in the poem's first half, as, paradoxically, the foundation for the new political individual imagined in the poem's later sections. Shortly before "To My Honour'd Kinsman" was published as part of the larger collection *Fables, Ancient and Modern* (1700), Dryden explained in a letter to the lord treasurer Charles Montague that he hoped to "have not only drawn the features of [his] worthy kinsman" in this late epistle, but to "have also given [his] Own opinion, of what an Englishman in Parliament ought to be" (quoted in Dearing 658). Although written to a member of William's government and thus clearly with a political purpose, Dryden's letter provides an essential insight into the poem by highlighting the way he applies the typological strategy that is so crucial to his early Restoration works to a distinctly nonroyal individual. By correlating his cousin's bare or basic life of rural retreat with the collective sovereignty embodied by the archetype of the "Englishman in Parliament," Dryden's poem redeploys the typological method in order to endow its addressee with the kind of doubled subjectivity that Dryden once reserved for kings.

Though "To My Honour'd Kinsman" remains suspended between the form of an ode and an epistle, its epistolary dimension has particular significance for the individual it helps construct because the epistle, in the early eighteenth century, perfectly embodied the paradoxical doubleness of this exemplary figure. As a public yet private letter composed in highly organized verse, Dryden's "To My Honour'd Kinsman" belongs to a tradition of eighteenth-century verse epistles that contain what Dowling terms a "double register," in that their form implies a community beyond the "epistolary exchange between letter-writer and addressee" (12). Authors of verse epistles, such as Pope, the Earl of Rochester, and Mary Leapor, responded to the modernization of English society by, in Dowling's words, "writing not merely epistles but verse epistles, poems in which the isolation symbolized by epistolary solitude is then opposed and redeemed by verse as an institutionalized mode of public utterance" (11). Dryden's "To My Honour'd Kinsman" helps inaugurate this tradition by articulating what is framed as a private letter to a family member in heroic couplets, the paradigmatic form of Dryden's broader English community.

Rather than simply opposing English modernity and the individualized life it heralds, Dryden, like the verse-epistle authors who follow him, relied on a particular rhetorical form to express the ambivalence of a solitude that at once isolates and ennobles. Dryden's turn to the verse epistle may in fact represent the crystallization of his lifelong effort to articulate a political faith that sees the private existence of the mortal body as the uncanny conduit for the public, political life of the nation. As a private letter that incarnates the collective identity of a community, "To My Honour'd Kinsman" manages to invest the implied solitude of the author as well as his addressee with the supremely public and sovereign status of the example. In this way, Dryden's poem embodies the paradox of exemplarity that Agamben describes in *Homo Sacer* as arising from the fact that "the example steps out of its class in the very moment in which it exhibits and delimits it" (22).

Dryden's poem uses the isolation and distance inherent in both epistles and rural spaces to construct a subject whose claim to sovereignty is grounded in the fact that he ultimately does not belong to either the private or public domains of mortal English life. Strange as it may seem, it is Dryden's political mysticism that makes him and not Milton the poet of England's future. While Dryden's model of the country gentleman clearly draws from key seventeenth-century traditions important to Milton—principally, civic republicanism and a kind of Christian Stoicism—the guiding intellectual light of Dryden's poem is English nationalism. The godly English nation becomes the principle upon which one exercises the self-governance of a republican Stoic hero. Other traditions do not so much disappear in Dryden as accumulate a new national purpose, a return, in a way, to the Stoic nationalism advocated by the great epic of imperial Rome, Virgil's *Aeneid* (29–19 BCE). Dryden's cousin emerges, then, from his poem as a hero simultaneously of Christianity, Stoic republicanism, and biopolitical nationalism.

Dryden opens "To My Honour'd Kinsman" by making a dual allusion to the first Psalm of Scripture and the second epode of Horace. Taken together, these allusions establish an opposition between divine authority and rural retreat that structure the withdrawn politics of the work as a whole: "How Bless'd is He, who leads a Country Life, / Unvex'd with anxious Cares, and void of Strife!"[27] Beyond the explicit biblical and Horatian allusions, the themes of rural retreat and moral contentment in this couplet echoes Dryden's earlier translations of fragments from Lucretius's *De rerum natura* and Virgil's *Georgics*, both of which appeared alongside his Horatian translations in the collection *Sylvae* (1685). While "To My Honour'd Kinsman" clearly continues Dryden's long-standing interest in classical celebrations of rural life, it lends further credence to Hammond's argument that "it is not primarily the rural life as such which attracts Dryden . . . rather it is the mode of life which the countryside makes possible, the life of freedom from care and disturbance" (171). Dryden effectively dematerializes the rural by transforming it into a symbol of the Epicurean and Lucretian notion of *ataraxia*, or the unperturbed state beyond pleasure and pain, that acts as the basis for his politics of engaged withdrawal.

By conferring a state of blessedness on this condition of withdrawn contentment, the opening couplet of "To My Honour'd Kinsman" grounds the pagan ideal of ataraxia in the Judeo-Christian realm of the divine. In doing so, it infuses rural life with the supreme sovereignty of a monotheistic God. Dryden uses the remoteness of the ancients, like the geography of the rural and the form of the private letter, as a means of simultaneously transcending and reinforcing England's modernizing post-1688 society. Dryden conceives of the patriot as opposed to present-day society only in order to ensure that he possesses the oppositional tension necessary to assume sovereignty over that society.

According to the logic of Dryden's poem, his cousin represents an exemplar of the collective and immortal sovereignty of the nation precisely because he pursues a calculated withdrawal from the very domains in which sovereignty is typically thought to reside. Beyond simply acting as an allegory for the political program envisioned in the second half of the poem, Dryden's depiction of his cousin's withdrawn relationship to the marital, judicial, medical, economic, and recreational domains of life in his poem's first half expresses the doubleness of an existence that is at once mortal and divine. In the first reference to Driden's crucial typological relationship to a prelapsarian Adam, Dryden suggests that his cousin's withdrawal from the marital state allows him to remain in the paradise of God's eternal garden:

> Promoting Concord, and composing Strife,
> Lord of your self, uncumber'd with a Wife;
> Where, for a Year, a Month, perhaps a Night,
> Long Penitence succeeds a short Delight:

> Minds are so hardly match'd, that ev'n the first,
> Though pair'd by Heav'n, in Paradise, were curs'd. (17–22)

The isolation of "Lord of your self" in the second line emphasizes that Driden achieves the reconciliation described in the first line only by refusing to assume the dynastic position of authority signified by the two secular definitions of "Lord" as the head of the state or household. To solidify his separation from the dynastic lineage that dominates the state and the home, Dryden correlates his cousin in the following section of the poem with the feminized and insurrectionary second son of Isaac in the Old Testament: "But you, like *Jacob*, are *Rebecca's* Heir" (43). As a bachelor and second son who inherited property from his mother, John Driden lent himself to Dryden's efforts to expand the dynastic sovereignty of the nation into the feminized and withdrawn domain of biological life.[28]

While my interpretation of "To My Honour'd Kinsman" is indebted to McKeon's "The Politics of Pastoral Retreat" (2004), I cannot endorse his assertion that the "displacement" of Dryden's cousin from "the paternal line" allows him to experience the "freedom entailed in the lineage of liberty" (103, 104). This assertion represents a crucial misreading of the poem because it overlooks the way the phrase "Lord of your self" maintains the unconditional sovereignty of the paternal line only in a new, biopolitical form. In democratizing divine sovereignty and immersing it in the private, biological recesses of everyday life, Dryden begins to sketch a political horizon in which all bodies are ideally sovereign subjects, free from all paternal authority except the divine one, that supreme kernel of premodern transcendence that endows every enfranchised body with its sovereign national core.

By typologically casting his cousin as the antitype of prelapsarian man, Dryden helps to inaugurate a modernity that is far from the unambiguous break with paternal sovereignty that McKeon's reading would suggest. In Dryden's early poems, the unity, innocence, and immortality of Eden emanate solely from the divine figure of the King, whereas, in "To My Honour'd Kinsman," they spring from both King and patriot. Dryden's correlation of his cousin's charity with God's gift of manna in *Exodus*—"so free to Many, to Relations most, / You feed with Manna your own *Israel*-Host"—recalls Dryden's earlier image in "To His Sacred Majesty" of Charles's generosity: "As Heav'n of old dispenc'd Celestial dew, / You give us Manna and still give us new" (48–49, 23–24).[29]

The withdrawn country gentleman joins the restored king as a novel site for the dispensation of God's grace.

The private individual is capable of being a new source of manna for the nation because his withdrawn relationship to the different domains of private life allows him to reside simultaneously in the paradise of Eden and in the fallen world of late seventeenth-century England. After his biblically and pagan-inspired panegyric on "country life" in the poem's first stanza, Dryden begins his depiction of his cousin's engaged withdrawal in the second stanza with a portrait of Driden's role as a justice of peace in Huntingdonshire that ironically centers on his renunciation of the legal system.[30] Just as the King exemplifies the law by exceeding it with transgressive acts of grace, cousin Driden stands as a paragon of justice by settling disputes without recourse to the "Expence of long Litigious Laws" (11). Dryden's celebration of his cousin's charity and domestic tranquility in the following two sections of the poem follow the same logic in that his withdrawal from the paternal roles of father, husband, and firstborn is precisely what allows him to perfect his paternal function as a divinely sanctioned leader of the body politic. While lauding his cousin's fidelity to the central Christian—and, especially, Catholic—value of charity, Dryden establishes the essential, causal link between his cousin's distance from patriarchal positions of authority and his proximity to the timeless space of the divine. The conjunction of this feminized second son's maternal inheritance and God's plan in the couplet "Heav'n, who foresaw the Will, the Means has wrought, / And to the Second Son, a Blessing brought" clarifies the religious significance of the restrained relationship to hunting and health that Dryden represents in the final two sections of the first half of the poem (41–42).

By referring back to his transgressive perfection of the legal and domestic spheres, Dryden's depiction of his cousin's restrained yet active relationship to hunting and modern medicine unify the first half of the poem in preparation for its culminating image of eternal Edenic life in the poem's second half. While the frequent hunting of Driden's youth works as a metaphor for his passion for justice and "the common good," the "restrain'd" hunting of his later years represents his fidelity to the habits of the "long-liv'd Fathers" of the Old Testament (53, 59, 88). Mirroring his relationship to the law, Driden perfects modern medicine by rendering it unnecessary: "Better to hunt in Fields, for Health unbought, / Than fee the Doctor for a nauseous Draught" (92–93). In exercising Epicurean restraint and not seeking "Pleasure thro' Necessity,"

Driden maintains an exceptional relationship to the expanding industries of recreation and health, both of which were a part of England's transformation in the late seventeenth century (68). This exceptional relationship, which Driden seems to cultivate with all the modernizing spheres of English life, endows him with a subjectivity whose doubleness renders it capable of existing both within and beyond the mortal realm of time.

Although Dryden's epistle draws heavily from Horace's second epode, particularly in the opening stanza, its transformation of the withdrawn space of rural paradise into an essential element of Dryden's political theology represents a significant departure from Horace's tale of an urban moneylender's failed attempt to adopt a country life. The central Edenic imagery of Dryden's poem translates the pastoral scenes of Horace's *Epode* into the timeless space of the divine:

> The Tree of Knowledge, once in *Eden* plac'd,
> Was easie found, but was forbid the Taste:
> O, had our Grandsire walk'd without his Wife,
> He first had sought the better Plant of Life! (96–99)

In withdrawing from the sensual domain of taste and the patriarchal realm of marriage, and thus avoiding the plight of Adam, the patriot Driden manages to gain access to the "Plant of Life," or the immortal realm of sovereignty previously reserved for kings alone.

Horace's second epode tells the story of a moneylender who ultimately fails to remain within a proverbial Epicurean garden, and what Dryden finds in this narrative is a positive possibility for blending rural innocence with urban power. Dryden uses the failure of Horace's moneylender as a means of infusing the rural private life of the English body politic with the supremely public force of sovereignty. In doing so, Dryden helps define the terms of a new biopolitical modernity, which, as Agamben argues, centers above all else on making indistinguishable "the classical distinctions between *zoe* and *bios*, between private life and political existence, between man as a simple living being at home in the house and man's political existence in the city" (*Homo Sacer* 187). Given that both law and medicine were associated in the late seventeenth century with England's burgeoning urban culture, Dryden's particular emphasis on his cousin's simultaneous perfection and transgression of these specifically urban professions suggests that the withdrawn yet engaged life of the first half of the poem perfects in advance the urban, political life of the poem's second half.[31]

As Alan Roper notes in *Dryden's Poetic Kingdoms* (1965), Dryden accomplishes the transition between the two halves of his poem by playfully reiterating the "ancient analogy between human and political bodies" (125). The separation of his cousin's individual body from the broader body politic serves in the following lines to legitimate his status as an exemplary member of that very body:

> You hoard not Health, for your own private Use;
> But on the Publick spend the rich Produce:
> When, often urg'd, unwilling to be great,
> Your Country calls you from your lov'd Retreat,
> And sends to Senates, charg'd with Common Care,
> Which none more shuns; and none can better bear. (117–22)

With the crucial verb "shuns," Dryden alludes to his earlier celebration of his cousin's decision to "shun the Married State" and thereby underscores the importance of his cousin's withdrawal from a domestic sphere that functioned in this period as an allegory—most prominently in the writings of the royalist Robert Filmer—for the unconditional and divine authority of the king (34). Dryden's insistence that "none more shuns" the burden of sovereignty only further emphasizes his cousin's exceptional relationship to the English body politic. By withdrawing from a position of paternal authority as well as from the professions of law and medicine, Driden achieves a level of separation from late seventeenth-century society that approaches that of the dynastic king. By gaining access to the "lov'd Retreat" of prelapsarian paradise, Driden's individual body is, like the medieval king that Kantorowicz uncovers, raised to the "angelic heights" of the "immutable within Time" (9, 8). The individual body of the withdrawn patriot achieves the status of exemplarity and joins the dynastic king as an at once singular and collective being. The repetition of consonants in the final couplet of the lines above—"And sends to Senates, charg'd with Common Care, / Which none more shuns; and none can better bear"—expresses the cohesiveness and fluidity of a nation sustained by a collectivity of exemplary individuals.

The arcadia Dryden imagines in the latter half of "To My Honour'd Kinsman" springs from the divine grace of both king and patriot. The Edenic imagery of Dryden's poem culminates only when the patriot completes the process of transforming the unruly elect into a cohesive whole:

> A Patriot, both the King and Country serves;
> Prerogative, and Privilege preserves:
> Of Each, our Laws the certain Limit show;
> One must not ebb, nor t'other overflow:
> Betwixt the Prince and Parliament we stand;
> The Barriers of the State on either Hand:
> May neither overflow, for then they drown the Land.
> When both are full, they feed our bless'd Abode;
> Like those, that water'd once, the Paradise of God. (171–79)

While McKeon is certainly right to observe that Dryden is "defining the terms of an emergent system of parliamentary democracy" in stanzas such as the one above, his assertion that parliament becomes "hard . . . to distinguish" from the "*national* collective" misses the real foundation of Dryden's call for sacred unity (108, 107). The first-person plural pronouns that, as McKeon notes, "proliferate" in this stanza construct a cohesive national collective not through the mediating work of Parliament, but through the exceptional and sacred foundation of the patriot's second body (107). With the indefinite article in the isolated phrase that begins these lines—"a Patriot"—Dryden portrays this exemplary figure as simultaneously singular and capable of limitless reproduction on a global scale. In balancing royal prerogative and parliamentary privilege, the patriot constructs "an emergent system of parliamentary democracy" that reinforces rather than undermines the global reach of the premodern sovereignty that had long elevated mortal English bodies to the angelic height of being an individual.

By articulating his new utopian political vision through the agricultural imagery of a running river, Dryden carefully recalls and rewrites the darker pastoral scene that the poet John Denham sketches in "Cooper's Hill" during the early stages of the English Civil War. Although the classical notion of *concordia discors*, or the harmonization of opposing natural forces, animates a yearning for political reconciliation in both poems, Denham chooses to undermine this utopian impulse by culminating "Cooper's Hill" with its "calm River" becoming a "Torrent" and then a "Deluge" (349, 356). Yearning for a harmonization that it ultimately portrays as impossible, "Cooper's Hill" exhibits a skepticism fitting for a monarchist work published just days before the start of the Civil War. In reproducing Denham's imagery of a river that threatens to "o'reflows th'adjoyning Plains," Dryden returns to the tumultuous 1640s in the hopes of articulating the definitive means of escaping them (350). To fulfill the utopian narrative that Denham leaves in a state of incompletion, Dryden adds the new figure of the "patriot" to a political landscape that had included only a king and his subjects. As he does on behalf of the King in "Astraea Redux" and "To His Sacred Majesty," Dryden uses the couplet's synthetic capacities to construct a mediating figure who, in this case, reconciles the opposing forces of the king and the people. While both Denham's and Dryden's models of political harmony rely on the ability of couplets to hold competing concepts in metrical unity, only Dryden exploits this formal capacity as an instrument for political innovation. Having solidified and perfected the preestablished figure of the king in Dryden's early work, the couplet becomes the means in Dryden's later poems for constructing a new political character. The patriot celebrated in the stanza quoted above fulfills Denham's vision of political moderation by incarnating the fraught doubleness of the couplet form itself.

As a figure of political moderation and sacralization simultaneously, the patriot stands on both sides of the canonical opposition between the metaphysical poetry of the early seventeenth century and the rhymed couplets of the century's final decades.[32] Although the rhymed couplet indeed seems to avoid the enthusiasm that springs from the internalized locus of truth in the metaphysical poetry and sectarian religious writings of the first half of the century, the patriot's proximity to the absolute space of the divine suggests that the late century couplet remains closer than it may at first appear to the preskeptical epistemology of the Civil War period. In Dryden's particular recovery of Denham's pastoral allegory of political moderation, the couplet indeed fulfills the possibility for harmonized discord, but it does so paradoxically by expanding the very forces of enthusiasm and absolutism that had long functioned as the enemy of political mediation and balance.

In the final couplet of the stanza quoted above—"When both are full, they feed our bless'd Abode; / Like those, that water'd once, the Paradise of God"—the patriot perfects a seemingly modern system of political mediation by extending rather than abandoning the premodern struggle to turn a collection of profane bodies into a sacred and unified whole. The essential function of the exemplary individual in accomplishing the sacralization of the national collective provides the clearest possible refutation of Zwicker's attempt to oppose "national election" to "individual grace" (*Dryden's Political Poetry* 120). Rather than marking the decline of Dryden's "faith in the nation as a covenanted people," as Zwicker claims, Dryden's turn to private individuals is precisely what allows him to rearticulate his vision of a harmonious body politic upon modified yet equally sacred grounds (102). With the phrase "our bless'd Abode," Dryden underlines the new importance of the withdrawn and prepolitical life of the home to this modified but still sacred national unity. The verb "feed" in the couplet's first line continues the agricultural imagery of the stanza, but also accentuates the foundation of the nation's theological identity, its "bless'd Abode," in the bare life of its individual members. Although it is "Prince and Parliament" that "feed" this "bless'd Abode," it is the engaged withdrawal of the patriot that blesses or consecrates this collective home as a sacred object capable of participating in a new political Eden. The patriot transforms the ominous river in "Cooper's Hill" that "knows no bound" into a symbol of the simultaneously technical and sacred management of the English body politic (358).

Despite the appearance of opposition, the exemplary patriot stands in the final three stanzas of "To My Honour'd Kinsman" as the ultimate guarantee of the king's right to suspend the law. As Dryden writes,

> Some Overpoise of Sway, by Turns they share;
> In Peace the People, and the Prince in War:
> Consuls of mod'rate Pow'r in Calms were made;
> When the *Gauls* came, one sole Dictator sway'd. (180–84)

Since the King retains his right to act as the "one sole Dictator" in states of emergency, the question is how to reconcile the preservation of absolute sovereignty with the rights and liberty granted to the patriot in the poem's final two stanzas. In contrast to the centrality of the King in the conclusions of "Astraea Redux" and "To His Sacred Majesty," the final two stanzas of "To My Honour'd Kinsman" instead celebrate the "Patriot Line" of the Dridens, who have over the course of several generations protected the "Birthright Liberty," laws, and "Common Cause" of the English people (195, 193, 190). Rather than representing some sort of logical lapse, the tension between the innate liberty of the individual and the continuing sovereignty of the King that Dryden expresses in these lines reflects the politics of his moment—namely, the development of a form of sovereignty that incorporates rather than opposes the liberty of its subjects.

With his vision of a body politic composed of free individuals who remain nevertheless subjected to the ultimate sovereignty of a single person in moments of crisis, Dryden sketches the terms of a new strategy of governance that takes the social body not as something that must be constructed, but that instead must be managed. In conceiving of the "Birthright Liberty" of the patriot as a part of the harmonization of the English body politic, Dryden outlines one of the key characteristics that Foucault, in *Security, Territory, Population* (1978), ascribes to the "mechanisms of security" that emerge in eighteenth-century Europe as a new means of managing the burdens of governance (8).[33] Rather than approaching the national collective as a product of state intervention, as the constitutionalists of the English Civil War period believed, the partisans of security insist on viewing the body politic as a civil society, which Foucault defines as a "specific field of naturalness peculiar to man" (349). The conjunction of individual liberty and greater social cohesion in Dryden's poem gives credence to Foucault's insight that, in spite of the appearance of opposition, civil society "emerges as the vis-à-vis of the state," a counterpart whose management marks the defining task of modern governance (349, 350). For this new mode of political management, "failing to respect freedom" and the "right of individuals legitimately opposed to power" becomes "not only an abuse of rights with regard to the law," but also, and most important, a demonstration of "ignorance of how to govern properly" (353). Although Foucault will characterize the development of this modern state as a move away from theological notions of sovereignty, Dryden's vision of a new political Eden rooted in the prepolitical life of its populace underlines the persistence of theology in a process of politicization that entails subsuming social constituents within the sovereignty of kings (247).

Making the Individual, Saving the Nation, and Fearing the Prostitute

While the relationship of "To My Honour'd Kinsman" to the transformation of the art of governance in late seventeenth-century England could be approached from many directions, I would like to briefly touch on its connection to the Societies for the Reformation of Manners (SRM). As evangelical groups that sought to impose juridical rather than ecclesiastical mechanisms of justice upon specifically urban vice, the SRM dramatized the theological underpinnings of the secularization of political authority in this period. Active from 1690 to 1738, the SRM used a network of informants to encourage the prosecution of vice associated with a rising urban population, particularly in London.[34] The SRM reflected, according to the sociologist Alan Hunt's *Governing Morals* (1999), a "theological trend" of focusing on the "responsibilisation of the laity" (30). With their grassroots network of legal informants, the SRM sought to ensure that the members of the elect nation were obeying the intertwined spheres of national law and God's covenant.

Responding to the same theological and political dilemma that animated Dryden's late turn to the figure of the patriot, the SRM sought to transform the mobile and often unruly urban poor into individuals who exemplified "manners," which in this period connoted "not only the rules of moral conduct, but [also] the dispositions, attitudes, and practices that marked civilized conduct and theological conformity" (Hunt 30). As their printed handbooks and sermons attest, the SRM unified a diverse group of members, including dissenters as well as Anglicans, around a shared commitment to seeing secular and religious law as indistinguishable. Published as a pocket-sized book in 1698, the prominent Anglican divine Josiah Woodward's *An Account of the Rise and Progress of the Religious Societies in the City of London* typifies the way SRM preachers viewed human law as synonymous with God's order: "And where the Informer, or the Magistrate, fails in their respective Duty, Justice is obstructed, the Efficacy of the Law null'd, Iniquity cherished, and the Wrath of God provoked" (67–68). The universality of God's authority not only transforms the enforcement of civil laws into a religious duty, but also effaces the distinction between public officials and private citizens, since both are equally subject to the totalizing authority of the divine. Through grounding the laws of the state in the sovereignty of God, Woodward and other SRM-affiliated preachers construct a distinctly modern political theology that emphasizes the importance of an individual's behavior in the private sphere to the cohesion and salvation of the nation as a whole. While high-church members of the SRM such as John Mapletoft, godson of the revered Nicholas Ferrar of Little Gidding, will continue to insist that "God is more properly . . . honoured by . . . our Common and united rather than by our Private Addresses," the SRM's actual activities display an unambiguous preoccupation with individuals' private conduct (12). By subsuming both private and political life in the totalizing scope of God's authority, the SRM, in the words of Hunt, "engaged in the regulation of 'social before the social'" (29).

In conceiving of England as a potentially global population bound together by the universal sovereignty of the divine, the sermons of the SRM invest the individual members of this body politic with the task of achieving the doubled existence of an exemplary individual who both resides in and exceeds the private domains of economic life. Although John Mapletoft holds to the canonical insistence on the necessity of public devotion, he locates the basis of this public devotion in the very much private act of internalizing the power of the divine. In the same sermon in which he privileges "Common" forms of worship over privates ones, Mapletoft asserts: "We do then honour God, when all the inward Affections and Dispositions of our Souls are centered upon God, ... when we live under a constant, awful Regard to his All-seeing Eye, ... When we esteem and love him as the Sovereign Good" (7). Through internalizing the "All-seeing Eye" of God, a previously undifferentiated member of the body politic becomes an exemplary individual endowed with the doubled existence of an at once mortal and immortal being. Mapletoft underlines the exemplary function of the true believer with his emphasis later in the sermon that "we do honour God most signally, when we make that Regard we have for him ... evident to others" who then "may be brought over to the Obedience of the Faith" (9, 10). By encouraging his followers to become public exemplars of an internalized faith, Mapletoft, a staunch Anglican, demonstrates the stubborn persistence of enthusiasm within even the most polite forms of Protestant thought. Once living under the "constant ... All-seeing Eye" of God, the English layperson achieves the elevated and enthusiastic existence of one in direct contact with absolute truth. Despite attempting to combat the potentially destabilizing effects of religious enthusiasm, the SRM, like other Protestant groups, cannot resist calling on its members to act as the unmediated representatives of divine truth.

While Mapletoft clearly perceived the exemplary individual his sermons helped constitute as a political and theological necessity, it was left to lower-church SRM ministers such as John Woodhouse to more clearly enunciate the stakes of creating this new entity. At the conclusion of a sermon that begins with the blunt assertion that the "exemplary piety" of SRM members shows the "World that Divine Service is not confined to Consecrated Places," Woodhouse articulates the essential political function of the modern individual within a truly harmonized

English body politic: "If you will not up to your Work, for God's sake, for your Neighbor's sake, for your Nation's sake, for Posterity's sake, do it for the King's sake: For if we still do wickedly, *Both we, and our King shall perish*" (5.50). Woodhouse's sweeping sermon sketches the providential economy of a modern era in which the "immaterial labor" of subjectivity, as the Italian philosopher Maurizio Lazzarato terms it, becomes responsible for preserving the collective sovereignty of the nation (133). By constituting themselves as individuals subjected to the authority of God, the previously undifferentiated members of the English laity transform the political theology of the nation into the sovereign principle of their being.

Although committed in theory to converting every English body, the SRM exhibited grossly disproportionate attention in practice to the single figure of the female street prostitute. Records from the over one hundred thousand prosecutions that the SRM pursued during their active years indicate that that the majority of these prosecutions targeted "lewd and disorderly practices," an offense that most likely referred to female street prostitution (Hunt 28, 45). In dedicating his account of the SRM to the citizens of London, Josiah Woodward asks them to view their city's sex workers as the greatest threat to national salvation: "How long shall those worse than *Midianitish Women* be a Plague and Reproach to your City? How long shall they be tolerated to spread their Nets in the very Streets, yea, before the Sun; and to bring their Rottenness into the very Bones of so many Persons and Families?" (vi). While the potential for prostitutes to spread syphilis and other diseases into the "very Bones" of good English families warrants, for a moral reformer like Woodward, some concern, it is their significance to political theology that truly captures the attention of the SRM. By encouraging the elect nation of Israel to begin worshipping multiple, foreign gods, the Midianite women of the Old Testament threatened its covenant with a singular God.[35] Woodward equates the prostitute with these pagan seductresses because they challenge the monotheism of God's new elect nation with the pantheism of the economic system they heralded: commercialism.

Like the figure of the slave discussed in chapter 4, the prostitute represents a constant object of fascination for eighteenth-century British authors, a foil against which a new conception of the self is made. From Dryden's patriot to the SRM's vigilant believer, the aim of eighteenth-century individualism is to transform the amorphous early modern body politic into a collection of self-possessed subjects—"Lord of your self," in the words of Dryden. Within such a framework, the prostitute, like the slave, appears as a portent of commercial dispossession. As Laura Rosenthal shows in *Infamous Commerce* (2006), the prostitute provided contemporary onlookers with "both an assuring alterity and anxious potential for self-recognition" (7). Prostitutes were roving signifiers of an economy in which people and things were measured by abstract economic value rather than custom. "Prostitution becomes," as Thomas Laqueur writes in *Making Sex* (1990), "like usury, a metaphor for the unnatural multiplication not of things but of signs without referent" (232). The prostitute signifies the pantheism of the commodity form, a phenomenon that later inspires Marx to represent the commodity as an occult figure, a *gespenstige Gegenständlichkeit*, or "phantom objectivity," that seduces consumers into mistaking its dazzling appearance as the source of real value (*Capital* 128). Like the mob that menaced Dryden throughout his career, the commodity is a sign of anti-individualist dispossession, and it is against this threat that authors ranging from Dryden to Edgeworth will build a new and modern definition of the British subject.

The Effigy of the Modern Self

In the final stanza of "To My Honour'd Kinsman," Dryden represents the higher second body of the patriot as a living effigy to the immortality of the nation. Having absorbed the sovereignty of the Church, this higher second body is what allows the patriot to participate in a commercializing society while nevertheless remaining safely beyond it. The national soul of the patriot is a work of art, and in the conclusion of his poem, Dryden emphasizes the poet's role in fashioning it:

> For ev'n when Death dissolves our Humane Frame,
> The Soul returns to Heav'n, from whence it came;
> Earth keeps the Body, Verse preserves the Fame. (206–9)

The opposition of corporeal mortality and ethereal transcendence in the first two lines establishes the expectation that the evenly balanced final line will neatly summarize the duality of body and soul. By establishing this expectation, Dryden highlights the incongruity of his final phrase, "Verse preserves the Fame," which opposes the mortality of the body to the constructed immortality of "Fame" rather than to the purely transcendent immortality of the heavens.[36] Dryden in effect moves from repeating Ecclesiastes's statement against vanity ("All go to one place"), invoked in the first line of this triplet, to echoing Horace's distinctively pagan assertion of fame as a monument "more enduring than bronze" (Ecc. 3:20). In suggesting that verse preserves the immortality of fame, Dryden portrays his poem and indeed writing in general as a means to perpetuate the immortality of the patriot's both mortal and transcendent second body.

Dryden thus infuses writing with the same "secular magic" that the literary critic Joseph Roach ascribes to the rituals and regalia that endow the monarch with "two bodies, the body which decays and dies, and the body cinematic, which does neither" (3, 36). The withdrawn self of the patriot that remains forever in the prelapsarian garden assumes responsibility for the national collective once it adorns its mortal frame with the regalia of the modern individual. And throughout his late writing, from the "Ode to Anne Killigrew" in 1686 to "To My Honour'd Kinsman" in 1700, Dryden aims to provide his readers with precisely such garb. Dryden offers the monument of a poem to anybody willing to incarnate the doubled being of its language.

Although Dryden clearly touches on the ambiguity of a divine immortality embodied in mere things, the "secular magic" of the king and the modern subject remains in the end dependent upon the transcendent domain of the divine. From his early Restoration poems to his later poetic addresses to individuals, Dryden pursues different rhetorical strategies for securing the unity of the English body politic on transcendental grounds not in order to demystify the sovereignty of God, but to give it a new world in which to play. And this is the lesson with which this book begins: the modern subject and the sovereignty of kings are one and the same. In Dryden's poetry, one witnesses the formation of a modern individual upon the foundation of the king. Dryden invests his patriot with the same transcendent "Common Cause" that gave Charles his "more Sacred head."

In our twenty-first-century moment—with Guantanamo Bay, extrajudicial wars and assassinations, and emergency laws in France, the United Kingdom, and the United States—it is clear that the sovereign state of exception, in which a single person suspends the law in the name of saving the law, represents an essential element of modern Western governance. The continuity of the patriot and the king in Dryden's poetry illuminates from the vantage point of Western modernity's origins what the new titles of "Prime Minister" and "President" have obscured:

that the antidemocratic sovereignty of kings persists in our supposedly democratic present. Beneath the appearance of opposition, the leader who decides on the state of exception and the rights-bearing liberal individual are part of the same political matrix. While the third and fourth chapters of this book delineate the freedom that this modern subjection makes possible, these opening two chapters on Dryden and Pope are dedicated to tracing its early formation in the conservative antimodern verse of the British Tory Augustans.

2

The Domestic Novel's First Heroine

Alexander Pope and the Construction of a National Theological Subject

Dryden, Pope, and the Domestic Novel

In the two poems at the center of these opening two chapters, Dryden's "To My Honour'd Kinsman" and now Pope's "Windsor Forest," Dryden and Pope create neoclassical heroes—the patriot and the poet, respectively—whose subjectivities anticipate one of the great figures of individualism in all of eighteenth-century British writing: the protagonist of the domestic novel. The domestic novel has many origins, but a central aim of this chapter will be to demonstrate that a crucial and overlooked source for the selfhood at the center of these works is the heroically individuated, discursively defined, and thoroughly nationalized identities of the English Tory Augustans. In the previous chapter I represented Dryden's patriot as a paradoxical figure of modern subjecthood because he embodies an increasingly individualistic culture by remaining apart from it. The patriot shuns marital and "civil strife," opting instead for a "country life," a position that ironically endows him with the self-possession and independence necessary to exemplify the individualistic values of the very modernizing society he eschews (3,1). Like the heroines of domestic novels from Samuel Richardson's *Clarissa* to Fanny Burney's *Cecilia* (1782), Dryden's patriot cultivates an exemplary, modern self through his struggle to maintain the integrity of his rural, premodern virtue.

What separates Dryden's patriot from the protagonists of Richardson and Burney, however, is that he maintains a prenovelistic relationship to language. Although Dryden concludes "To My Honour'd Kinsman" by asserting the immortality of verse, declaring that "Earth keeps the body [while] Verse preserves the Fame," he nevertheless retains a subordinate image of language as a secondary reflection of a nonlinguistic original (209). In the final stanza of "To My Honour'd Kinsman," Dryden celebrates verse while also addressing his cousin as its extradiscursive point of origin:

> Vouchsafe this picture of thy soul to see;
> 'Tis so far good, as it resembles thee:
> The beauties to th' Original I owe,
> Which, when I miss, my own defects I show. (197–200)

Dryden thus hails the moral and aesthetic value of his verse as a monument not to language, but to the "Original" that inspires it (198–99). While the patriot's at once withdrawn and exemplary subjectivity undoubtedly helps to carve out the interiority of domestic novel protagonists, he nevertheless stands at a distance from epistolary heroines who use their "natural talent" for letters to constitute rather than reflect reality (*Clarissa* 1368). It is, in other words, an ideology of language as representation that separates the patriot from his domestic novel successors. The heroines of domestic novels are characters who both inspire and compose language, a position they exploit in order not only to constitute ideal readers, from Mr. B to John Belford, but also, and even more important, to remake themselves as exemplary subjects of virtue.

In this chapter, I move to the poetry of Pope because it is Pope's self-reflexive figure of the poet who turns the oppositional subjectivity of Dryden's patriot into a proper domestic novel protagonist. From the early panegyric "Windsor Forest" to the biting satires of the 1730s, Pope spends his career extending the royal bifurcated being of the patriot to the supremely withdrawn yet triumphantly engaged figure of the author. I focus on "Windsor Forest" because it is here that Pope most clearly ties the heroically individuated and discursively centered subjectivity of the author to the theological destiny of the British nation, a conjunction that is essential to the new conception of the subject that emerges in this period. Originally written alongside his youthful pastorals sometime between 1704 and 1707 and then expanded to commemorate the impending Treaty of Utrecht in 1713, "Windsor Forest" has struck many readers as a clumsy work of Tory propaganda, a tired reiteration of the oft-repeated trope of England as God's new Israel. While Pope certainly draws from the nationalized theological rhetoric that flourished in the seventeenth century, he also innovates by rearticulating the poetics of biblical typology through the protomodern frame of a heroically individuated and embodied author. Pope opens and closes "Windsor Forest" with self-conscious figurations of the poet who, like Dryden's patriot, stands at the nexus of modern English individualism and a theology of national election.

Moving from the "Savage [Forest] Laws" of England's eleventh-century Norman invaders to the Edenic early eighteenth-century forest regime of the Stuart queen Anne, Pope constructs a scriptural narrative of redemption in "Windsor Forest" that takes the governance of the royal forest at Windsor as a synecdoche for the political fate of the nation as a whole (45). Like many English poets before him, from Ben Jonson to Andrew Marvell, in "Windsor Forest" Pope uses natural description to make a political argument; Pope's argument, however, culminates with a distinctly modern vision of a world redeemed through the combined forces of humanist individualism and scriptural nationalism. This chapter pays particular attention to the central activity of hunting in "Windsor Forest" because it is through hunting that Pope imagines the democratization of the king's two bodies. Drawing upon the widespread humanism of his moment, Pope rewrites the binary between the deified and the mortal that had set the king apart in the newly popular terms of an elect humanity counterposed against an abandoned animality destined by God for sacrifice and subjection.

From the mid-1990s to the early 2000s, a series of studies by critics including Helen Deutsch, Paul Hammond, and Catherine Ingrassia challenged the once-canonical opposition between conservative English Augustans and the modernizing culture they derided. This was a transformative moment in English Augustan criticism that left us with a new image of Pope in particular as a highly ambivalent figure who, in the words of Ingrassia, "simultaneously resisted and embraced those cultural forces" he condemned as "feminized" (11). Building upon such interpretations, this chapter addresses the still-unanswered question of how a nuanced understanding of Pope, as simultaneously opposed to and illustrative of modernity, changes the way we think about modernity itself. In eighteenth-century studies, the idea of a strict opposition between Tory Augustan poets and British modernity has long served a Whiggish agenda; it has allowed generations of scholars to depict Anglo-American modernity and its preeminent literary form, the novel, as distinct from the theological and nationalist concerns of the tradition-minded Augustans. At the center of this chapter is the competing contention that the modern individualism long associated with novels is born of a history shaped by nationalism, theology, and verse. Pope's authorial persona occupies an important position within this history because it is explicitly steeped in a centuries-old poetic tradition of sacralizing the English nation and yet, at the same time, also represents an early instance of modern novelistic subjectivity.

Eighteenth-Century England's Ascendant Theology Was the Nation and Pope Was its Isaiah

Why would a literary study of the modern individual begin with the work of two Catholics? In *The Protestant Ethic and the Spirit of Capitalism* (1904–5), Max Weber famously represents Puritanism as "the most important" factor in the "development of . . . rational bourgeois economic life," labeling it the "cradle of . . . modern economic man" (174). While the Reformation was undeniably an important condition in the making of the modern English subject, it was never its sole "cradle." Although one might be inclined to think of England with its Reformation Church and early entrance into capitalism as the quintessential case study for Weber's argument, its history, as "Windsor Forest" helps demonstrate, in fact departs from Weber's Protestant-centric model. The dissemination of divinity indeed was an essential condition for the emergence of a new individual in early modern England; however, this process of distributing the transcendent power once held exclusively by churches and kings occurred through not only the medium of the Reformation, but the political theology of the nation as well. Weber draws convincing connections between the "worldly asceticism" of Puritanism and the "pure utilitarianism" of early twentieth-century capitalism, yet he fails to give an adequate account of the historical change that separates them, leaving readers with the impression that the modern subject simply issued forth from early modern Protestant thought (181, 183).

What Weber misses is that, at least in England, the modern individual emerges as the product of a nationalized synthesis of two key ideologies of late medieval and early modern Europe: divine kingship and Reformation Christianity. Although Protestant militants and royalist believers were on competing sides of the major conflicts that shook England in this period, these two camps held nationalist assumptions in common, and, unbeknownst to themselves and in spite of their stated intentions, they acted together to refashion the worldly collective of England as the chosen vehicle of God. From either end of the political spectrum, low-church radicals and high-church monarchists defined the terms of political debate in early modern England along stridently nationalist lines.

In the first of the Renaissance-era legal cases with which he opens *The King's Two Bodies*, Kantorowicz recounts the debate over Queen Elizabeth's liability for a lease that her predecessor Edward VI had signed while still a minor for land long designated as the private property of Lancaster monarchs. As the Queen's Catholic advisor Edmund Plowden explains, crown lawyers upheld the legitimacy of Edward's lease despite the fact that he made it before reaching legal age because "no act which the King does as King, shall be defeated by his Nonage" (212a). Crown lawyers, in other words, decided against Elizabeth but in favor of the sovereignty she embodied. In a royalist formulation at the center of Kantorowicz's study, Plowden elaborates that the monarch has "two Bodies, viz., a Body natural, and a Body politic," and it is the latter that "includes" and "magnifies" the former, raising it to the angelic heights of an entity "utterly void of Infancy, and old Age" (212a).

Royalists like Plowden relied on a doctrine of legal exceptionalism that was in fact taken up by and elaborated upon by Protestant radicals who began to cast the English body politic and all of its individual constituents in the kingly terms of the sacred—that is, as persons "set apart" by God as his privileged agents in the world (*OED* n3). In "The Locusts," an epic verse work that exemplifies the nationalist fever of Puritan thought in the years preceding the English Civil War, Phineas Fletcher reiterates Plowden's faith in the sacredness of the English body politic, while departing from Plowden and other royalists in depicting the collective rather than the king as the ultimate agent of divine authority. Although he pays tribute to Charles I as a "Greate Prince" and more generally casts the monarch as a mediator modeled after the "great Umpire" God, Fletcher nevertheless maintains a distinction between England's king and the immortal sovereignty he bears (5.38.1, 5.26.3). According to Fletcher's mythopoetic account of early seventeenth-century English history, moderate Anglicans were allied with the demonic forces of the Catholic faith who conspired to assassinate King James I in the 1605 Gunpowder Plot insofar as both represented obstacles to the eschatological fulfillment of history through the worldly vehicle of English nationalism. Combating the "rising Babel seed" is not one fight among many for Fletcher; instead, it is the struggle through which all other conflicts are understood, the war that gives meaning to nations, individuals, and history itself (5.40.4).

In Fletcher's model, England derives its significance from the role it plays in a divine economy of salvation, and it is the unity provided by this position that transforms a premodern body politic divided by regional, class, and other clannish affiliations into a single essentialized protomodern nation. What is often lost in discussions of the English Civil War is the fact that the very nature of the conflict—over who would govern the elect nation—expresses a unifying and expansionist faith in the idea of England as a single entity whose identity was grounded in the essentializing presumption of God's favor. When it comes to England, in other words, the privileging of national belonging over other forms of affiliation occurred through the medium of a new political theology, one centered on the idea of election. From Fletcher's perspective, Charles may represent a privileged subject, but he is a subject nevertheless, obliged like every other to respond to the holy war embedded within his divine second body. Imploring Charles to launch a new war against the Catholic powers of Rome and Spain, Fletcher refashions royal prerogative not as a unique subjectivity, but as a heightened form of responsibility. It is Charles who must ensure that God's gift of election is not wasted upon the new Israelites of England:

> 'Tis not in vaine, that Christ has girt thy head
> ... 'tis not in vaine,
> That in thy Realmes such Spirits are dayly bred,
> Which thirst, and long to tug with Rome, and Spayne:
> . . . .
> Only this warre's a match worthy thy Realmes, & Thee. (5.39.1–9)

Rather than depicting the King's actions as synonymous with the law itself, as Plowden does, Fletcher implores Charles to acknowledge his position as a kind of ur-subject, indebted to an even greater degree to a law and an economy that forever exceed even the kings they ennoble.

In the opening invocation of "The Locusts," Fletcher demonstrates his common ground with Plowden by translating divine authority into strictly national terms. Fletcher's epic narrator begins by asking God for guidance:

> Thou world's sole Pilot, who in this poor Isle
> (So small a bottome) hast embark't thy light
> and glorious self: and stear'st it safe, the while
> ....
> Steare me poor Ship-boy, steare my course aright. (1.1.3)

With the synecdochal slippage between the poet and the nation, the "Ship-boy" and his "bottome," Fletcher expands Plowden's model by placing the nonmonarchical believer in the kingly position of an essentially national and sacred subject. Fletcher refers to this at once collective and individual subject as both a "poor Isle" and a "small ... bottome"—an island as well a ship—in order to configure England as a radically singular yet mobile nation, set apart by God, and for this reason expected to move with the aim of fulfilling his global apocalyptic promise. On opposite sides of the early modern political spectrum, Fletcher and Plowden nevertheless come together in articulating the source of England's unity as something beyond formal alliances or shared geography. This surprising point of coincidence offers a fresh perspective on the expansion of the English state in the late seventeenth and eighteenth centuries since it suggests that this development is not entirely novel, as most historians contend, but is instead the institutionalization of a preexisting faith constructed by earlier partisans of almost every variety.

With "Windsor Forest," Pope facilitates the movement of English national theology from its origins in Protestant exceptionalism and royalist mysticism to its eighteenth-century status as a unifying faith in the sovereignty of a radically singular and expansionist nation. Pope's work helps fill in what Weber's *The Protestant Ethic and the Spirit of Capitalism* leaves out: the centrality of nationalism to the emergence of the modern English individual. What Weber misses and Pope's vision of England's "golden Years" makes clear is the essential role that nationalism plays as an ecumenical medium capable of translating competing ideologies into a common political language (92). Weber demonstrates his inattention to nationalism with the relatively scant analysis he devotes to the crucial notion of a chosen people, which he mentions only in passing as one of the many factors contributing to the "formalistic, hard, [and] correct character" of the Puritan believer (166). The identification of early modern England as God's elect nation was neither an exclusively Protestant conviction nor simply one idea among others; rather, it was the cornerstone of a pan-Christian national theology that brought royalists and

Parliamentarians together around their shared faith in England's exceptional nature.

A word of caution, however, is needed at this juncture, since it would be a mistake to think that the development of this new unifying political faith was the only or even the predominant mode of affiliation in early eighteenth-century England. As Hoppit notes, England during the reign of Anne from 1702 to 1714 remained a "disunited kingdom" whose "political and religious divisions" frustrated the Queen's efforts "to unify her people in a common cause" (276, 278). In the words of one political observer, amid rumors of the Queen's failing health the Parliament of 1713 "gave up the distinction of Whig and Tory" and instead concentrated on the "new distinction between the Tories themselves, as Hanover Tory and Pretender's Tory, English Tory and French Tory, for trade and against it" (Hoppit 308). All of this is to say that England did not emerge from the Glorious Revolution of 1688 as a miraculously cohesive nation. By the end of Anne's reign, fears of a new civil war reached such heights that a French envoy to England assured Louis XIV in Paris that "affairs are moving in such a manner that civil war is becoming inevitable" (309).

While the only book-length study of Pope's poem, Pat Rogers's *The Symbolic Design of Windsor-Forest* (2004), focuses on the Stuart sectarianism evident in Pope's verse, I believe one finds a less ambivalent articulation of Pope's allegiance to the "French Tory" or Stuart cause in his first work of national prophecy, the "Messiah" (1712). In the "Messiah," Pope constructs an unambiguously royalist narrative that provides a clearer example of the Stuart millenarianism that Rogers locates in "Windsor Forest." Presented as an imitation of Virgil's "Pollio," Pope's "Messiah," much like Dryden's "Astraea Redux," synthesizes Virgil's messianic "Eclogue IV" with the book of Isaiah, depicting both as types awaiting their fulfillment in the arrival of a Christic antitype. While Anne certainly plays a role in "Windsor Forest," proclaiming at one point "Let Discord cease!" as the "World obey'd," she remains of secondary importance to the humanist subjects and animist objects that act as the primary agents of England's redemption in this work (327, 328). In contrast, the "Messiah" organizes its vision of national salvation around the royalist and Christ-centered figure of an "auspicious Babe . . . the promis'd Father of the future Age" (22, 56). Dependent upon the arrival of a child "from Heav'n descend[ed]," the "Messiah" exemplifies a model of politicized biblical typology that translates Scripture into contemporary political terms while still fulfilling the original aim of biblical typology, which was to harmonize the Old and New Testaments (20).

Pope takes the tradition of politicized biblical typology in a different direction in "Windsor Forest," by turning his analogical attention from the expectation of a transcendent savior to the immanent yet equally theological force of an elect nation. Bypassing the dual function of biblical typology in the "Messiah"—namely, to politicize and Christianize its Old Testament sources—"Windsor Forest" instead directly interpolates eighteenth-century England into a Judaic narrative of national election and pastoral redemption. From the book of Isaiah, Pope borrows a theological model of authorial and national identity as well as a bucolic vision of the apocalypse as that which brings these identities to their extreme point of perfection. Near the opening of Isaiah, the narrator portrays national cohesion as a matter of responding to the spiritual essence that distinguishes the bodies of Israelites from their surroundings. Crying "O house of Jacob, come ye, and let us walk in the light of the LORD," Isaiah represents the elect political collective of Israel in the fleshly and economic language of a single "house" or family, a protoracial model of political affiliation through shared ancestry (2:5).[1] Like Pope's poet in "Windsor Forest" who sings of truths nature already embodies, Isaiah fashions himself as the prophet of an immanent promise and implores his brethren to affirm the redemption that their existence itself already contains. At once a directive and a description, Isaiah rallies a "sinful nation" to accomplish what has already happened, a tension he expresses later in his book by announcing, "Arise, shine, for thy light is come [Jerusalem], and the glory of the LORD is risen upon thee" (1:4, 60:1).[2] The at once prophetic and apostolic function of Isaiah's narrator is important for "Windsor Forest" because it provides Pope with a model for constructing his poetic self as a visionary interpreter of what already exists. The glory of Pope's poetic persona turns on his capacity to sing of the future that lies within the present.

Where "Windsor Forest" departs from the book of Isaiah is in its radicalization of God's immanence. Unlike Isaiah, Pope writes of God as an entirely immanent force, a cause indistinguishable from his effects rather than a subject who precedes the economy of redemption he governs. In Isaiah, God speaks to the narrator and the nation he embodies as instruments of his preexisting will. As Isaiah explains, "The LORD hath called me ... and he hath made my mouth like a sharp sword ... and said unto me thou art my servant, O Israel, in whom I will be glorified" (49:1–3). With telling emphasis on his authorial "I," God elaborates, "In an acceptable time I heard thee, and in a day of salvation have I helped thee: and I will preserve thee, and give thee for a covenant of the people, to establish the earth, to cause to inherit the desolate heritages" (49:8). The syntactical repetition in "I heard" and "I helped" accentuates the distinctness of God's status as the subject whose actions in the past have allowed Israel to ascend in the present. Although he clearly valorizes himself as a prophet of God, the narrator of Isaiah occupies a secondary role in a representational process that begins with the primordial voice of a creator. For Pope, on the other hand, God stands entirely within the landscape he inspires. The prophetic poet of "Windsor Forest" who sings of a nation's "long-expected Days" is no mere instrument of a preexisting will; instead, he is the agent of a language that simultaneously uncovers and accomplishes the immanent promise of history's end (434).

Pope's Humanism as English Nationalism in Global Form

If Pope had published the version of "Windsor Forest" that he penned alongside his youthful pastorals between 1704 and 1707, his poem would have culminated with a self-aggrandizing panegyric on the divinity of English verse, but it would have lacked the published poem's explicit reiteration of the book of Isaiah and the Old Testament model of election that it articulates. Although the final stanza of Pope's work remains the same, save for the addition of a single couplet, Pope's closing moment of self-constitution and the broader self-conscious narrative frame of "Windsor Forest" assume new meaning when what they frame includes a rewriting of the Old Testament in which the ascendant colonial empire of eighteenth-century England stands as God's chosen agent for the final fulfillment of scriptural prophecy (434).

Anticipating the end of the War of Spanish Succession (1701–14), Pope added a 290-line penultimate section to "Windsor Forest" that depicts the rise of the British Empire as the beginning of a new apocalyptic age. Far from a mere rhetorical flourish, Pope's synthesis of eighteenth-century politics and biblical prophecy reveals something that is frequently overlooked in discussions of Western humanism. Though twenty-first-century criticism tends to assume humanism's opposition to theology, Pope's "Windsor Forest" helps illustrate the fact that humanism emerges as a continuation of rather than a departure from scriptural narratives of redemption. Beginning with William the Conqueror, who made "his trembling Slaves the Royal Game," Pope develops a mythopoetic account of English history in "Windsor Forest" that hinges on the idea that the restoration of those who have been treated like animals to their rightful position as sovereign human subjects will bring about a state of permanent global peace (64).

Pope makes every effort to underline the global reach of the redemption he heralds in "Windsor Forest," declaring, "Oh stretch thy Reign, fair *Peace!* from Shore to Shore, / Till Conquest cease, and Slav'ry be no more" (407–8). And, yet, as many critics have noted, his poem is published to commemorate a treaty that marked England's ascent as Europe's new preeminent slave-trading power. By the end of the War of Spanish Succession, the dream of uniting France and Spain, Europe's two major Catholic Empires, was dashed, and, perhaps even more important, France and Spain were compelled to make numerous territorial and commercial concessions, the majority of which benefited England. In negotiations from 1713 to 1715, England expanded its colonial holdings and won monopoly contracts to supply the expansive Portuguese and Spanish empires with everything from clothing to slaves. As Christopher Hill states, "At Utrecht England got all the pickings, at the expense of France [its enemy] and the Netherlands [its ally]," an outcome that signaled London's new status "as the centre of world trade," and, more generally, Britain's position as "greatest world power" (*Century of Revolution* 264, 2). Pope's emancipatory images in "Windsor Forest" appear even more awkward when one considers that a part of England's success in these negotiations was wresting the asiento contract from the French, granting England a monopoly right over the business of supplying slaves to the Spanish New World.

Rather than tactfully avoiding allusions to the Spanish New World, however, as one might expect, Pope intensifies the apparent tension at the heart of his utopian vision by singling out the victims of Spanish colonialism as exemplary beneficiaries of England's rise to power. Near the end of "Windsor Forest," Pope calls for England's "fair *Peace*" to extend

> Till the freed *Indians* in their native Groves
> Reap their own Fruits, and woo their Sable Loves,
> *Peru* once more a Race of Kings behold,
> And other *Mexico's* be roof'd with Gold. (407–12)

With the repetition of the grammatically unnecessary possessive pronouns—"their native Groves"; "their own Fruits"; "their Sable Loves"— Pope places a civic humanist emphasis on land ownership as the foundation of personal freedom. It is by repossessing "their Groves" that Native Americans will become able to act as independent agents capable of controlling their own agriculture, sex, and, most important, selves.

Like much of "Windsor Forest," Pope's image of a redeemed New World is constructed through a combination of neoclassical humanism and biblical prophecy. Pope's pastoral vision of Americas freed from bondage clearly calls upon the language of Isaiah, echoing prophecies such as "in that day shall the branch of the LORD be beautiful and glorious, and the fruit of the earth *shall* be excellent and comely for them that are escaped of Israel," for "they shall inherit the land forever" (4:2, 60:21).[3] Although Pope's model of humanity in "Windsor Forest" is intensely nationalist, it is not one that is organized by the opposition of Europe to its colonial others. Pope equates "the trembling slaves" of England's past with the natives of the Spanish New World in order to demonstrate that his nationalized definition of humanity is a potentially universal category (64). Pope's definition of the human is protoracial because it is essentially English, yet his model differs from the eugenicist theories of the nineteenth century in that it is rooted not in a semiotics of physical traits, but in the twinned concepts of England's national election and its constituents' ensuing right to humanist self-possession.

In *The Machiavellian Moment* (1975), Pocock argues that a central and irresolvable problem for early eighteenth-century English political thought was how one could imagine a citizen of moral autonomy "in a world of rapid and irrational change," where property itself, once the bulwark of personal independence, was merely another object of "symbolic value" to be endlessly speculated upon and exchanged (486). According to Pocock, this was an era when "the dominant paradigm for the individual inhabiting the world of value was that of civic man; but the dominant paradigm for the individual as engaged in historical actuality was that of economic and inter-subjective man, and it was peculiarly hard to bring the two together" (466). This conflict was reflected in the bitter division of early eighteenth-century English politics between a Country Party advocating the preservation of neoclassical value and a Court Party arguing for "historical actuality" and the changes it wrought.[4] While "Windsor Forest" certainly confirms Pocock's argument regarding the centrality of civic humanism to this period, Pope's poem also challenges Pocock's diagnosis of English Augustan thought as torn by the competing interests of value and history. Throughout "Windsor Forest," Pope synthesizes Old Testament prophecy and eighteenth-century mercantilism by representing contemporary developments such as "ascending [suburban] *Villa's*" along the Thames as signs of God's redemptive economy at work (355). Pope, in other words, endows the material changes occurring in England's increasingly urban and trade-based society with moral and theological purpose. In doing so, Pope not only undermines the dichotomy of theology and history at the center of Pocock's analysis, but also articulates a solution to the division of Court and Country Parties—namely, a theology of the modern colonial nation.

Rather than being a simple case of eccentric anachronism, Pope's solution to the problem of how to construe value in a commercial age was part of a larger historical process that saw the formation of what Steven Pincus has characterized as a "new kind of modern state" (3). During the twenty-five years from Pope's birth in 1688 to the publication of "Windsor Forest" in 1713, the English state assumed a hitherto unprecedented size, becoming a sprawling, if uneven, bureaucracy that enacted as well as symbolized the growing sense of England as a cohesive whole. On both a practical and ideological level, England was becoming an increasingly unified entity held together by trade, debt, and an expanding central government, as well as the national and commercial philosophies that inspired and arose from such changes. The driving force behind many of these developments—in particular the expansion of the state—was the expense incurred by a series of costly wars on the continent, beginning with the Nine Years' War from 1688 to 1697 and continuing with the War of Spanish Succession from 1701 to 1714. These military ventures dramatically increased state spending, which in turn spurred the development of more sophisticated systems of government taxation and borrowing, with the national debt rising from £3.1 million in 1691 to £54 million in 1721.[5] The formation of the Bank of England in 1694 is especially significant, since it institutionalized the national debt and thus made credit a permanent means of political unification.

While Pat Rogers has some basis for contending that "Windsor Forest" articulates "a conscious Jacobite program," Pope's poem as a whole, taken in all of its complexity, is far from the anachronistic work of sectarian longing that Rogers's interpretation would suggest (16). Despite the Jacobite allusions that run through it, "Windsor Forest" is on the surface and in essence a work of ecumenical nationalism perfectly in line with the innovative atmosphere of post-1688 England. Pope devoted much of his career to satirizing the supposedly foreign culture of finance that 1688 heralded, and yet, as "Windsor Forest" demonstrates, he nevertheless helped ensure that this very culture found a new source of meaning. When historians discuss religion in this period, they tend to look at matters such as the decline of communion rates or the decreasing use of ecclesiastical courts.[6] What "Windsor Forest" suggests is that these historians should instead turn to the English state if they wish to find the site of this period's truly ascendant faith.

For many scholars, such a reorientation may appear misguided, since for them the national theology at work in "Windsor Forest" represents nothing more than ideological mystification, beautiful lies fabricated to give a rising empire a false aura of universality. In her study *Alexander Pope* (1985), Laura Brown exemplifies this position by arguing that Pope's "*pax Britannica* is a subjective rewriting of history represented as an objective account of reality." Pope, according to Brown, reverses "the terms by which history is understood: usurpation becomes self-determination, oppression liberty, and violence peace" (44). The problem with such a reading is that it relies on a definition of reality as something that exists outside of and prior to ideology. While it might appear absurd to later critics to think that the British Empire possessed a divinely grounded and universal authority, it is a mistake to believe that this idea was a kind of ideological mist underneath which history was occurring.

To think that ideology does not belong in history is to approach works like "Windsor Forest" from the outside and, like Brown, to overlook what they have to tell us about a history that ideology helped make. Operating upon the assumption that liberty exists in opposition to oppression, Brown misses what Pope's poem reveals about these very concepts: that they emerge together, that humanist liberty is a product of colonial oppression. Challenging Pope's poem ought to mean interrogating what it clearly states rather than what it allegedly obscures. If one wants to hold Pope's feet to the fire, the question to ask is why a supposedly universal and self-determining mode of being, the human, requires the constitution of an explicitly unfree other, the animal. Pope develops the idea of a modern emancipated subject only by splitting life in two, between the sacred and the abandoned, and, about this, one can and ought to ask why.

Hunting, Sovereignty, and the Making of History as Race War

The nonhuman other emerges in "Windsor Forest" not from distant lands, but from the very forests of England, in the form of "Birds and

Beasts" who can be hunted and slaughtered without disrupting the "sacred *Peace*" of humanity's redemption (374, 355). "Windsor Forest," as Joseph Roach puts it in *Cities of the Dead* (1996), consists of a series of "dancelike" or "choric movements" from an initial "strophic assertion of Peace and Plenty" to an "antistrophic reply of displaced violence," and finally to a culminating "epode of the hunt, where nature's abundance offers up a copious portion of itself as sacrifice" (143). Roach's delineation of the narrative movement in Pope's poem is masterful, but, like Brown, he brings a "paranoid reading" to bear in interpreting it, arguing that the "pervasiveness of hunting imagery in 'Windsor Forest' underlines the theme of sacrificial violence that returns to the poet like the repressed" (140). Roach follows Brown by depicting "Windsor Forest" in the representational language of a Freudian dream, a condensed and distorted reflection that must be deciphered in order to uncover the historical truth lying beneath it. Proceeding from the position of a truth outside the text, such a perspective obscures what happens within it. Pope narrates the history of England through the prism of hunting in "Windsor Forest" in order to sketch a new form of sovereign violence that is compatible with his biblical utopia of a redeemed humanity living in perpetual peace.

Rather than effacing the sovereign power that medieval kings held over their subjects, Pope reformulates it as the universal right of humanity to exercise absolute authority over the animate yet nonhuman life that surrounds it. What no critic of Pope seems to have taken seriously is that Pope's vision of peace in "Windsor Forest" rests on the idea of a permanent "Sylvan War" between humanity and its animal others (148). Pope marshals the rhetoric of national election to depict England and its ascendant empire as responsible for uniting humanity around the divinely sanctioned task, in the words of the book of Genesis, of exercising "dominion over the fishes of the sea, and the fowls of the air, and the beasts, and the whole earth, and every creeping creature that moveth upon [it]" (1:26). The crucial distinction in "Windsor Forest" is between those capable of joining the elect fold of Britain—and thereby gaining the capacity to exercise self-possession over their "Groves," "Fruit," and "Loves," as Pope writes of the "freed *Indians*"—and those relegated to a domain of animality chosen only for sacrifice and death. In Pope's poem, the pheasant, the woodcock, and the perch occupy the same position as a contemporaneous African slave or English peasant who is deemed beyond the possibility of redemption, condemned to act as grist in the mill that makes the human.

In his 1976 lectures on the place of war in modern European societies, published under the title *Society Must Be Defended*, Foucault theorizes that the idea of history as "perpetual war" emerges not, as one might expect, in the work of Niccolò Machiavelli or Thomas Hobbes, but in the seventeenth-century writing of English Protestants. It is, as Foucault contends, in the "discourse of the Puritans . . . and the Levellers" that one finds the earliest formulation of a new idea of "war [as] the uninterrupted frame of history"—that is, war as that which occurs "beneath order and peace . . . [and] that undermines our society and divides it in a binary mode" (59). Foucault identifies this state of perpetual conflict as a "race war" that surfaces in the seventeenth century as a rhetorical weapon of "decentered camps" and that becomes in the two centuries that follow the "the discourse of power itself" (60–61). By locating the origins of what he describes as "state racism" in the seventeenth-century reformulation of history as an endless battle between the elect and the reprobate, Foucault complicates the conventional understanding of racism as a secular product of nineteenth-century thought. In Foucault's analysis, the appearance of state racism in the nineteenth century represents less of an innovation than an expansion of a preexisting theological discourse of divine election and imminent salvation (62). Against this backdrop, one could say that Pope's conception of the animal as a lawful object of violence expands rather than effaces Fletcher's depiction of Catholics in "The Locusts" as the "rising Babel seed" and hence legitimate targets of Charles's Christ-sanctioned wrath. Pope's poem exemplifies a moment when the idea of history as a never-ending conflict between the believer and heretic is reformulated as the war of humanity against its biological others.

Delivered at the same time that the critic Edward Said is composing *Orientalism* (1978), Foucault's lectures follow Said in placing representation at the center of Europe's encounters with its racial and colonial others. For both Foucault and Said, the colonial other is confronted not in the immediacy of experience, but in discourse. In his account of the history of Anglo-European representations of "the East," Said notes that the professional scholar or poet is "never concerned with the Orient except as the first cause of what he says," which, "by virtue of the fact that it is said or written, is meant to indicate that the Orientalist is outside the Orient, both as an existential and as a moral fact" (21). Said's emphasis on the essential exteriority of the Orientalist coincides with Foucault's contention that "the other race is basically not the race that came from elsewhere," but is rather a domestic product "constantly being re-created in and by the social fabric" (Foucault 61). While Said addresses a discourse that purports to talk about a particular region whereas Foucault addresses "power itself," the two analyses similarly highlight the domestic origins of otherness, an emphasis that Saree Makdisi, in *Making England Western* (2014), situates within the particular context of eighteenth- and nineteenth-century England.

Bringing together the work of Said and Foucault, and building upon the arguments of literary critics such as Ann Stoler and Susan Thorne, Makdisi depicts the history of British colonization as a two-stage process beginning with a "domestic Occidentalism" that functioned as "the necessary correlate of an eventually overseas-directed Orientalism" (10). Although many critics in the past several decades have drawn attention to the continuity, in the words of Stoler, of "bourgeois 'civilizing missions' in metropole and colony," Makdisi sheds new light on the conceptual and historical consequences of such a parallel (15). By reading the internal construction of an English identity alongside the broader civilization conflict staged by nineteenth-century Orientalists, Makdisi counters the "much narrower notions of national identity [that] have dominated eighteenth-century and Romantic studies for some time now" and instead defines the new model of affiliation emerging in this period as "racial and civilizational" rather than national (17). According to Makdisi, the familiar "we" forming in eighteenth- and nineteenth-century England is civilizational from the start, and it is for this reason that this ascendant identity rejects populations both at home and abroad before coalescing around a newly purified notion of England as white and Western in the latter half of the nineteenth century.

While Makdisi is right to argue that it was not until the Romantic period that England first became capable of joining a "putative West" standing against a "dialectically counterposed" East, he runs astray in attempting to isolate this moment from the rest of the eighteenth century (17). Makdisi contends that it is "disabling to try to collapse the Romantic period into a 'long eighteenth century'" and upon this basis depicts England's Romantic-era Western identity as distinct from the nationalism that preceded it (18). In "Windsor Forest," Pope casts England as an at once particular and universal nation, a paradoxical combination that lays the conceptual groundwork for broader Romantic-era models of belonging such as the West, Europe, and cosmopolitanism itself. These larger cultural formations have a tendency to represent themselves as endowed with an apocalyptic responsibility for ensuring the world's redemption, a self-presentation whose origins can only be understood if they are placed within a history that includes the nation.

By hailing England as "the World's great Oracle in Times to come," Pope undermines efforts to place the national and the cosmopolitan in opposition, suggesting instead—as my final chapter makes clear in its discussion of Kant—that the idea of a global or cosmopolitan state is national theology in newly civilizational terms (382).[7] While Immanuel Kant will speak of Europe, or "our continent," as the chosen agent of "nature's intention" in his "Idea for a Universal History with a Cosmopolitan Purpose" (1784), Pope addresses England as the subject responsible for the fulfillment of an equally immanent and apocalyptic plan for global salvation (52, 42). Beyond merely demonstrating a parallel, the continuity of these two formations highlights the essential fact that the model of the West from the nineteenth through the twenty-first century is a product of nationalisms steeped in the absolute prerogative of God.

Although Foucault and, building upon him, Agamben both highlight the centrality of racism to modern European power, they each fail to devote adequate attention to the question of race, since to do so they would have to contextualize their studies within particular nation-states. For Foucault and Agamben, racism is the means through which modern European societies preserve the distinction between the sovereign and the subjected that Foucault identifies as a defining attribute of premodern power. In an important point for his overall revision of Foucauldian biopolitics, Agamben convincingly shows how Foucault's own theory of racism poses a fundamental challenge to his chronology of modernity since it places a supposedly anachronistic form of sovereign violence at the center of modern power (*Kingdom and Glory* xi, 76). Yet what both Agamben and Foucault overlook is that if racism "becomes the discourse of power itself" in modernity, then a primary vehicle for its development, the nation, must be addressed on an individual basis (*Society Must Be Defended* 61). Neither Foucault nor Agamben pay much attention to particular nations; instead, they speak of "power in the West" or simply "power" as if these generalities existed (*Discipline and Punish* 27; *Kingdom and the Glory* xi). As a result, they neglect the very aspect of modern governance that their work exposes as essential. This oversight is even more glaring in the work of Agamben since he, in the now nine volumes that make up his *Homo Sacer* series, has done more than anybody else to illuminate the conjunction of the sovereign and the biopolitical that both he and Foucault identify as the site of racism's emergence.[8]

Pope's "Windsor Forest" is important for this conversation because it elucidates how the rhetoric of early British nationalism informs the development of European racism. Pope constructs a protoracial narrative by imagining national human subjects achieving Scripture-foretold redemption in the space of a forest, a territory embodying monarchical power. As Pope's Twickenham editors E. Audra and Aubrey Williams note, a "forest" was "a legal rather than a topographical term in the eighteenth century and referred specifically to land outside (*fortis*) the common law" (135). Forests were a spatial representation of the king's exceptional authority and were devoted to royal uses, including hunting, celebratory spectacles, and the harvesting of wood.[9] In the space of a forest, one could find woods, heaths, and marshlands, as well as towns and villages, all of which were governed by a patchwork of royal officers responsible for imposing the king's law. On both a practical and symbolic level, forests embodied the sovereignty of the king, and Windsor Forest had been especially important ever since William the Conqueror chose it as the site for Windsor Castle, a strategically placed royal home on a hill overlooking the vital waterway of the Thames.[10] Pope thus situates his poem in Windsor Forest in order both to celebrate royal sovereignty and to see its power disseminated among newly fashioned national subjects, a protoracial conception made manifest by the central activity of hunting in Pope's poem.

In "Windsor Forest," hunting is the means by which one distinguishes the subjects and objects of God's immanent economy. For Pope, hunting brings nationalism and animalization together and in the process helps shape what Foucault describes as a "race war" model of history (*Society Must Be Defended* 60). From the perspective of conventional definitions of war, Pope's assertion that an ascendant colonial empire will be free of "War or Blood" seems nonsensical (371). Placed within the broader context of his poem, however, Pope's vision of peace makes sense: it is the reformulation of violence along protoracial humanist lines. In the prophetic present tense, Pope proclaims,

> The shady Empire shall retain no Trace
> Of War or Blood, but in the Sylvan Chace,
> The Trumpets sleep, while cheerful Horns are blown,
> And Arms employ'd on Birds and Beasts alone. (371–74)

Pat Rogers cautions against believing that "Pope is writing about 'ordinary men' here" since only "courtiers" or "local worthies" could reasonably be thought to be in the train of a "royal huntress" (151). Rogers is more right than he knows. Pope's humanist utopia rests upon the elevation of nonmonarchical bodies to the kingly position of sovereign subjects who, even upon royal land, can kill with impunity those creatures set aside by God as the means of their redemption.

Pope converts the familiar idea of hunting as a moral substitute for war into a biopolitical principle of erasing all violence from the world save that which is necessary for the perpetuation and flourishing of that life deemed human. The partridges, pheasants, larks, and trout that populate "Windsor Forest" serve as the means through which an Anglicized humanity establishes itself as Israel incarnate. Whether it is "the bright-ey'd Perch with Fins of *Tyrian* Dye" or "the vivid Green" of a pheasant's "shining plume," animals appear in "Windsor Forest" as aestheticized objects whose meaning derives from their subordinate role within an immanent economy of human salvation (142, 117). The pathos Pope exhibits in his depiction of these animals' deaths has prompted critics such as Brown and Roach to interpret them as displaced figures for the victims of imperial violence. In Brown's terms, Pope's treatment of hunting "both conceals and reveals the violence of imperial war" (38). As the following portrait of the pheasant's demise demonstrates, however, Pope undermines the pathos expressed in his representations of creaturely death by couching such depictions in the self-conscious and aestheticizing language of spectacle:

> Short is his Joy! he feels the fiery Wound,
> Flutters in Blood, and panting beats the Ground.
> Ah! what avail his glossie, varying Dyes,
> His Purple Crest, and Scarlet-circled Eyes
> The vivid Green his shining Plumes unfold
> His painted Wings, and Breast that flames with Gold? (113–18)

With a series of painterly terms, from the "glossie, varying Dyes" to the "painted Wings," Pope not only casts this dying bird as first and foremost an object of representation, but also situates it within his poem's broader narrative of humanist aesthetics.

The image of the dying pheasant's "blood," which Brown too quickly reads as a signifier of "imperial violence," foreshadows the later proclamation of "Father *Thames*," who announces near the end of Pope's poem that "no more my Sons shall dye with *British* Blood / Red *Iber*'s Sands, or *Ister*'s foaming Flood" (39, 330, 367–68). Alluding to two scenes from the War of Spanish Succession, "*Iber*'s Sands" and "*Ister*'s foaming Flood" recall recent battles in which British bodies—that is, ordained human subjects—were used as mediums of representation and thus treated like objects. Blood that God had rendered sacred through national election was used to paint the sandy shore of a Spanish river and the surface of the German Danube. Like earlier Norman forest laws that imposed the death penalty for poaching on royal land, these battles ignored a scripturally sanctioned distinction between the subjects and objects of God's economy. Far from a victim, then, of a regrettable act, the dying pheasant with his "glossie, varying dyes" is a sign of humanity's rightful restoration. The pheasant is an object of death that is not death. His plight is to be bemoaned and enjoyed like a tragedy upon a stage, a drama to be seen by the chosen subjects around him as a figure of woe sketched upon God's canvas.

Pope poses the sentimental question of "what avail" the dying pheasant while simultaneously placing this creature beyond the purview of care. Drawing upon the first definition of the verb "avail," which is "to have force or efficacy for the accomplishment of a purpose," Pope allows the missing object of the intransitive "avail" to remain absent in order to register the pheasant's purposelessness, a state ironically stemming from the role it plays within a larger economy of purpose (*OED* n2). With the painterly language of a self-conscious artist, Pope represents the pheasant as a medium for reflecting a value designated by God for humanity alone. The creature, even in its death, is a tool for producing the meaning and purpose that only the human artist can hope to possess.

Painting and the Ambivalent Agency of the Human Subject

Amongst the various attributes with which Pope endows his pheasant, its "painted Wings" are unique in that they exceed the aestheticization evident in the rest of Pope's portrait of this radiant bird's "Purple Crest," "Scarlet-circled Eyes," and "Breast that flames with Gold" (118). With "painted Wings," Pope instead names the process of creation itself, a departure that begs the question of who exactly is doing the painting in "Windsor Forest." This is a moment of heightened self-consciousness, and it is far from the only one in Pope's poem. From the "blushing *Flora* [who] paints th'enaml'd Ground" near the opening of Pope's work to the final stanza's self-reflexive image of its author's "humble Muse [who]

Paints the green Forests and the flow'ry Plains,'" "Windsor Forest" is suffused with allusions to painting that all draw attention to the figure of the human artist as well as the ambiguous question of his or her agency (38, 427–28). This question is at the heart of "Windsor Forest," but, as the rest of this chapter demonstrates, it is a question that Pope resolutely refuses to answer, for it is within this space of undecidability that humanity itself resides. Elected and subjected, Pope conceives of humanity as distinguished by a sovereignty and a language that are ultimately not its own.

Pope mobilizes the oppositional harmony of the couplet form to enunciate the competing powers of human agency and historical determination without privileging either. In the final two lines of "Windsor Forest," Pope leaves his readers with an image of the poet as an ironic hero, one who both creatively exercises and readily submits to God's providential economy: "Enough for me, that to the listning Swains / First in these Fields I sung the Sylvan Strains" (433–34). Pope organizes this last line around a caesura that joins the heroism of the "First" "I" to the modesty of singing that the sylvan woods already contain, which is to say that Pope concludes "Windsor Forest" by depicting human creativity's place within history as a mock epic, a saga of heroic ambition that cannot but fail.[11]

Pope is an important figure for political theology because of the artfulness through which he uses rhyming verse couplets to express the irresolvability that is at the core of this movement. Pope in fact articulates an anticipatory rejoinder to one of the more influential recent accounts of political theology, Kahn's *The Future of Illusion* (2014), which asserts a very different conception of poetry and human agency from Pope's as well as from the broader discourse of political theology. For Kahn, poetry signifies the possibility of resolving the opposition between human agency and history that Pope's couplets stubbornly maintain. Kahn argues that Kantorowicz begins and ends *The King's Two Bodies* with Shakespeare and Dante because he "finds in literature an exemplary self-consciousness, about the symbolic dimension of human experience, about the human capacity to make and unmake symbolic forms" (60). Literature is the means by which one achieves an unambiguously heroic position of control over the mythology of the past; the poet, according to Kahn, manipulates inherited thought at will, at times engaging in "ideological critique" and at others exploiting the "enabling fictions of human community" (60). Though Kantorowicz pays little attention to the question of his method in *The King's Two Bodies*, he does disclose in the introduction that his intention is to "outline the historical problem ... of the 'King's Two Bodies'" by situating it in "its proper setting of medieval thought and political theory" (6). This seminal work in political theology, in other words, makes one guiding normative commitment, and it is to history. While Kahn notes the difficulty of assigning much in the way of philosophical commitment to Kantorowicz's work, she nevertheless projects a critical and demystifying intention upon *The King's Two Bodies*, a book that in truth follows in the tradition of Pope. Pope's poet, like Kantorowicz's, belongs to rather than makes history; he aims not to accomplish the heroic and ultimately futile task of overcoming every myth that has preceded him and instead focuses his creative energies on the question of how he ought to inherit them.

"Windsor Forest" is a profane poem, but it is not a godless one. It marks an early moment in Pope's lifelong struggle to inherit the Judeo-Christian tradition along fiercely material and national lines. Pope aims not to heroically efface all residue of the myths that preceded him, but rather to strategically organize them as the immanent mythos of a rising imperial nation. When Pope, for instance, addresses the "Woods" of Windsor as miraculously animate near the end of his poem, he does so in order to depict them as objects enlivened by an imperial economy of salvation:

> Thy Trees, fair *Windsor!* now shall leave their Woods,
> And half thy Forests rush into my Floods,
> Bear *Britain's Thunder*, and her Cross display,
> To the bright Regions of the rising Day. (385–88)

From the perspective of secularist critics, Windsor's moving forest can appear only as a ruse for human power, a mask in the words of Brown for the real "agent of imperialism," which is the "English navy" (30). The problem, however, is that within Pope's poem these trees are no mere metaphor for some underlying historical process; they are objects made truly animate by God's new plan.

Following his initial address to the "Trees" of "fair *Windsor*," Pope proceeds to list a series of animate objects around the globe, from bleeding "Balm" to "ripening Ore" (392, 396), before finally articulating the scriptural prophecy to which these things belong:

> The Time shall come, when free as Seas or Wind
> Unbounded *Thames* shall flow for all Mankind,

> Whole Nations enter with each swelling Tyde,
> And Seas but join the Regions they divide. (397–400)

In these lines, Pope brings the apocalyptic landscape of the book of Isaiah into the things of Windsor, echoing Isaiah's pledge that "in the last days . . . the mountain of the Lord's house shall be established in the top of the mountains, and shall be exalted above the hills; and all nations shall flow unto it" (2:2). What Pope adds to Isaiah in this instance is only the presumption of a second election, which he articulates through the synecdochal transformation of the Thames into a chosen vehicle for God's final descent into the world. Pope calls upon the language of Isaiah to announce the imminence of an imperial apocalypse, and, in doing so, he brings the transcendence of Scripture into the material politics of Britain.

What Pope's poem helps demonstrate is that the development of British modernity meant bringing the theological transcendent into the flesh of the particular. This is the couplet that McKeon, Kahn, and so many others exclude from their analysis, a decision that not only obfuscates theology's persistence within Britain's so-called secular age, but also unwittingly supports the political claims made upon this false basis from the eighteenth century to today. By reducing political theology to the myth-making capacities of a human subject, Kahn establishes the groundwork for her own Edenic vision of "art bringing about a new, secular cosmopolitanism" (79). Kahn imagines her secular golden age to be divorced from the transcendental claims of earlier eras, but this is only because she has mistaken an effect of modern political theology for its cause. Viewed from the perspective of Pope's poem, one could say that Kahn's effort to locate an alternative to theology in the creativity of the secular human subject represents an unknowing articulation of theology's reach in a humanist era. Kahn asks us to free a secular human subject who is in truth a product of theology, and what she loses in the process is an opportunity not to imagine a life without theology, but to debate how theology ought to be inherited.

Pope as Meta-Author

As a poem dedicated to endowing a piece of English landscape with scriptural significance, "Windsor Forest" resembles earlier works in the country house verse tradition such as John Denham's "Cooper's Hill,"

Andrew Marvell's "Upon Appleton House" (1651), and Dryden's own "To My Honour'd Kinsman." By convention, it is Ben Jonson's "To Penshurst" (1616) that initiates this tradition, which consists of poems that celebrate a rural seat of power by unearthing its metaphysical basis in the nature that surrounds it. The pastoral estates at the center of country house poems, in the words of Jonson, "joy'st in better marks, of soil, of air, / Of wood, [and] of water" because it is in the economy of nature that these symbols of human *technē* find their supposedly unalterable foundation (7–8). In the pastoral, country house poets discover a national identity and a model of order legitimated by time and guaranteed by God. Poets in this tradition thus privilege nature above castles, kings, and parliaments in order to refashion the English body politic instead of abandoning it. While appearing to celebrate the timelessness of pastoral life, country house poets in fact work to represent the amorphous collection of provincial communities and peoples that was the premodern English body politic in the newly cohesive and radically singular terms of God's new Eden, a status Marvel enunciates quite clearly in "Upon Appleton House" when he hails England as "the garden of the world ... [the] Paradise of four seas, / Which Heaven planted us to please" (322–24).

Largely ignoring the potent royalist symbol of Windsor Castle, Pope follows his country house predecessors by opening "Windsor Forest" with a call to nature—"Thy Forests, *Windsor!* and thy green Retreats"—and then proceeding to locate the foundation of England's imperial ascent in the divine economy of nature itself (1). Where Pope, however, departs from precedent is in placing an author at the center of this landscape. What truly distinguishes Pope's poem is not the historical process it reveals, but the subject it fashions. Turning to the moments of authorial assertion that open and close Pope's poem, the rest of this chapter is devoted to delineating what Pope does in "Windsor Forest" to cast his own poetic persona as the quintessential subject of England's national theology. Written alongside his youthful imitations of Virgil, the narrative frame of "Windsor Forest" places Pope's authorial self at the center of a pastoral landscape wrought with divine language. Although Pope never writes another work quite like "Windsor Forest," he devotes much of his career to elaborating upon the paradoxical combination of heroic self-assertion and pious self-effacement that make up its authorial identity. While many early modern poets dreamt of an ascendant England accomplishing the prophecies of classical and scriptural golden ages, it was Pope alone who imagined the hero of this process to be an embattled individual defined by the at once transcendent and material virtue of language. It was Pope, in other words, who took the various mysticisms of early modern England as an opportunity to construct for himself the character of an eighteenth-century domestic novel heroine.

After calling on the muses for inspiration, Pope begins the second stanza of "Windsor Forest" with a self-conscious figuration whose significance has been lost by critics. Marshaling a host of literary allusions, Pope transforms humanity's original state of paradise into a metalanguage kept alive by the pens of heroic subjects like him:

> The Groves of *Eden*, vanish'd now so long,
> Live in Description, and look green in Song:
> *These*, were my Breast inspir'd with equal Flame,
> Like them in Beauty, should be like in Fame. (7–10)

With the assonant rhyme scheme in these lines, from "long" and "Song" to "Flame" and "Fame," Pope constructs a tightly organized metrical frame designed to unite the opposing poles that constitute the two central dichotomies of his work: divine origin versus discursive determination, and transcendent authority versus mortal authorship. The caesuras neatly dividing the first two lines reinforce the unity of the opposition between the lost paradise of Eden and its representational legacy in verse. The irregularity of the third line, with its punctuated opening syllable "*These*," marks with a belabored pause the difficulty of the transition between these oppositions, from the bygone era of divine immediacy to the present discourse of inspired yet mortal mimesis.

Despite the metrical pauses and conditional tense, these two couplets accomplish a movement from the transcendent to the earthly that contradicts Pope's own later allusion to these lines at the end of "The Rape of the Lock": "*This Lock*, the Muse shall consecrate to Fame, / And midst the Stars inscribe *Belinda*'s Name!" (2.191–92). In both iterations of "Fame," Pope calls upon the Horatian adage of verse as a "monument more lasting than bronze," but only in "Windsor Forest" does Pope actually attempt to fix in history the dichotomy of immorality and matter that structures Horace's oft-repeated phrase (30.1). Steeped in biblical allusions and articulated with a sincerity not found in the depthless irony of "The Rape of the Lock," Pope's authorial persona in "Windsor Forest" comes closer to the narrator of John Milton's *Paradise Lost* (1667) insofar as both represent themselves as divine mediators capable of translating the "Beauty" and fullness of humanity's Edenic origins into the shadows of mortal representation. From this perspective, Pope's authorial "I" seems less an innovation than an imitation of Milton's epic narrator, who, after all, was "taught by the Heav'nly Muse to . . . see and tell / Of things invisible to mortal sight" (3.19, 54–55). Yet what distinguishes Pope's poem is that it engages theology but abandons the illusions of orality that underpin the authorial identities of authors like Milton and Dryden who represent their inspired writing in the more modest terms of seeing and telling. Distinguished from "The Rape of the Lock" by the earnestness of its political and theological commitments, "Windsor Forest" nevertheless stands apart from its religiously inclined predecessors because, like "The Rape of the Lock," it is molded by the irony of literary self-consciousness.

Each of the couplets in Pope's opening act of self-representation in "Windsor Forest" is made up of overt allusions to earlier texts. Pope's "I" thus emerges from these lines not as a mediator of divine presence itself, but as a translator of an already mediated divine filtered through a supernaturally elected tradition of English writing. In stating that the "Groves of *Eden* . . . Live in Description [and] look green in Song," Pope playfully implies an original, a primordial signified lying beneath his descriptions and their mimetic representations of fecundity, while at the same time denying precisely this sentiment by expressing it through the words of a previous text. As a piece of neoclassical rhetoric, the invocation of the muse is in itself a contradiction since it asks for extralinguistic inspiration through the hyperlinguistic means of a formal trope. Instead of reproducing the paradox of linguistically invoking the extralinguistic, Pope parts from convention by making this contradiction explicit. He borrows his suggestion that the "Groves of *Eden* . . . Live in Description [and] look green in Song" from the first lines of Edmund Waller's "On St. James's Park" (1661), which begins "Of the first paradise there's nothing found; / Plants set by Heaven are vanish'd, and the ground; / Yet the Description lasts" (1–3). Written to celebrate Charles II's restoration of St. James's Park and the nation more broadly, Waller's poem casts England in the typological glow of Old Testament Israel, yet, unlike "Windsor Forest," Waller posits this aura of divinity as beyond the reach of language and its authors. Pope employs biblical typology to precisely the opposite effect by depicting the author as the central agent in a process of election that occurs within rather than beyond language. Throughout "Windsor Forest," Pope depicts ideas of pure presence, whether they are of humanity's origin or God's transcendence, as inescapably immersed within the mediating categories of discourse and authorship.

Having established paradise as an irretrievably discursive entity, in the couplet beginning "The Groves of *Eden*," Pope turns to representing his authorial identity as heaven's exemplary heir: "*These*, were my Breast inspir'd with equal Flame, / Like them in Beauty, should be like in Fame." With deceptive modesty, Pope describes divine inspiration in the conditional tense of "were my Breast inspir'd" while simultaneously making an allusion that transforms the subjunctive mood of this first conditional into the zero-conditional certainty of a performative utterance. Pope takes the sentiment and rhyme scheme for this couplet from Denham's "Cooper's Hill" and thus speaks in these lines from the perspective not merely of writing, but, more precisely, from a national tradition of writing cast in the previous couplet as God's one true medium.

In the midst of its royalist survey of England's landscape and history, "Cooper's Hill" analogizes the contested origins of Windsor to the debates surrounding the birthplace of Homer, whom it is said seven Greek cities claimed as a native son. Speaking to the unknown progenitor of Windsor Castle, Denham writes, "Like him [Homer] in birth, thou shouldst be like in fame, / As thine his fate, if mine had been his flame" (71–2). Though opposed to the radical abstraction and interiority of earlier metaphysical poets, Denham nevertheless opens "Cooper's Hill" with a self-conscious representation of the poet as a miraculous figure of creation on par with the king. Poets for Denham made "Parnassus" and "Helicon" just as surely as "kings the court" (2, 3, 5). Given his emphasis on the constitutive function of poetry and his ensuing deification of Windsor, Denham's confession that he is not the Homer Windsor warrants appears to be an instance of false modesty. Denham bows before Homer while at the same time creating a national mythology that succeeds the Homeric. By hailing Windsor as a site sanctioned by God to bear the "pompous load" of royal authority, Denham subtly valorizes his language as the source of the world's new Olympus (50). Denham thus provides Pope with something beyond rhyme and sentiment: he establishes a model of ironic enactment that Pope intensifies through a set of strategic allusions (50).

Pope helps make the domestic novel possible because he takes the literary self-consciousness of seventeenth-century verse to the point of self-constitution. Going beyond Denham and his peers, Pope uses allusion to craft his authorial self as the bearer of a national identity preserved in writing and grounded by God. The understated yet central authorial "I" of "Windsor Forest" emerges from a fissure in English history that the critic Earl Wasserman, in his important essay "Nature Moralized" (1953), locates in the eighteenth century, since it was then that truth began to shift from an a priori theological domain to an a posteriori psychological plane of individual experience. Wasserman argues that "in the eighteenth century . . . there is to be found the last significant vestige of the myth of an analogically ordered universe" in which "all created things are explications of God" and thus "analogous to each other and the divine original" (42–43). The poet plays an essential role in such a universe, given that it is through imaginative acts of language—of correspondence, analogy, and typology—that humanity learns to read the things of this world as imbued with spiritual value (66). In Renaissance and early modern English society, the sensory universe of human experience was a divinely grounded text awaiting poetic illumination; by the period in which Pope writes, however, the combined forces of "science, skepticism, and rationalistic deism" had prompted many to question "whether the basis of figurative language lies within or without man" (40, 61).

Pope's "Windsor Forest" at once confirms and complicates Wasserman's image of the eighteenth century as a period of transition from the divine ontology of nature to the secular psychology of individuals. Pope's poem possesses the bipartite structure of figurative representation and didactic interpretation that Wasserman identifies as symptomatic of an age in which analogies could no longer be taken for granted. Having once been simply implied through moving descriptions, divine analogies now had to be consciously created through didactic explanations of nature's significance. Wasserman depicts the eras on either side of the eighteenth century as separated by an irreducible "breach" (75). He characterizes the coming age as one devoid of the absolutism of God, one in which "associational psychology . . . served to explain . . . relationships between the material world and qualities of the mind, not the relationship of the physical, moral, and spiritual" (68). And yet, when Pope cries "my Breast" in the opening self-representation of "Windsor Forest," he marks the impossibility of Wasserman's neat distinction, since the body he inserts into the poem stands as an inherently discursive and nationalized medium of God rather than a source of particularized, secular meaning.

The intersection of myth and matter that constitutes the Renaissance-like sensuality of Pope's poem extends beyond the portraits of animate rivers and blushing flowers: it includes Pope's own authorial body. Pope's attention to self-constitution in "Windsor Forest" is both linguistic and corporeal. The doubleness, however, of his meta-authorship is lost on those who view the early eighteenth century in the stagiest and teleological terms of a transition between two distinct periods. Read from the perspective of Wasserman and the mode of historiography he practices, Pope's self-consciousness in "Windsor Forest" appears to be merely another instance of the dual and sometimes-contradictory allegiances present in moments of change. As such a reading would have it, Pope posits two competing foundations for truth, nature, and a poetic individual, because he, in the words of Wasserman, participates in "that divorce of head and heart, of object and value, that accompanied the approaching end of the Renaissance" (39). The problem is that the Renaissance conception of nature was not some kernel for Pope to discard in the forward march of history; instead, it was the very substance of Pope's new individual, a kernel of absolutism that is internalized rather than effaced.

Pope never stops grounding his authorial persona in the transcendent sovereignty of God, a characteristic he exemplifies with particular vigor in the second "Epilogue to the Satires" (1738), where he hails his writing as a "sacred weapon . . . / To all but heaven-directed hands denied, / The muse may give . . . but the God must guide" (212, 213–14). While many of Pope's works craft a doubled authorial self suspended between the earthly and the transcendent, "Windsor Forest" is unique in dramatizing the origins of Pope's protonovelistic identity in the Renaissance landscape of natural ontology. Pope constructs a heroically individualized and discursive self out of the medieval and Renaissance assumption that it is God's sacred and nationalized language that gives animation and purpose to nature's many objects, from fields to rivers to authors. Synthesizing past and present, Pope develops an alternative narrative of the movement from divine ontology to individual psychology in the early eighteenth century. For Pope, the individual, far from abandoning God's order, subsumes it as an at once transcendent and discursive principle of being.

The Embodied Author and the Theology of National Matter

In "Windsor Forest," Pope constructs a narrative self that stands within rather than before the sacred landscape he describes; Pope's narrator is thus both more discursive and more embodied than his seventeenth-century predecessors. Rejecting the distinction between an Edenic origin and its later representations, Pope depicts his authorial self as a subject who embodies Eden not only in his self-conscious verse, but also in his linguistically rich flesh. Stricken by tuberculosis of the spine while still a child, Pope was marked by the age of twelve with a hunchbacked body that never reached more than four and half feet in height and a face that bore the strained countenance of disease. In the words of his biographer Maynard Mack, "By the time [Pope] began to be known as a successful poet he was already established in his own mind and in the minds of others as a dwarf and a cripple" (153). Deutsch's *Resemblance and Disgrace* (1996) is a crucial work in the study of Pope because it was the first to take Pope's exceptional body as a serious literary problem. Among Pope scholars, the overarching consensus had been to separate Pope's corporeal particularity from his verse. Mack, for example, describes Pope's writing as a "sword . . . that gleams so brightly inside its decaying scabbard" (158). Following Deutsch, I counter that the body for Pope was not some external condition of his poetic practice; rather, it was his first word, his most immediate and intimate connection to the art of representation—"a mode of conceiving," in the words of Deutsch (4). While persons read as normal in the eighteenth century may have been able to imagine their bodies as existing beyond language, Pope's strained face and hunchbacked frame solicited discourse.

In the opening of "Windsor Forest," Pope reinforces the corporeal dimension of his poetic persona by alluding to his own authorial "Breast": "*These*, were my Breast inspir'd with equal Flame, / Like them in Beauty, should be like in Fame" (9–10). The definition of "breast" in the *Oxford English Dictionary* ranges from the unambiguously physical ("the front of the thorax or chest . . . lying between the neck and the belly") to the intensely figurative ("seat of affections and emotions; the repository of consciousness, designs, and secrets; the *heart*, hence, the affections, private thoughts and feelings") (n2, n5). Pope draws on both valences, creating a subjective space of interiority grounded in both the flesh and the language of God it incarnates. Set against the backdrop of the discursive Eden invoked in the previous couplet—"The Groves of *Eden*, vanished now so long, / Live in Description, and look green in Song"—Pope proceeds to enact the possibility of an Edenic return occurring through the newly fleshed-out figure of the embodied author (6–7). And Pope stages this return by interjecting a body part, the breast, classically associated with the swelling of pride and, in Pope's case, with its shameful imitation.

Described by Voltaire as "protuberant before and behind" and by Pope himself as a "Spider," Pope's body was marked by a breast that was fixed in the hyperlinguistic position of the permanently ironic, signifying at once pride and its debasement (quoted in Deutsch 1, 2).

Acting as a kind of metateratologist, Pope seizes upon his own frame as an opportunity to pursue a state of self-possession rooted in language. Rather than attempting to obscure or overcome the discourse his body solicits, Pope takes it as a source of valorization, a condition that imbues with linguistic value those parts of his authorial self that seem most outside discourse. As part of a Tory Augustan culture that celebrated the autonomy made possible by owning guns and land, Pope, as Catherine Ingrassia notes, "regarded his poetry as a type of property," and, one could add, a weapon as well (486). Barred from owning land as a Catholic but intent on achieving the republican ideal of self-possession, Pope develops a mode of virtue fit for a new financial age.

Though fashioned from the principles of civic humanism, Pope's authorial persona is nevertheless available to characters such as crippled Catholic poets as well as their feminine domestic novel successors. In an era when, as Pope asserts in his "First Epistle of the First Book of Horace," not a single person "has it in his power / To act consistent with himself an hour," his poetry works to recast virtue as a matter of submission to the ennobled medium of divinely sanctioned English verse (137). It is no coincidence that three stanzas following the previous quote, taken from his "Epistle to Bolingbroke" (1738), Pope alludes to his own "half beau, half sloven" body (161).[12] It is, after all, Pope's body that ironically marks his self-possession in a world he redefines as plagued by its alienation—not from arms or lands, but language and the transcendent truths it carries. Upon the marvelous swerve of his own monstrosity, Pope constructs an immanent yet theological mode of being that anticipates the physically besieged yet discursively empowered heroines of domestic novels. In his hands, the discursively overdetermined body of the monster becomes the basis for a new self, one defined by its devotion to the doubled medium of text. Within and without a Renaissance landscape of divine analogy, Pope's authorial self is the monstrous possibility of a new norm.

Confusing distinctions between the metaphysical and the natural, the Renaissance and the modern, the divine and the secular, Pope's final act of self-constitution in "Windsor Forest" builds upon the corporeal dimension of his opening self-figuration by situating the "Breast" of his authorial self within the "Strain" or race of the English nation. In a characteristic gesture of false modesty, Pope begins the final stanza of "Windsor Forest" by subordinating his "humble Muse" to the "Verse" of his poem's dedicatee, George Granville, an aristocratic poet and privy councillor who helped negotiate the Treaty of Utrecht (427, 425). Granville was a favored advisor of the Queen, and it is thus "*Granville's* Verse" that promises to give "the thoughts of Gods . . . / And bring the Scenes of opening Fate to Light" (425–26). Pope's deference to Granville would make sense in Dryden's early panegyrics and other works in which the monarch alone holds the key to salvation, but in "Windsor Forest" something more is at work.

Imitating Virgil, who ended his *Georgics* by echoing the opening of his *Eclogues*, Pope concludes "Windsor Forest" with a reiteration of the start of his own youthful pastorals. What separates Pope's conclusion from Virgil's is that Pope's authorial self stands at the end of "Windsor Forest" not simply as a symbol for a pastoral way of being, but as a hero of the nation, closer to the epic protagonist Aeneas than the lounging Tityrus of the *Eclogues*. At the beginning of his poem's final stanza, Pope makes a number of allusions to the *Aeneid* while describing those subjects fit for "*Granville's* verse": lofty themes such as the "fair Fame of *Albion's* Golden Days," "the Thoughts of Gods," and "the Scenes of Opening Fate" (424–26). While appearing to mark a distinction between the pastoral universe of his poem and the epic sphere of Granville, Pope in fact engages in a characteristically ironic strategy of poetically enacting what the content of his verse deems impossible. Pope infuses the broader and more abstract vocabulary of the epic into the immanent particularity of the pastoral by following his invocation of the abstract themes of national fate and glory with a final rendition of the bucolic imagery running throughout "Windsor Forest."

Having attributed the act of painting to gods, trees, and Granville himself at earlier points in the poem, Pope takes the conclusion of "Windsor Forest" as an opportunity to identify his authorial persona as the primary agent of artistic creation: "My humble Muse, in unambitious Strains, / Paints the green Forests and the flow'ry Plains" (38, 216, 285, 427–28). By placing his poetic "I" in the position previously held by "blushing *Flora*," "floating forests," and Granville's "lofty numbers," Pope develops the expectation that his authorial self will emerge from the final stanza of his poem as the ultimate cause of Windsor's beauty (38, 216, 287). Pope prepares his reader for the revelation that his claims to modesty up to this point in the poem have been false, since they served as a mere mask for the sly construction of himself as the secular source of Windsor's charm. This secularized image of the author builds through the concluding lines of Pope's work, gaining momentum in the enjambed form and heroic content of the last couplet, until the final contracted five syllables of the poem unequivocally dispel it: "Enough for me, that to the listning Swains / First in these Fields I sung the Sylvan Strains" (433–34). Pope borrows this concluding line from the opening of his first pastoral, "Spring" (1709), which begins: "First in these Fields I try the Sylvan Strains." Substituting "sung" for "try," Pope finishes "Windsor Forest" by cementing the status of his authorial self as a glorified object of God's language and not an autonomous subject of secular beauty. Pope's poet sings what already exists, and in the piety of this submission lies the transcendent heights and heroic individuation of his life as a parishioner of national verse.

Disabled and Catholic, Pope could neither look nor act like an enfranchised member of the English political system, yet in the final couplet of "Windsor Forest" he represents himself as one of its truest subjects. The pastoral objects of Windsor's landscape—its "green Forests," "flow'ry Plains," and authorial "breast"—find their principle of animation and inner purpose in an immanent language of election. Pope characterizes this language as made up of "Sylvan Strains," a description that captures the at once transcendent and corporeal nature of English national theology. Signifying "a thread, line, [or] streak," the noun "Strains" is used by Pope as a means of figuratively representing both the sequential harmony of his verse and the essentialized model of nationhood that it articulates (*OED* n3). "Strains" is a word that lends itself to metaphor, and its signification ranges from the poetic to the concrete, from the harmony of verse to issues of "begetting and generation," such as, in the words of the *OED*, the "the germinal vesicle in the yolk of an egg," or, more broadly, the lineage of a "race, stock, [or] line" (n1). With "strains," Pope emphasizes that he is constructing a nation that is both theological and biological. It is a collective whose identity is grounded in the supposed unity of a "stock" chosen by God as the means of global redemption. While "Strains" names the physical side of this equation, "Sylvan" expresses its mythological import.

Drawn from the annals of ancient Greek and Roman precursors, "Sylvan" not only marks the classicism of Pope's verse, and its particular indebtedness to Virgil, but also the liminality existing at the heart of Pope's authorial self. Connoting "a being of the woods"—whether it be a human "rustic," an "animal," or an "imaginary" creature such as a nymph or satyr—the adjective "Sylvan" is used to describe the forms of life borne of wooded domains beyond the more ordered spaces of cities and fields (*OED* n1). By adding "Sylvan" to "Strains," Pope clarifies that the thread of ancestry and verse dominating the objects of his landscape emanates from a literal and metaphorical outside. In a sylvan space of withdrawal, a *locus amoenus*, Pope's narrative "I" exists as a liminal creature inhabiting that state conceptualized by Epicurus as ataraxia, a condition where "the body is free from pain and the mind from anxiety" ("Letter to Menoeceus" 57). Beyond the aleatory oscillation of happiness and worry, and thus beyond happiness itself, Pope's poet stands in the penultimate couplet of "Windsor Forest" in a position of Epicurean serenity: "Ev'n I more sweetly pass my careless Days, / Pleas'd in the silent shade with empty Praise" (431–32). Happily estranged from the fortune-driven spheres of public opinion, Pope occupies the subjectivity of an individual who has risen above the whims of chance.

While Epicurus and many after him characterize the state of ataraxia as a "simple life" beyond the realm of political power, Pope moves in precisely the opposite direction and posits the perfection of one's political fidelity as the foundation of sylvan ease (57). Pope's final two couplets in "Windsor Forest" allude to the most influential moment from Dryden's much-celebrated 1697 translation of the *Georgics*. Characteristically broadening the philosophical scope of his Virgilian original, Dryden's second *Georgics* exclaims not "all terrors cast, and death's relentless doom," as another translation puts it, but states, "His mind possessing, in a quiet State, / Fearless of Fortune, and resigned to Fate" (Rhoades 57; Dryden 700–701). As Hammond notes, Dryden "brings Virgil closer to Lucretius" by endowing his metaphorical depictions of pastoral life with Epicurean significance (204). In his translation of Virgil's works, Dryden achieves what Hammond describes as "a dematerialization of the Virgilian pastoral" (202). Dryden's philosophical interpretation of the rural exercised a profound influence upon a literary public that increasingly included those who could read neither Virgil nor Epicurus in the original (Hammond 200).[13] Dryden's "happy" rustic "decks the Bow'rs / Of Sylvans, and adores the Rural Pow'rs," and thereby rises above "the Purple Slavery ... of Courts" (702–3, 705, 704). Pope, on the other hand, plumbs the philosophical meaning of pastoral retreat in order to discover, instead of depoliticized contentment, the supremely political task of manifesting and submitting to the immanent destiny of a nation. Pope maintains the dematerialized idealism of Dryden's translation while simultaneously rematerializing its concepts within the particularity of pastoral objects, in a way that builds on Dryden's own strategy in "To My Honour'd Kinsman."

Dogged by accusations of deism throughout his life and accused by Johnson of "confounding words with things," Pope was a poet bent on finding discursive meaning, divine and otherwise, in material things (Russell 242). A Catholic throughout his career, Pope nevertheless was the poet who wrote a *Universal Prayer* (1716/1738) that ends not with the a plea to Christ to "lead [him] safely through Death," as in the case of Pope Clement XI's 1721 version, but with an invocation of a fleshly Lord, "whose Temple is all space, / Whose alter earth, sea, and skies" (Pope Clement XI 66; Pope 49–50). While such statements led Pope's contemporaries as well as many of his later readers to suspect him of deism, the critic Chester Chapin helpfully notes that such conclusions tend to rest on the false assumption that "Roman Catholic teaching was as monolithic, as unified, as clearly a defined body of doctrine in Pope's day ... as it seems to have become in the next two centuries" (411). Chapin attempts to bring Pope back into the Christian fold and makes a convincing case for understanding him as an "ecumenical" Catholic modeled after the Renaissance humanist and Dutch theologian Erasmus (423). Chapin is right, but not exactly in the way he intended.

Departing from Erasmus, Pope nationalized the "ecumenical" promise of Scripture, incorporating it into the sinews and oaks of a particular sectarian nation. To ignore this in favor of a more palatable image, as Chapin does, is to miss the essence of Pope's theological practice. Pope was a political theologian and teratologist as well as a poet, and he took his own monstrous body as the exemplary first word of a "Strain" that turned the universality of Christ's promise into the prerogative of an ascendant imperial nation.

Pope, Clarissa, and the Ambiguous Legacy of the Domestic Novel

No scholar of Pope should ignore the blood on his verse. Pope's vision of "*Albion*'s Golden Days" came to fruition with the United Kingdom's nineteenth-century transformation into the world's largest-ever empire, encompassing one-fifth of the global population at its height and bearing responsibility for unprecedented massacres, famines, and mass enslavements, crimes ranging from the starvation of the Irish in the 1840s to the widespread torture and internment of the Kenyans in the 1950s (424). Amid the great diversity of horror spawned by over three centuries of British imperial rule, there is a single thread that unites it all, a point of conceptual continuity present in "Windsor Forest" and succinctly expressed by the historian Philip Morgan in the context of Britain's Caribbean colonies: "White West Indians accepted the naturalness of Africans as slaves . . . [by] likening them to animals" (381). Pope's vision of a perpetual peace secured by the long-prophesized ascent of a God-loved humanity is predicated upon anticipatory acts of dehumanization. Such acts are the other side of his "Sacred *Peace*" achieved through permanent "Sylvan War;" they express the violence that is committed upon "Birds and Beasts alone" and that is therefore no violence at all (355, 148, 374). It is the threat of being expelled from the nationalized boundaries of a God-grounded humanity that has menaced everyone, from enslaved West Africans and imperiled novelistic heroines to embattled Tory poets.

Late in life, decades after the height of his political clout and years after his withdrawal to the suburban village of Twickenham, Pope devoted himself to writing bitter satires in which his authorial persona appeared as a heroic exception to a culture he depicted as overcome with the dehumanizing experience of commodification. In the first of his epilogues to these 1730s satires, Pope envisions "*Vice*" as a goddess of pure matter who "in golden Chains the willing World she draws," as "thronging Millions to [her] Pagod run, / And offer Country, Parent, Wife or Son!" (141, 147, 157–58). Against a majority given over to the lure of life without virtue, Pope proclaims at the end of his poem: "Yet may this Verse (if such a Verse remain) / Show there was one who held it in disdain" (171–72). However different this may appear from "Windsor Forest," in truth Pope's moving finale to this epilogue represents a reiteration of his earlier image of his authorial self as a singer of "Sylvan Strains" (435). Whether laced with the bitterness of age or lifted by the promise of youth, Pope casts his authorial self as a subject saved from enslavement and animality by the conjoined forces of God, writing, and the nation.

When the eponymous heroine of Richardson's *Clarissa* faces her own threat of degradation, she dramatizes the potential emancipation that lies within the subjectivity that Pope spent his career cultivating. In the following chapter, I trace Clarissa's response to this dehumanization, which is remarkable in part for the simple reason that Clarissa refuses to indulge in the fantasy of a humanity that exists somewhere beyond a history shaped by theology. Clarissa commits herself to a process that the critic Cesare Casarino describes as "running the risk of transcendence" (xxxiii). What she shows is that since theology cannot be avoided, it instead ought to be inherited strategically, for only then can one dream of redirecting it away from the blood-soaked landscape of nations and toward the promised land of a universal elect.

3

"Beyond What the Crown Itself Can Confer"

Clarissa and the Antinomian Heart of the Modern British Subject

Clarissa as King

Critics generally know what to do with Richardson's first novel, *Pamela* (1740). Its tale of a young servant girl who tactfully manages to convert the libertine lust of her gentlemanly master into a respectable desire for matrimony indeed seems to neatly signal the emergence of the domestic novel from the more chaotic universe of early eighteenth-century fiction. Rather than circulating through the global landscape of England's newly commercial society, like the protagonists of earlier novels such as Daniel Defoe's *Moll Flanders* (1722) or Eliza Haywood's *Fantomina* (1724), *Pamela*'s eponymous heroine remains confined within the rural, upper-class home of her employer as a kind of captive commodity. Pamela exploits this state, by transforming her patriarchal employer/first customer into a husband; in doing so, she articulates a specifically domestic strategy for managing the disorientation of a market-driven society. With a heroine who relies on the bourgeois arts of delayed gratification, lawful negotiations, and marriage to escape the danger and excitement of early capitalist England, *Pamela* participates in the ideology of domesticity that to this day tells us we can escape the inhumanity of commodification through the sentimentality of our domestic relations.

In his second novel, *Clarissa*, however, Richardson does something different. At once within and beyond the domestic novel tradition,

Clarissa demonstrates the possibility of using the conjoined ideologies of domesticity, individualism, and nationalism as tools for rebellion rather than submission. Though similarly held as a captive, first by her family and then by her libertine suitor, Robert Lovelace, *Clarissa*'s eponymous heroine refuses to follow Pamela and so many other domestic protagonists in pretending that marriage represents a real solution to the crisis she faces. In one of their many confrontations over the course of the novel, Lovelace describes the heroine he courts, kidnaps, and rapes as stubbornly ennobled, animated in fact by the same otherworldly persona that once elevated apostles, popes, and kings above the realm of the merely mortal: "She gave distinction to everyone related to her, beyond what the crown itself can confer.... The noble creature proceeded; for I could not speak.... Her whole person was informed by her sentiments. She seemed to be taller than before. How the God within her exalted her, not only above me, but above herself" (852–53). Mortal yet exalted, Clarissa stands alongside Pope's poet, Dryden's patriot, and Pamela herself as a modern-day king, but, unlike these others, Clarissa uses "the God within her" to oppose rather than sanctify the sovereignty of secular British society.

Clarissa rejects her family's choice of husband, the vulgar Mr. Solmes, as well as Lovelace's belated proposal, and instead embarks upon a campaign to use the theological foundation of her modern national self as a weapon of emancipation. Despite living in a fiercely patriarchal culture and being imprisoned by a succession of politically powerful men, Clarissa manages to achieve by the end of Richardson's novel a state of sovereign, self-governing independence. While critics have endlessly interpreted the fact that Clarissa eventually dies as a result of her hardships, far less attention has been given to what she accomplishes in anticipation of her demise. Long disparaged by scholars, and misunderstood by Richardson himself, it is *Clarissa*'s prolonged conclusion that represents the most significant section of the novel, and it is here that this chapter focuses, on the glorious period Clarissa spends beyond the authorities of this world and before the reach of the next one.[1]

Richardson's heroine passes the final weeks of her life in a simple London apartment above a glove shop where she is surrounded by friends and free to dedicate herself to activities of her own choosing, principally an epistolary religious practice best described as a kind of modern monasticism. In this period, living as a fully sovereign subject, Clarissa shows the emancipatory power that the modern national self contains. Trapped in a marriage plot that is itself steeped in the secularized theology of an ascendant empire, Clarissa embraces the marriage plot and the individualism it cultivates as the means of both her subjection and potential emancipation. Clarissa, in a sense, becomes a failed and yet also perfect subject of marriage and the nation. She stands not as the saint of a fading Puritan world—as Leo Damrosch and many other critics suggest—but, rather, as a national hero, a beacon of what the secularized theology of Britain could become.[2]

Clarissa and Political Theology

Like contemporaneous Methodist leaders of the 1730s and 1740s who declared themselves "more orthodox than the orthodox," Richardson's heroine rebels against eighteenth-century social order not by rejecting its values, but by exemplifying them too well (Clark 285). In the eighteenth century, marriage was a simultaneously religious and political act that signified one's incorporation into the national theology of imperial Britain. The vast majority of eighteenth-century weddings, whether regular or clandestine, were conducted in churches by ministers using the *Book of Common Prayer* in a ceremony that asked man and wife to publicly devote themselves to God and country, pledging "to live together after God's ordinance" within a political body repeatedly identified by the *Book of Common Prayer* as the bearer of "true religion" (136, 238).[3] Marriage, according to this ceremony, was "not by any to be enterprised, nor taken in hand, unadvisedly, lightly, or wantonly, to satisfy men's carnal lusts and appetites, like brute beasts that have no understanding." Instead, marriage represented an opportunity to fulfill typologically "the mystical union between Christ and his Church," the latter being for eighteenth-century Britain the Church of England. Marriage, in sum, was an object of holy nationalism; it was, as the *Book of Common Prayer* states, "instituted by God in the time of mans innocency" in order to set human life apart, and it was not therefore to be traded or calculated upon as if the subjects it engendered were not fully human—or, in other words, British (135).

Clarissa resembles countless other domestic novel protagonists, from Frances Burney's Evelina to Jane Austen's Fanny, in that she develops her capacity for individualism and self-governance through the struggle to protect the sacrality of marriage. Just as Pope cultivates himself as a national hero of virtue by battling an increasingly commercial culture with the timeless truths of his pen—"Yes, the last pen for Freedom let me draw!"—the heroes and heroines of domestic novels constitute themselves as fully fledged subjects only by opposing the materialism of those who seek to instrumentalize the sacred nationalism embodied by marriage ("Epilogue to the Satires II" 420). Clarissa, however, remains so faithful to the virtue of marriage that she cannot have one. She resists the successive efforts of her family and Lovelace to profane marriage, the first by commodifying it and the second by outright violating it, and, in the process, she stumbles upon a high-church path to antinomian insurrection.

Such a strategy for emancipation might appear, at first glance, radically insular. Richardson's heroine is, after all, a kind of loyalist rebel who is able to revolt in the name of England's most treasured values only because she begins her story as unquestionably Anglican and English. One would be justified in asking whether Clarissa's struggle is relevant to those who are not Anglicans living in the normatively Anglican society of eighteenth-century England. What such doubts overlook, however, is the essential fact that Clarissa is first and foremost a national rather than an Anglican protagonist. She emerges in the first pages of Richardson's novel as an exemplary subject of the nation, and she becomes a figure of renegade Protestant virtue only by retheologizing the national belonging she bears. In this chapter, I take the discussion of religion in Richardson's novel in a new direction by framing its heroine in the worldly terms of political theology, an approach that opens the possibility of viewing Clarissa as neither entirely religious nor secular and, in a sense, both at the same time.[4]

Although she offers an opposing definition of political theology, Victoria Kahn's diagnosis of the Heideggerian origins of the definition I use is important for this chapter, as it helps clarify the Heideggerian dimensions of Clarissa's struggle for freedom. From Kahn's perspective, by positing political theology as antisecular while simultaneously drawing from Kantorowicz, my book follows a wave of recent critical theorists—first and foremost Agamben—in projecting upon Kantorowicz's work an "existential relativism" smuggled from the thought of his contemporary Heidegger and, in particular, his idea of *Geworfenheit*, or "thrownness," the experience of being involuntarily cast into existence (80). Kahn's account is revealing in what it overlooks because what it misses is something that Heidegger in fact has in common with Richardson—namely, an antirelativist conception of death as a living phenomenon that allows mortals to puncture the relativism of *Geworfenheit* and in the process access the transcendent. In *Being and Time* (1927), Heidegger reconceives of death not as a material biological event, but as an inescapable internal possibility for no longer existing, "*an eminent* imminence" that connects life to the transcendent domain of being that underlies it (245). Being in the world or "Da-sein" must have "*the courage to have* Angst *about death*" because doing so allows it to apprehend the transcendence of being and thereby come to terms with itself "in its own *higher* power, the power of its finite freedom" (235, 351). Heidegger depicts the world as at its foundation transcendent, and yet also finite and secular, a presentation he can make only because he operates within a metaphysical realm that claims to lie outside the particularities of historical determination. In *Clarissa*, Richardson anticipates Heidegger's idea of death but does so in historical terms, and the result is that the transcendence death discloses can no longer be represented as either finite or secular.

Clarissa pursues a strategy that on one level is proto-Heideggerian insofar as she actively anticipates death and in the process transforms it into a tool of human freedom. However, on another level, Clarissa departs from Heidegger in that the transcendence she mobilizes has a history, and it is both infinite and religious. Clarissa uses the imminent possibility of death to access the particular Protestant transcendence that lies embedded within her secular national community. Clarissa's strategy centers on subordinating her mortal body to the overlapping tasks of writing letters and contemplating death, all of which she does in order to better incarnate the same otherworldly power that distinguished kings before her.[5] Clarissa frames her activities as mere "preparation" for the hereafter, and, by doing so, she manages to obscure what they accomplish in the here and now: a state of independence authorized by the very theological power that the British state claimed as its own (1118).

In the following lines from a posthumously delivered letter that Clarissa writes in expectation of her death, she exemplifies her tactic of using writing and death to achieve a divine independence in this world while appearing merely to anticipate it in the next one:

> I take this last and solemn occasion to repeat to you my thanks for all your kindness to me at a time when I most needed countenance and protection.
>
> A few considerations I beg leave, as now, at your perusal of this, from the dead, to press upon you, with all the warmth of a sincere friendship. (1367)

These two sentences are separated by the biological moment of Clarissa's passing, and yet the language of embodiment runs through both. Having needed her addressee's "protection" in the past tense of life, Clarissa writes, "as now," in a kind of anticipatory present tense from the triumphantly independent position of the already dead. Defined by Johnson as either "support" or "a form of the face," "countenance" establishes a thread of corporeality that Clarissa imagines intensifying after her death when she expects her discursive body "to press upon" her friend John Belford "with all the warmth" of the living (1.494). While Clarissa's anticipation of death is clearly oriented toward a beyond, it also has an effect on the living body of the author, and this latter point is the one that has long escaped the attention of critics. Clarissa's religious practice is a living political strategy that consists of using the inevitability of her death to access a divine perspective that she folds back onto her self through the practice of writing.

Interpretations of Clarissa's monastic withdrawal—deconstructionist, Marxist, Foucauldian, psychoanalytic, and less easily classifiable recent studies by authors such as Vivasvan Soni and Laura Rosenthal—have varied widely, but they have tended to agree on the one point that it is tragically anachronistic. These critics, as well as Richardson himself, have failed to appreciate the political alternative that Clarissa embodies during her final weeks because they have interpreted them according to a false dichotomy between the transcendent concerns of England's religious past and the material life of its modern secular future. Refusing this opposition, this chapter represents *Clarissa* as both a critique of secularism and a defense of the freedom that a nonsecular understanding of British modernity makes possible. In a message that reverberates in his own time as well as our own, Richardson's novel highlights the possibility for a sovereign, emancipated existence not in some extratextual "hereafter," but rather in the very heart of Britain's modernizing present (*Clarissa* 1205).

Captivity Memoirs and Clarissa as the Excessive Exemplar

With its stories of exemplary young women using letter-writing to endure a captivity that ends happily in marriage, the eighteenth-century domestic novel indeed seems to owe, as Nancy Armstrong and Leonard Tennenhouse argue in *The Imaginary Puritan* (1992), its protagonist and narrative structure to the captivity memoirs of colonial American women abducted by New World natives. Due to the popularity of these memoirs on both sides of the Atlantic, as well as their association with female authors, the figure of the "exemplary captive," in the words of Armstrong and Tennenhouse, "existed for the early eighteenth-century reader as a kind of epistolary heroine whose ability to read and write, more than anything else distinguished her from her Indian captors" (204). Organized around stories of "exile and return," captivity memoirs possessed, as Armstrong and Tennenhouse demonstrate, an uncanny capacity to make the effects of their narratives appear as if they preceded all such acts of writing (25). When the protagonists of memoirs such as Mary Rowlandson's *Sovereignty and the Goodness of God* (1682) win their freedom, they return not simply to their communities of origin, but more specifically to their spouses and the "restored" domestic sphere that this reunion signifies. These tales of bondage and liberation thus produce not only a new model of the British subject as a "literate individual" and the family as a nuclear unit, but also the illusion that these innovations represent timeless qualities of their heroines' original communities (204).[6] Writing functions in these stories, as Derrida says of the trace in *Of Grammatology* (1967), as "the origin of the origin" (61).

Armstrong and Tennenhouse convincingly show how *Pamela* exemplifies the uncanny rhetorical power of the captivity narrative by representing the products of its heroine's letters—her sacralized self, marriage, and dramatic class ascent—as ironically beyond the purview of language. Functioning within the story essentially as a character in themselves, Pamela's letters are what ultimately persuade her master, Mr. B, to accept her as a wife, and his even more status-conscious sister to forgive this scandalous act of class condescension (250, 456). With characters making frequent allusions to the "pretty Novel" they are enacting, *Pamela* can be read until the point of its denouement as a self-conscious meditation on the constitutive power of discourse (232). All this, however, changes with the emergence of the editor in the novel's conclusion: "Here end the Letters of the incomparable Pamela to her Father and Mother. For, as they arriv'd at their Daughter's House on *Tuesday* Evening in the following Week, she had no Occasion to continue her journal longer" (498). With the union of Pamela's new conjugal family and the family of origin from whom she had been forcefully kept, Richardson illustrates the way domestic novels strategically reinterpret the narrative structure of seventeenth-century captivity tales. Rather than returning to her original community, Pamela effectively civilizes the New World of the premodern gentleman, thereby rendering his estate amenable to the virtuous family she left behind. In synthesizing old and new, civilized and uncivilized, domestic novels provide readers with the means of reconciling new and threatening models of the self and the family with earlier, more communitarian modes of being. Domestic novels, in other words, mobilize a narrative of "exile and return" to make the new appear as synonymous with the old. Once firmly established in the position of a heroically individuated national subject and dutiful wife, Pamela, as Richardson's editor insinuates, is so natural that she exists beyond language; there is "no Occasion" for any further acts of epistolary self-constitution.

While Armstrong and Tennenhouse are right to take *Pamela* as a quintessential captivity tale, their suggestion that *Clarissa* belongs to the same tradition overlooks the simple but essential fact that its heroine refuses to return. Clarissa uses the individuating experience of captivity not to introduce her original community to a new model of the individual, but to recover the divine foundation of her heroically isolated and discursive self. Clarissa is the "exemplary captive" who chooses the divinity of her origins over the comforting arms of a husband. Eschewing formal and theological heresies, *Clarissa* paradoxically achieves a singular status within the domestic novel tradition by remaining militantly faithful both to the developing structure of the novel and the foundational tenets of the Reformation. In terms of its form, *Clarissa* in truth merely perfects the captivity narrative by refusing to collapse its exemplary heroine and epistolary narrator into an extratextual beyond, which would undermine the constitutive role that such narratives assign to writing. Heroically defending her identity from the opening letter of the novel, Clarissa is unusual only in that she brings the figure of the captive heroine to its extreme limit of perfection.

Whereas *Pamela* begins with its heroine declaring herself a figure of suffering and virtue, *Clarissa* opens with the public calling upon its heroine to perform the role of moral exemplar.[7] Writing as a representative of England's burgeoning community of literate individuals, Anna Howe delivers the following challenge to her friend: "You see what you draw upon yourself by excelling all your sex. Every individual of it who knows you, or has heard of you, seems to think you answerable to *her* for your conduct in points so very delicate and concerning. Every eye, in short, is upon you with the expectation of an example" (40). Anna places Clarissa in the simultaneously glorified and debased position of an objectified subject who, by standing apart from and "excelling" her counterparts, renders herself vulnerable to their judgment. With the phrase "you draw upon yourself," however, Anna subtly articulates the masochistic and narcissistic strategy through which Clarissa will oppose this overbearing public, for she exists within this phrase as the simultaneous subject and object of a violence she both draws and suffers. Rather than refusing the oppressive demands of eighteenth-century English society, Clarissa counterintuitively seeks her emancipation by declaring this violence her own and affirming her mortal frame as its appropriate object.

Clarissa pursues a militant epistolary practice that centers on masochistically submitting herself to writing as that medium that houses transcendent truths in mortal life. Clarissa's spiritual struggle through the novel is, in other words, also a formal one, since it involves her coming as close as possible to being the exemplary epistolary self that her community imposes upon her. Tasked with being at once a body and an ideal, Clarissa develops an absolutist strategy for collapsing the former into the latter. When Anna looks upon Clarissa's corpse at the end of the novel, she marks the culmination of this absolutist campaign by identifying Clarissa's body as a purely narrative object: "Oh my blessed friend . . . my sweet companion!—my lovely monitress—kissing [Clarissa's] lips at every tender invocation. And is this all!—is it all of my CLARISSA's story! . . . . Repeating, This cannot, surely, be all of my CLARISSA's story!" (1402–13). Anna touches the body of her friend with "every tender invocation," and yet, at this late point in Richardson's narrative, Clarissa's mortal frame is inescapably discursive, part of a "story" rather than a single, unambiguous moment between bodies. Over the course of their prolonged separation, Anna had taken not only to understanding her friend in the doubled terms of a linguistic sign, both signified and signifier, but also to privileging the latter. She began to diagnose the health of Clarissa's mortal body through the symptoms of her written one, noting at one point that Clarissa's epistolary "style and sentiment are too well connected, too full of life and vigor to give cause for so much despair as the staggering pen seems to threaten" (1348). Once reunited in the flesh, it thus is fitting that Clarissa's mortal body stands as a lifeless object, and Anna's response is to express both heartfelt woe and disbelief that this thing, this "it," could threaten the exemplary "story" it made possible.

To Anna's initial challenge that she "put the whole of her story" into letters, Clarissa responds with an excessive affirmation. She usurps the power of the society that speaks through Anna by appropriating and intensifying its demands. Taking herself as the object of the orders she now utters, Clarissa commands herself to perfect the role of exemplar and live as fully as possible within the sacred wake of language, death, and the transcendence they incarnate. Lovelace, Clarissa's rapist and suitor, is correct to suspect that Clarissa "refuses [him] in view of another lover"—namely, "DEATH"—but what he misses is that Clarissa turns the transcendent possibility of death into an erotic object only through the worldly means of writing (1097). Over the course of her final weeks, Clarissa ignores repeated pleas from friends and doctors to lessen her epistolary activity and instead insists on clinging to her "staggering pen" and continuing to "write too much for her health" (1127). In the words of her friend John Belford, "she was always writing" (1368). As a figure of simultaneous obedience and subversion, Clarissa embodies the model of the exemplary epistolary heroine so well that she detaches it from the society it was supposed to help fortify.

While the judgment of one's original community may have always been an impetus for captive heroines to put their stories into letters, it seems particularly important in the domestic landscape of the novel, where the line between captor and friend is never very clear. From the position of a captive author, object and subject at once, Clarissa writes not only to maintain, in the words of Armstrong and Tennenhouse, "her own identity among the heathens," but also to defend herself against the seemingly merciless judgment of her own community (210). In *Harm's Way* (2010), Sandra Macpherson interprets the strikingly harsh moral standard apparent in the very first letter of *Clarissa* as further proof that the realist novel shares the same "'tragic' law of responsibility" that inspired eighteenth-century jurists to begin ignoring humanizing questions of intention when deciding liability (4). By declaring individuals responsible for unknowingly causing injury, the strict liability laws of the eighteenth century, according to Macpherson, mirrored the novel's effort to reformulate causality and responsibility as independent of human consciousness or intention. Although Clarissa certainly did not intend to cause the duel between Lovelace and her brother, James Harlowe, which directly precedes the beginning of Richardson's story, her community, as Anna makes clear, will hold her nevertheless responsible. To be an exemplary subject, Clarissa ironically must accept that she stands before events she unwillingly causes as a culpable object.

Anna depicts letter writing as the best means through which her friend can handle the scrutiny of a public that looks upon her as both an exemplary subject and guilty object: "Write to me therefore, my dear, the whole of your story from the time that Mr. Lovelace was first introduced into your family; . . . And pray write in so full a manner as may gratify those who know not so much of your affairs as I do. If anything unhappy should fall out from the violence of such spirits as you have had to deal with, your account of all things previous to it will be your justification" (40). The language of accountability in this passage frames Clarissa's emergence as an epistolary subject in the legal terms of liability. Writing "the whole of her story ... in so full a manner as may gratify" unknown spectators gives Clarissa an opportunity to rise to the challenge of becoming, as Anna later puts it, "answerable" to the individuals that look upon her (40). The first definition of "answerable" in the OED is "responsible" in the sense of a "legal or moral obligation" that renders one "liable to be called to account" or "to answer to a charge." With the use of this particular adjective, as well as the related terms of accountability throughout his novel's opening letter, Richardson introduces his heroine as doubly subordinate in that she is not only accountable to the authority of any individual in her community, but also "liable to be called to account" for the unintended effects of her actions or mere existence. By urging her friend to accept responsibility for the violence of the men fighting to possess her, Anna initiates the narrative arc of *Clarissa* by challenging its heroine to accept the moral framework of a world in which subjects exist as objects of harm.

While Macpherson's reinterpretation of Clarissa as a tragic object illuminates a genuinely new dimension of her character, her attempt to universalize Clarissa's position has the very different effect of obscuring the distinctly heroic and exemplary role she plays in Richardson's novel. In opposition to a history of reading *Clarissa* and the broader novel tradition as part of the rise of a newly modern and supposedly self-conscious individual, Macpherson contends that "the novel form ... treats human subjects (victims and wrongdoers alike) as that most alien of others, the object" (23). According to Macpherson, *Clarissa* exemplifies this tradition in taking heroine and villain alike not as subjects that err to a greater or lesser extent, but as objects that cause harm regardless of knowledge or intention. Richardson's heroine stands out from other characters because she openly accepts the unlimited and tragic ethic of responsibility that governs a world in which every character and creature exists as an involuntary subject of violence. In reading Clarissa's heroism, however, as an articulation of the overarching logic of Richardson's novel and, even more expansively, as the condition of being itself, Macpherson takes the crowning achievement of Clarissa's theological practice as an ontological given.

Like other object-oriented theorists and critics such as Bill Brown, Jonathan Kramnick, and Quentin Meillassoux, Macpherson dismisses the idea of a self-conscious individual as if it were a mere philosophical misunderstanding entirely divorced from the historical experience of modernity. Rather than emerging from and existing within an ahistorical vacuum, the ideological image of the liberal individual is an actually existing thing produced by a real historical process. While critics have debated whether changes in economics, politics, or sex were most responsible for the emergence of this idea, it is worth recalling Louis Althusser's summation of Blaise Pascal's instructions on faith: "Kneel down, move your lips in prayer, and you will believe" (168). If we follow Macpherson in seeing Clarissa's object existence at the conclusion of Richardson's novel as merely a self-conscious iteration of "each of the characters . . . who populate the novel," then we lose track of the deceptively simple truth that Clarissa is fundamentally not like everyone else (96).

Clarissa's Modern Monasticism

Richardson only wanted to make virtuous heroes. He represented the protagonists of his other two novels, *Pamela* and *The History of Sir Charles Grandison* (1751), as, in the words of the latter, "the very Christian in practice" (1.440). Despite these intentions, Richardson ultimately sacrifices the purity of these other exemplars to the great bourgeois cause of constructing a modern sense of the English family and nation. Although only *Pamela* is a proper captivity tale, both it and *Sir Charles Grandison* participate in the captivity novel's effort to reconceive of England's premodern body politic as, in the words of Armstrong and Tennenhouse, "a nation made up of [conjugal] families that are in turn made up of literate individuals" (213). England's increasingly urban and commercial landscape appears in the typical eighteenth-century domestic novel as a source of disorientation capable of subjecting protagonists to the condition movingly articulated in the following terms by the heroine of Burney's *Evelina* (1778): "I found myself in the midst of a crowd, yet without party, friend, or acquaintance" (194).[8] A new conception of the nation and the family stands at the end of these stories as a home offering wayward heroes and heroines the illusion of escaping the alienating and individuating forces that animated their journey.

Richardson's second heroine stands apart from this tradition not only in choosing God over a husband, but also in pursuing her redemption by affirming rather than simply trying to escape the disorienting forces of eighteenth-century commercialism. After escaping the brothel in which Lovelace had held her captive, Clarissa seeks refuge in "Mr. Smith's, a glove shop, in King Street, Covent Garden," where she hopes to begin "a life of severe penitence, for corresponding, after prohibition, with a wretch who has well justified ... [her family's] warnings and inveteracy" (974, 901). Significantly, Clarissa chooses to pursue her new monastic life in the upstairs quarters of a commercial venue in a neighborhood of London that had become synonymous with the city's eighteenth-century transformation into the financial and trade capital of Europe. Once the property of the abbey of St. Peter, who used its open fields for pasture, Covent Garden by the mid-eighteenth century was home, in the words of the historian Roy Porter, to a thriving "fruit and vegetable market" in addition to the more recent arrival of "taverns, coffee-houses, gambling-dens, and brothels" (6). The magistrate and half-brother of Henry Fielding, Sir John Fielding, remarked at the time that "one would imagine that all the prostitutes in the kingdom had picked upon the rendezvous" of Covent Garden's central square, which was designed by Inigo Jones on grounds adjacent to St. Paul's Church (Porter 6). When the heroine of the notoriously erotic novel *Fanny Hill* (1748–49) first enters London, her employer brings her to a shop in Covent Garden "where she [buys] a pair of gloves" for the latest addition to her nearby brothel (45). That Clarissa decides to embark on a life of extreme religious devotion in the very sort of shop that an eighteenth-century reader might expect a prostitute to frequent underlines the stubbornly commercial dimension of her theological practice whose mixture of piety and modernity has still not been adequately appreciated by scholars.

Though it may seem outdated, Ian Watt's *The Rise of the Novel* (1957) remains the foundational work for reading *Clarissa*'s conclusion as a cautionary tale on the perils of antimodernism. According to Watt's sweeping—and, it must be stated, compelling—interpretation, the tragedy of Richardson's novel stems from the fact that both Clarissa and Lovelace hold to a dichotomy of "the flesh and the spirit" that is at odds with the critical turn in seventeenth-century European thought (237). Watt identifies critical philosophy and the eighteenth-century novel as "parallel manifestations of ... that vast transformation of Western civilization since the Renaissance which has replaced the unified world picture of the Middle Ages with ... one which presents us, essentially, with a developing but unplanned aggregate of particular individuals having particular experiences at particular times and at particular places" (31). From the perspective of this great transformation, Clarissa and Lovelace represent transitional figures whose commitments to the theological universals of an earlier era cause them to interpret sexual desire as a moral failing. A militant believer on the one hand and a skeptical libertine on the other, Clarissa and Lovelace darkly mirror one another in that they each deny the possibility of spiritual purity coexisting with fleshly reality, a refusal that Richardson portrays, knowingly or not, as tragically anachronistic.

For Watt, Clarissa's allegiance to supposedly outmoded religious beliefs obstructs her development into a critical and secular subject of modernity. As a result, Clarissa is condemned to live, according to Watt, in the undermodernized position of a narcissistic masochist: "Clarissa's tragedy reflects the combined effects of Puritanism's spiritual inwardness and its fear of the flesh, effects which tend to prevent the development of the sexual impulse beyond the autistic and masochistic stages." Historically and psychologically stunted, Clarissa's libidinal energy becomes directed toward death, from which she, in the words of Watt, derives a "narcissistic" and "self-consuming" sense of pleasure (234). While Clarissa undoubtedly exemplifies, as Watt states, a Puritan commitment to "spiritual inwardness," his assumption that such religious conviction entails a "fear of the flesh" is simply incorrect. What Watt and the many critics who have followed him miss is that Clarissa's at once worldly and theological practice exemplifies the essential synthesis of the spirit and the flesh that grounded Martin Luther's seminal Reformation call for the internalization of religious authority. Opposing the dichotomy of the spirit and the body, Luther asked his followers to look upon the hypostatic union of the divine and the earthly in Christ as the basis for a very modern reformulation of society, laypersons and clergy alike, as imbued with spiritual forces. Luther's injunction to his followers to remember Christ's profession that "I live in the flesh, I live in the faith of the sonne of God" underscores the capacity for devoted subjects to access the Godly realm of pure transcendence within a fallen universe of bodies (889).[9]

That critics continue to read Richardson's heroine as anachronistic is more of a reflection of present-day ideological images of secularism than of anything to be found in Richardson's novel. Whether acknowledged or not, much of this criticism hinges on a liberal model of secularism and progress that conceives of the present as the fulfillment of a grand narrative movement from the darkness of Europe's religious past to the clarifying light of its modern, rational future. Richardson's heroine must be condemned from such a perspective because she lacks the qualities that are said to mark the beginning of this story—that is, she fails to exhibit the traits of a nascent liberalism whose teleological point of culmination supposedly occurs with the triumphant secularism of the United Kingdom, the United States, and the broader configuration of "the West" in the twentieth and twenty-first centuries. What this ideology of secularism has obscured is the timeliness of Richardson's novel both within his mid-eighteenth-century moment as well as our twenty-first-century one. *Clarissa* articulates a contradictory mixture of religious orthodoxy and political rebellion that was and is a foundational point of fragility for Western empires from the eighteenth century to the present. At the time Richardson was writing *Clarissa*, in the early 1740s, Luther's call for democratizing Christianity was far from a bygone sentiment; in fact, it was being rearticulated on both sides of the Atlantic by a popular Protestant movement that aimed to bring the Christian word of God to those whom both Dissenters and high-churchmen had become accustomed to ignoring—namely, the poor and working classes.[10]

Known as the "Evangelical Revival" in Britain and the "Great Awakening" in the American colonies, this movement had its "*annus miralibis*" in the words of the historian Paul Langford in 1739 when skeptical churchwardens of an outer London church "denied the pulpit" to the revivalist Church of England minister George Whitefield, who responded by delivering his sermon "from a tombstone in [the] Islington Church-Yard." With this, Whitefield inaugurated the practice of "field-preaching," a method quickly taken up by other revivalists, most prominently among them John Wesley, who, as Langford reports, began preaching to large crowds in "open spaces best known for highwaymen and horse-races, Moorfields, Kennington, Common Hackney Marsh, Marylebone Fields" (244). Just as Clarissa seeks to intensify her faith in an apartment linked to prostitutes, revivalists attempt to save Christianity by bringing it to those spaces most strongly associated with the fallen world of eighteenth-century English commerce.

In their authoritative biography *Samuel Richardson* (1971), T. C. Duncan Eaves and Ben D. Kimpel caution against reading Richardson's heroine in mystical terms since, according to Eaves and Kimpel, she belongs to a distinctly antimystical seventeenth-century Puritan tradition of "right reason supported by revelation" (283). Eaves and Kimpel justifiably object to the 1960s and 1970s "tendency to think of religion as always mystical," but, in the fervor of their reaction, they miss the way in which the rational overlaps with the mystical in both *Clarissa* and the contemporaneous evangelical movement it reflected. Richardson's heroine is not, as Eaves and Kimpel suggest, a figure for a fading age of Puritan rigidity; instead, she is the embodiment of a present-day orthodox Protestant movement that brought the Reformation tenets of the Church of England to their antinomian point of perfection.

Evangelical leaders like Whitefield, Wesley, and Lady Huntingdon used the sufficiency of scripture and justification by faith, mainstream Lutheran principles enshrined into the Church of England's *Thirty-Nine Articles*, as the basis for a popular Protestantism that ultimately rejected the authority of the Church. Revivalists gave laymen and women the power to preach and established parallel religious societies that vacillated from the very beginning between saving the Church of England and separating from it. The evangelical movement was a revolt in the name of loyalty, and, as such, it dramatized the explosive and potentially revolutionary contradiction at the heart of Britain's eighteenth-century political establishment: it depended on a God that could never be entirely its own.

Although the conventional starting point for the evangelical revival is high church by association—John and Charles Wesley's 1729 formation of the "Holy Club" at Oxford—the movement was an ecumenical phenomenon bound together by a shared sense that the pervasive deism, skepticism, and rationalism of the early eighteenth century had put Christianity itself into jeopardy, and that all believers, whatever their denomination or training, had a duty to save it.[11] Richardson himself perfectly encapsulates the evangelical ethos of his time when explaining his reason for writing *Clarissa*: "Religion never was at so low an Ebb as at the present: And if my Work must be supposed of the Novel kind, I was willing to try if a Religious Novel would do good" (Eaves and Kimpel 222). While Richardson certainly had reservations regarding "the enthusiastic parts of Methodism," as he puts it in a letter criticizing the evangelical minister James Hervey, Richardson's novels, and *Clarissa* especially, clearly participated in the evangelical struggle to disseminate Christianity in a newly popular and sentimental form (554). With impassioned sermons emphasizing the personal connection of an individual believer to the emotional experience of faith, the revivalists sought to cultivate, in the words of John Wesley, "a religion of the heart" (*An Earnest Appeal* 206).

Despite Richardson's presumably moderate intentions, *Clarissa* represents a nuanced engagement with perhaps the most enthusiastic idea of the evangelical movement: Wesley's conviction that true believers could achieve a life beyond sin. As Wesley explains in the late sermon *On God's Vineyard* (1787), he envisions being born again as only the beginning of a spiritual journey culminating with one's worldly ascent to saintly perfection: "At the same time that a man is justified, sanctification properly begins. . . . For when he is justified he is 'born again'. . . . [and] the new birth implies as great a change in the soul as was wrought in his body when he was born of a woman: Not an outward change only, but . . . an inward change from all unholy, to all holy tempers . . . in a word, from an earthly, sensual, devilish, mind, to the mind that was in Jesus Christ" (205).[12] Wesley believed that one truly could be "born of the spirit," and when Richardson describes his heroine in the midst of her monastic devotions as a "WOMAN in her charming person" but an "ANGEL . . . in her mind," he lends further credence to Wesley's conviction (1299). Though he undoubtedly would have rejected Wesley's notion of perfectionism as unacceptably enthusiastic, Richardson nonetheless seconds Wesley's model with his own theory of perfectionism centering on the subordination of one's life to death, writing, and the incarnation of transcendence that they make possible.

In the midst of her monastic withdrawal, Richardson underlines the living function of death within his heroine's pursuit of spiritual perfection by having her begin to use a coffin as a piece of furniture, a symbolic repurposing that turns a repository for the dead into an emancipatory instrument of the living. While Clarissa claims to order the coffin merely as "preparation" for her death, the very active role that it plays in her life as a writing table and a surface for inscription suggests that something beyond diligent planning is at work (1304). One of the inscriptions Clarissa engraves on the top of her coffin is a premature date of death, and, in explaining this marking to friends, Clarissa subtly portrays herself as someone inhabiting the sovereign position of the spiritually perfected: "The date April 10 she accounted for, as not being able to tell what her closing-day would be; and as that was the fatal day of her leaving her father's house" (1306). In choosing "the fatal day of her leaving her father's house" as the date of her demise, Clarissa declares herself dead several weeks before her monastic phase of life even begins, which begs the question as to what form of existence she actually leads during her final weeks. The double meaning of "father's house" only further emphasizes the importance of this question, for it endows Clarissa's alienation from her family home with the additional metaphorical significance of the book of Genesis. Continuing the play throughout his novel between mortal and divine fathers, Richardson represents his heroine's alienation from her mortal father's house as a repetition of humanity's originary expulsion from the primal father's home that was Eden.

It is possible that Clarissa writes a premature date of death in order to depict her time beyond the walls of the Harlowe family home as a kind of doubly lapsarian existence severed not only from the paradise of humanity's origins, but also from Christ's offer of redemption. However, it is equally possible—and, indeed, more justified by the totality of Richardson's text—to read Clarissa's inscription from the other direction. Clarissa may prematurely mark the end of her life in order to distinguish her previous mortal existence from the sanctified state she begins to achieve once born anew. From this perspective, Clarissa abandons her mortal father and dies to the society of men in order to enter the company of angels and to begin mediating between the finitude of life and the eternity beyond it. Given that several of Clarissa's friends describe her during her final weeks as "one just entering into a companionship with saints and angels," it seems that Richardson means to encourage this latter interpretation that his heroine indeed succeeds in bringing the static transcendence of eternal life into the dynamism of her mortal being (1275).

With his portrait of Clarissa, Richardson attempts to reconcile Wesleyan perfectionism with the orthodox doctrine of sin maintained by other major evangelical leaders, including Whitefield and Lady Huntingdon, by focusing on a point that they all hold in common: the certainty of assurance and the ensuing sovereignty of the true believer.[13] While Wesley's notion of perfectionism clearly departs from one of the Church of England's key principles, that of the inherently sinful nature of humanity, Richardson's text suggests that it does so only to reinforce the integrity of another key principle, the worldly power of the saved. Richardson strives to demonstrate that the seemingly heretical idea of perfectionism is nothing more than an articulation of the power that every good Anglican grants to those of faith. "Godly persons," as article 17 of the *Thirty-Nine Articles* contends, "feel in themselves the working of the Spirit in Christ" (7). Although a complete synthesis would be impossible, Richardson brings perfectionism and an orthodox model of sin as close together as one can by depicting his heroine as an involuntary subject of sin who nevertheless is capable of sanctification. Clarissa's moment of alienation from her family's home is thus "fatal," a word signifying both fate and death, because it is an inevitable effect of Adam and Eve's expulsion from their own father's house, which was the product not of Adam's choice, but, as the *Thirty-Nine Articles* states, of "the fault and corruption of the Nature of every man" (5). And yet Clarissa is also ennobled, "exalted ... above herself" by an "assurance" that both Wesley and his more orthodox allies characterize as the conviction that, in the words of Whitefield, "those whom God has once justified, he also will glorify" (Richardson 853, 1247; Whitefield 18).[14]

Before her expected union with God in the next world and after her escape from the patriarchal authorities in this one, Clarissa attains the same life that Dryden and Pope envision for their gentlemanly patriots, an existence simultaneously fallen and sanctified. When Clarissa says that she cannot "tell what her closing-day would be" in explaining her decision to choose a premature date of death, she uses a commercial expression, "closing day," as a synonym for her death, a turn of phrase that metonymically associates her life with the glove shop she calls home during her final weeks (1306). Over the course of his novel's conclusion, Richardson places increasing emphasis on both the purity of his heroine's faith and the various objects that connect her state of monastic withdrawal to the commercial activity flourishing everywhere around her.[15] Richardson makes the interrelationship between commerce and religious devotion particularly clear when he has Clarissa acquire her coffin through the symbolically rich means of selling clothes: "She discharged the undertaker's bill after I was gone, with as much cheerfulness as she could ever have paid for the clothes she sold to purchase this her *palace* [the coffin]: for such she called it; reflecting upon herself for the expensiveness of it" (1306). Clarissa gains the capital necessary to purchase the central object of her monastic practice by selling some of the most ostentatiously visible and commented-upon signs of England's expanding consumer society in the early to mid-eighteenth century (1306).[16] While Clarissa, as Rosenthal argues, certainly aims to infuse commodified objects with "sentimental rather than market value," her efforts should not be understood in the antimodern terms that Rosenthal and others assign to it (152).

By representing the sale that allows Clarissa to purchase her coffin, Richardson identifies the crowning symbol of his heroine's faith, the object that reminds her "that there is such a vast superiority of weight and importance in the thought of death," as a commodity and hence the potential equivalent of modernity's most profane objects from clothes and gloves to prostitutes and joint-stock shares (1306). At the time of

Clarissa's publication, England was witnessing the emergence of a mass fashion market that would reach such heights by the century's end that gentlemen, as the fashion historians C. W. and P. Cunnington explain, "began to adopt the styles of dress and actual garments of the working man," and to look for other, subtler ways of distinguishing themselves (14).[17] Far from opposing this movement, Clarissa participates in it, but with the goal of redirecting its dizzying powers toward the theological domain, where she finds the possibility of at once exemplifying and undoing the values of commercial England.

Like contemporaneous field preachers, Clarissa aims to imbue a fallen commercial society with new religious value. She depicts her life as wholly commodified yet at the same time dedicated to "higher contemplations" (1254). Clarissa in a sense becomes the human equivalent of those infamous open fields that revivalists treated as chapels: she is a space dedicated to sin that nevertheless can be made holy.

To Be So Modern You're Sacred: *Clarissa* Contra Weber

While *Clarissa*'s relationship to contemporaneous evangelicalism is certainly important, Richardson's novel—and, indeed, evangelicalism itself—can be understood only if placed within a much broader history of Protestantism and its relationship to the social transformation of England from the sixteenth through twentieth century. At once binding her to and detaching her from early market society, the militant Protestantism of Richardson's heroine anticipates as well as complicates Weber's seminal argument that the secular individual of modern capitalism develops from the worldview of early modern Protestant reformers. Published between 1747 and 1748, Richardson's novel has a complicated relationship to the emergence of a modern British individual from the social disarray of the early eighteenth century, a period in which a new consumer market and a growing middle class dissolved the visible hierarchy of premodern English social order. The sudden impossibility of using physical appearance to determine class status provoked endless condemnation from the organs of England's expanding print culture, such as the *World*, which reported in 1755 that "we have not such thing as common people among us ... Attorneys' clerks and city prentices dress like cornets of dragoons ... every commoner ... treads hard on the heels of quality in dress" (quoted in McKendrick, Brewer, and Plumb 54). The birth of a mass fashion market was a scandal because clothing in the early eighteenth century, as Dror Wahrman explains, was "still taken to have constitutive power but the authorities that had previously shaped and controlled [it] did not" (178). In exchanging her clothes for a coffin, Clarissa signals the rise of a new strategy for managing England's social order, one that rooted difference in the immaterial domain of sensibility rather than the newly democratized world of sartorial appearance.

However distant this transition may appear from religious issues, Weber's *The Protestant Ethic and the Spirit of Capitalism* provides the crucial reminder that it was Protestantism that brought this immaterial domain of sensibility into the interiority of the early modern individual. In their struggle to democratize the transcendent authority of the Church, sixteenth- and seventeenth-century religious reformers endowed individual bodies with the once highly centralized responsibility of regulating their behavior according to the disembodied moral code of the Christian faith. By carrying "asceticism ... out of monastic cells" and "into everyday life," Protestants created a new model of identity that privileged the immaterial domain of faith and reason over the material world of good works and appearances (181). Weber asks his readers to consider the possibility that "other-worldliness asceticism ... and participation in capitalistic accumulation ... might actually turn out to be [in] an intimate relationship [*innere Verwandtschaft*]," since both demand that individuals view their actions, and in particular their labor, as driven by abstract ideals rather than physical needs (42). For Weber, the seemingly opposed figures of the Puritan and the capitalist were in a relationship of continuity, and while *Clarissa* generally confirms this argument, it also suggests that the largely literary character of the sentimental protagonist should be added to this list of analogous early modern social types. Whether it is assurance of salvation, money, or the prestige of cultivated sensibilities, all three of these figures—the Protestant, the capitalist, and the sentimental protagonist—signify an ascendant tendency to view one's activity in the world as an end in itself. These three seemingly disparate characters turn out to be close kinsmen (*innerlich verwandt*) because they subject their everyday lives to the internalized rule of abstract principles.

With her exquisite sensibility, bourgeois concern for frugal accumulation, and heroic piety, Clarissa represents a near-perfect embodiment of these three major figures. The animating question of *Clarissa* is whether this exemplary figure of the eighteenth century's three major valences of abstract life—religious, economic, and sentimental—can be converted into an ideological subject of modernity. Richardson's narrative, consciously or not, uncovers a paradoxical capacity to dissolve the modern structure of selfhood by perfecting one's fidelity to its own immaterial principles. Clarissa's heroic virtue is tragic because it is too modern for modernity. She refuses a series of opportunities to marry and effectively surmount her transitional state of selfhood because these opportunities fall short of the sentimental perfection she exemplifies. Her exquisite sentiments, as well as her piety, demand, for example, that she oppose the husband her family has chosen for her since his physically repulsive body and crass mind render him a sentimentally and religiously unfit partner. This Mr. Solmes, as Clarissa explains, has "but a very ordinary share of understanding, is very illiterate, knows nothing but the value of estates and how to improve them, and what belongs to landjobbing, and husbandry" (62). The same commitment to maintaining her faith in all three of modernity's abstract registers inspires Clarissa to resist the suggestion of her family's reverend, Dr. Brand, to "go in some *creditable* manner to some of the foreign colonies" in order to save "her *own credit* and *reputation*" as well as her family's (1294).

Clarissa rejects the possibility of renewing her "credit" in the colonies as little better than the prospect of marrying the decidedly unsentimental Solmes because it too would turn her exemplary modern self into a crude, one-dimensional reflection of market forces. If Clarissa were to pursue her moral and financial renewal in the colonies, she would come to inhabit the transparently presentimental position of earlier heroines, such as Defoe's Moll Flanders, who achieve happy conjugal lives by embracing a global market of exchange. The final and most promising option for converting Clarissa into a properly modern heroine would be a marriage with her kidnapper and rapist, Lovelace, a union that her piety opposes. Although this opposition, as Rosenthal argues, reflects Clarissa's refusal to commodify her sexual relations, the crucial element of Clarissa as a character, and the underlying motivation for this refusal, is her commitment to affirming rather than opposing modernity's most treasured values (130).

Clarissa is a perversely modern rather than antimodern figure because she achieves her withdrawal from modern society by affirming the democratization of divine authority that made the emergence of this society possible. In using the internalized sovereignty of God to pursue a life beyond the domain of worldly authorities, Clarissa not only suggests that the divine remains accessible to modern subjects, but also that it can be wielded as a tool of liberation. Richardson's heroine provides an anticipatory rejoinder to Weber's pessimistic announcement that capitalism in the early twentieth century no longer has any need for the Protestant theology that helped bring it into existence. Weber explains that "today the spirit of religious asceticism ... has escaped from its cage ... but victorious capitalism, since it rests on mechanical foundations, needs its support no longer" (181–82). According to Weber's narrative, modern men and women practice what were originally Protestant values—such as the belief in a single calling, the moral obligation of self-denial, and the abstract and hence insatiable necessity of hard work—out of a secularized and mechanistic sense of compulsion. Industrial capitalism appears at the end of *The Protestant Ethic and the Spirit of Capitalism* as a totalizing structure that determines the lives of "all individuals who are born into ... [its] mechanism ... with irresistible force" (181). From the perspective of *Clarissa*, Weber's portrayal of the production of subjects as a totalizing and thus an inescapable process stems from the false idea that this process can ever be divorced from its theological origins.

As a paragon of Anglican virtue and yet an enemy of the society it underpinned, Clarissa dramatizes the heretical separatism lurking within the Church of England's very foundation. In *The World Turned Upside Down* (1972), Christopher Hill proposes that there were two revolutions during the English Civil War, one that actually occurred and that hastened the rise of a capitalist society, and "another revolution that never happened, though from time to time it threatened" to embark on the separatist path of "reject[ing] the protestant ethic" in favor of a society founded on the principle of "communal property" (15). Interestingly, it is in an article on *Clarissa*, "Clarissa Harlowe and Her Times" (1955), that Hill complicates his own overly neat opposition between the seventeenth century's "two revolutions" by suggesting that they are not so much opposed as dialectically intertwined, with the revolution that did not happen persisting within the one that did as the haunting possibility of the negation of the negation that would disclose the communitarianism that modern capitalist society had long harbored. From this perspective, Clarissa does not so much resurrect England's seventeenth-century past as show that it never left. As Hill states, Clarissa "break[s] through the social conventions of her time by pressing to its ultimate implications the religious orthodoxy of her society" (337). Clarissa rebels from the inside by excessively devoting herself to the founding principles of the very society she forsakes. Though he never explicitly states it, Hill's "Clarissa Harlowe and Her Times" is pregnant with the idea that Richardson's heroine embodies not the legacy of a dying age, but the enduring dialectical possibility of a new one.

While Hill's interpretation of *Clarissa* is illuminating, particularly in the way it challenges his own effort to separate the moderate from the radical legacies of the English Civil War, his analysis ultimately supports the familiar idea that *Clarissa* is anachronistic. According to Hill, Clarissa exemplifies the religious values of her period and yet can find approval only in heaven, a tragic plight that demonstrates "the breakdown of the noblest aspirations of Puritanism in the face of the realities of bourgeois society" (338). The exemplar of a faith that is supposedly supplanted by the economic system to which it gives rise, Clarissa stands for Hill as a powerful symbol of the ultimate incompatibility of mainstream Protestant theology and early capitalist society. As important, however, as seventeenth-century Puritanism is to Clarissa's struggle, she is not simply the saintly embodiment of values supplanted by modernity. Instead, Clarissa manifests the persistence of Civil War–era thought within the foundational doctrines and institutions of eighteenth-century imperial Britain. *Clarissa* dramatizes in fiction what John Wesley, George Whitefield, Lady Huntingdon, and many other revivalists were demonstrating in fields, pamphlets, and pulpits: that England's most treasured imperial values were replete with the potential for rebellion.

"We Christians Are Kings": Clarissa as a Figure for the Antinomian Luther

Through the struggle of his heroine to achieve an alternative form of modernity, Richardson represents the Protestant origins of capitalism as always accessible through death. Although death may appear to be thoroughly ahistorical, it in fact assumes new meaning following the early modern democratization of divine authority. For medieval kings, high-church officials, and select aristocrats, death existed within life as a reminder of the fact that these figures already lived apart from mortal life. When medieval and Renaissance crowds gathered at royal burials to cry "The King is dead! Long live the King!" they were proclaiming, in the words of Kantorowicz, the "perpetuity of a kingship" whose inner truth becomes apparent only in death (412). In announcing to her friends that she has come to "enjoy . . . the thought of death," since contemplating death "annihilates all other considerations and concerns," Clarissa positions herself as the heir to the doubled being of the dynastic king who also looked upon death as the sovereign principle of being (1306). Beneath the "mechanism" that entraps individuals in the political-theological structures of modernity, Richardson discovers a privileged mode of being that is democratized by the overlapping forces of nationalism, capitalism, and the Reformation. Once seen by the vast majority of the population as simply beyond the grasp of mortal life, death becomes available to the members of the British body politic as the means through which they can achieve a sovereign existence in this life. Clarissa contemplates death with the assurance of a king.

The development of a modern self hinges on the conversion of a kingly mode of being into the gendered subject of commercial society. In *Clarissa*, however, Richardson imagines a heroine who uses her kingly post-Reformation aura to become an angel rather than a wife. Clarissa assumes the angelic and kingly role of a divine mediator, but stands apart from her medieval predecessors by withholding her immortal second body from the cause of political unity, leaving her in the doubly liminal position of a failed or detached mediator. Richardson develops the character of Clarissa, as he explains in his novel's postscript as well as in his private correspondence, in order to provide a society he perceived as increasingly sinful with a model of Christian virtue so nearly perfect that "heaven *only* could reward [it]" (1498). In the story that follows, however, Richardson's narrative exceeds his presumably good Anglican by culminating with his heroine becoming an exemplary figure for the antinomian possibilities lying within the foundational Protestant doctrine of salvation through faith. Formulated by Luther, this doctrine rested on the idea that that all believers could through faith alone (*sola fide*) assume the shape and sovereignty of God.

Luther's *sola fide* was at the center of the eighteenth-century evangelical movement, the "capital doctrine of the Gospel," in the words of the revivalist John Venn, and although revivalists would never deny the additional necessity of God's grace, it was increasingly subordinated to faith (quoted in Langford 237). In a world where God predestined the elect and the reprobate in advance of creation, grace was less a gift to be anticipated than an already established fact to be deduced from the integrity of one's conviction. Enshrined in the *Thirty-Nine Articles* under Elizabeth, predestination entailed a paradox of double motivation in which, in the words of article 17, the chosen "through Grace obey the calling: they be justified freely" and, in turn, "feel in themselves the working of the Spirit in Christ, mortifying the works of the flesh, . . . and drawing up their mind to high and heavenly things" (7). What one confronts in Richardson's heroine is the potential lawlessness of *sola fide* for a self-proclaimed elect. At once subjected and profoundly ennobled, Clarissa was, and is, a living evangelical call to arms, a declaration that if individuals retheologize the secularized sovereignty they bear as national British subjects, they can use it as the basis for revolution.

When addressing his followers in the seminal Reformation treatise *On Christian Liberty* (1520), Luther demanded that they see something more in Christ than the momentary miracle of the divine taking mortal form; he asks them to believe in Christ as a very present mode of being, similar, in fact, to the one Clarissa comes to inhabit. In his critique of historicist preachers, Luther portrays Christ as a synecdochical representative of the doubled being assumed by any person of faith: "But Christ ought to be preached to this end, . . . that it is not enough that there is a Christ, but that he may be Christ (which is a Savior) unto thee and unto me: And that he does worke the same in us, which is mentioned of him. . . . And this cometh to pass, where Christian libertie . . . is truly taught: and by what means we Christians are Kings and Priests wherein also we be Lords over all" (837). Those satisfied by the pure actuality of the statement "There is a Christ" fail to understand that Christ represents not one miraculous occurrence or event among others, but instead marks the very possibility of the historical event itself. Christ, in other words, is for Luther the ur-event that first demonstrates the possibility of the transcendent incorporating itself into the material world.[18] Luther insists on the phrase "he may be Christ unto thee and unto me" because it captures the conjunction of the potential and the actual that occurs when the perfected being of the divine endows the potentiality of the mortal believer, signified by the modal verb "may," with the aura of full actuality. The lay believer thereby assumes the *character angelicus* once reserved only for the premodern ruler of the church or the state whose perfected second body of divine actuality ensured, in the words of Kantorowicz, that the sovereign "never dies; that he is free from the imbecility of infancy and the defects of old age; that he cannot sin or do wrong" (495). The medieval guarantors of social order grounded their right to rule in an antinomian or lawless space of transcendence to which they alone had access. It was a space beyond all law that gave the law its foundation.[19] What Luther seeks to demonstrate is that the Christ event names the capacity for every mortal body to be raised to this lawless source of all law.

The sovereign privilege of lawlessness becomes in Luther's theological system the common condition of every Christian believer: "Christian liberty ... is spirituall, and true, making our hearts free from all sinnes, from all laws, and commandments (as *Paul* witnesseth in his first Epistle to *Timothy*, the first Chapter, *The law was not made for the just man*)" (850). Inheriting the doubled being of Christ, popes, and kings, the once undistinguished member of the Christian polity becomes a sovereign individual whose access to the transcendent source of all law renders sacred whatever he or she may choose to do in this no longer profane world. Although Luther invents "antinomian" as a pejorative term for his contemporary Johanna Agricola's outright rejection of the law, Luther's struggle to endow each individual believer with an angelic subjectivity was a decisive influence for contemporary as well as later antinomian heretics. When Luther states, "Good works do not make a good man, but a good man doth make the works to be good," he elucidates the socially disruptive element of a theological system that will inspire later followers to assert that Christ's presence within their souls frees them from all law and, in some cases, even sin itself (842). Despite the horror with which he would greet this association, Luther stands alongside Calvin as a forefather of the many heretical sects that emerged in the midst of the English Civil War and Interregnum, groups such as the Ranters who staged ritualistic orgies of swearing and sex in an effort to demonstrate the irrelevance of law to a world that already has been saved. While the substance of the particularly notorious Ranter Abiezer Coppe's declaration that "Sin and Transgression is finished and ended" certainly strays from Luther's model, his justification for this assertion is in fact merely a reiteration of Luther's insistence that Christ remains present within the souls of his followers: "That excellent Majesty, which dwels in the Writer of this Roule, hath reconciled all things to himself" (81, 86).

The lawless potential of mainstream Protestantism persists well into the eighteenth century as an essential point of instability within the secularized theology of British political order. When a Church of England minister, Dr. Nicholas Carter, writes an angry letter to Lady Huntingdon, a key evangelical leader, asking, "Who gave you leave to send your *preaching-fellows* into my parish?," he touches on the antinomian presumption that, however much revivalists denied it, was indeed at the heart of their movement (quoted in Langford 276). Women were banned from the ministry in the eighteenth century, to say nothing of assuming positions of authority beyond it, yet Selina Hastings, the Countess of Huntingdon, acted as her own bishop, presiding over a religious society that she founded and that during her lifetime rivaled Wesley's in terms of size and significance. Encompassing a vast network of traveling preachers, over sixty chapels, and a college, Lady Huntingdon's "Connexion" was a monument to evangelicalism's emancipatory disregard for Church law.

Although Lady Huntingdon, like Luther, would have balked at the antinomian label, she and her fellow revivalists were exactly that, as they privileged their own internalized religious authority above that claimed by the intertwined powers of the eighteenth-century English Church and state. Strictures such as the declaration in the *Thirty-Nine Articles* that "it is not lawful for any man to take upon himself the office of public preaching ... before he be lawfully called" meant little to evangelicals who believed that, as Lady Huntingdon states, the *"true Church* ... belongs not to this world" (article 23; Crossley and Seymour 626).[20] Rather than ignoring the law in the name of Christ's return like the Ranters, evangelicals such as Huntingdon take a more orthodox route to the same antinomian conclusion by using the Church of England principle that Christ indeed has not returned as justification for rejecting the authority of the Church. For eighteenth-century evangelicals, it is the stubborn absence of Christ that makes his sovereignty impossible ever fully to possess and, paradoxically, for that very reason an object of communal possession. This is a negative absolutism in which demonstrating the impossibility of ever completely incarnating Christ becomes the best means of embodying Christ in this world.

From Oliver Cromwell and Abiezer Coppe to John Wesley and Lady Huntingdon, Luther's emphasis on the immediacy of a believer's connection to Christ left a deep antinomian mark on early modern English history. And Luther was conscious of the potential for this legacy, an awareness he demonstrated with his ultimately futile efforts to contain the consequences of his idea that true believers could live as Christ, that is, above "all sinnes," "all laws," and all "commandments" (850). Luther begins *On Christian Liberty* by attempting to temper it with a reiteration of the Pauline ideal of nonresistance:

1. A Christian man is a most free Lord of all, subject to none.
2. A Christian man is a most dutifull servant of all, subject to all. (821)

Luther uses identical syntax to reinforce the supposedly unbreakable bond between the status of the believer as a truly sovereign and emancipated subject and, at the same time, dutiful "servant" to the secular authorities that govern his or her community. Since the believer comes to resemble Christ after being "raised by faith up above himself," it seems logical to Luther that he or she also would follow Christ in freely and lovingly giving his or her self to society and its norms (862).

Tying together transcendent liberty and earthly submission, Luther articulates the internal tension that the contemporary philosopher Étienne Balibar notes in the word "subject." As Balibar explains, the French and English form of subject "retains in the equivocal unity of a single noun" the distinct Latin terms *subjectum* and *subjectus*: the former signifying that which underlies and bears an attribute and the latter an entity subjected to some higher authority (38). In portraying political obedience as an effect of the transcendent freedom one bears in a post-Reformation world, Luther seeks to reconcile these competing forms of subjecthood in a pact that Clarissa ultimately undoes not by outright rejection, but, like her evangelical contemporaries, by a hyperorthodox insistence upon the separation of God from the political rulers of this world. While Luther can assert that "out of Faith floweth" a concern for the fate of worldly society, the fact remains that within his theological system this specific moral demand is both chronologically and essentially second to the emancipatory condition of faith (850).

By devoting herself absolutely to the word and to death, Clarissa manages to transform the political relationship implied by the normative second clause of Luther's prescription for subjecthood (*subjectus*) into an interiorized and masochistic relationship with the divine sovereignty that she bears as a post-Reformation subject (*subjectum*). Richardson imagines a subject, in other words, who refuses to allow the relationship of obedience implied by the possession of a divine attribute to flow into the secular realm of a political community. His heroine escapes the secular and modernizing authority of her brother, James Harlowe, and her potential husband, Robert Lovelace, in the hopes not of avoiding sovereignty and submission altogether, but rather of making them a purely internal and transcendent affair. In their depictions of Clarissa's monastic period, Richardson's epistolary narrators emphasize her "angelic" nature as well as her masochistic insistence on "sacrificing her health" to writing and religious devotions (1103, 1100). Clarissa achieves the transcendent position of an angel, both within and beyond this world and thereby fulfills Luther's promise that we may through faith alone allow God "to write his law in our hearts" (463). Clarissa accomplishes this transformation by narcissistically withdrawing into herself in order to intensify and perfect her submission to the interiorized authority of God and his word. Clarissa displaces her subjection from the secular domain of a modernizing Britain to the theological context of her psyche and its relationship to the word.

Just as Luther assured his followers, Clarissa comes to "dwell in God" by transforming herself into a subject of language, only she refuses to comply with the accompanying demand to be "throwne down beneath [her]self, toward [her] neighbor by love" (850). As she explains to the friends who surround her during her final weeks, Clarissa instead directs her love toward death: "I must say I dwell on, I indulge (and, strictly speaking, I enjoy) the thoughts of death. For believe me ... that there is a vast superiority of weight and importance in the thought of death, and its hoped-for happy consequences, that it in a manner annihilates all other considerations and concerns" (1306). Clarissa privileges the "thought of death" as the essence of a religious practice that she realizes through writing. Masochistically committed to writing and the thought it makes possible, Clarissa embodies Luther's convictions that "the sacred word of God ... only and alone" is necessary to attain "life, righteousness, and Christian liberty" (823, 822). Her devotion to the word coincides with a fixation upon death because it is death that allows the word to travel from the transcendent domain of God to the interiority of Clarissa's mortal life. As the potential for material life to assume the immaterial form of not being, death is a living possibility that joins the transcendent and the earthly into a vital relationship that language incarnates.

The deconstructive moment in *Clarissa* criticism in the late 1970s and early 1980s never quite captured the significance of language to Richardson's text because it insisted on portraying the determinative function that Derrida assigns to language in a secular light. Given Derrida's highly influential turn to political theology later in his career, culminating with his assertion in *Specters of Marx* (1993) that "deconstruction is perhaps ... a structural messianism" (74), it no longer seems possible to support the unambiguously secular depiction of deconstruction in works such as Terry Castle's *Clarissa's Ciphers* (1982). What deconstruction-inspired criticism succeeded in clarifying is the centrality of writing to Clarissa's religious practice and in particular to her final demise, an event that makes her, in the words of Castle, "like a letter in an envelope" (139). Once deceased, Clarissa enters the coffin she had been using as a writing table and surface for inscriptions, returning to her family's home as one of the many texts she has left behind. As the lifeless interior of the marks her coffin bears, Clarissa personifies, as Castle notes, the chasm that separates language and writing from any "'natural' point of origin" in the intention of a living author (145).

Clarissa, in other words, gives dramatic form to the "hermeneutic situation" that prompts theorists as wide-ranging as Jacques Derrida, Roland Barthes, Michel Foucault, and Louis Althusser to proclaim the death of the author in the late 1960s (Castle 145). For Castle and other deconstructive critics, Clarissa's death figuratively represents the ascent of a properly modern understanding of language as a secular space in which signifiers create meaning independently of God, man, or prediscursive things. The problem with such a reading is that it obscures the originary place of theology within the ascendant domain of language that subsumes Richardson's heroine. The old opposition between Lovelace as the deconstructive hero of linguistic determinism and Clarissa as the anachronistic saint of prelinguistic meaning vanishes once one acknowledges the fundamental continuity of God and language in Richardson's text.

As is the case for Luther as well as, ultimately, for Derrida, language in Richardson's novel can never be entirely self-contained because it remains forever bound to the transcendent. In order to place the "thought of death" at the center of her life, Clarissa spends her final weeks using writing to dwell within the nothingness she will become. Clarissa's final confidante and executor, Belford, reports that she "was always writing" during her time at the Smiths', and, in the many posthumous letters she leaves behind, Clarissa explicitly positions herself in the transcendent position of death (1368). While Clarissa sometimes expresses merely "hope" in attaining eternal life, she confides to her beloved nanny Mrs. Norton that she in fact "knows[s] ... all will be at last happy" (1368, 1168). Given her distinctly Protestant assurance in her own salvation, Clarissa's masochistic dedication in her final weeks to writing from the perspective of the dead represents an effort to bring the anticipated aura of eternity into her mortal life. In the will she leaves for her estranged family, Clarissa writes from the perspective of one who can no longer write: "So much written about what deserves not the least consideration and about what will be nothing when this writing comes to be opened and read" (1413). The triumphant irony of Clarissa's statement lies in the fact that it is precisely the "nothing" of death that allows her to be endowed with the sovereign authority of the divine. As an immanent mark of transcendence, death exists within individuals, language, and the world they create as an originary interruption that instills within all three the promise of an extradiscursive beyond, and it is by organizing her life around the supremacy of this other world that Clarissa becomes able to declare her independence in this one.

Domestic Fiction after *Clarissa*

During the final weeks that she spends beyond the reach of fathers or suitors, Clarissa lives among merchants in a seedy section of London where she rarely makes it to Church services, particularly toward the end of her life, and yet it is in this period precisely that Clarissa most clearly inhabits the subjectivity of a "saint"—that is, one who, in the words of Wesley, has experienced "a renewal of the heart in the whole image of God, the full likeness of him that created it" (*Clarissa* 1299; *Plain Account of Christian Perfection* 46). Clarissa opposes patriarchal representatives of eighteenth-century imperial Britain in the reappropriated name and sovereignty of God. Through her struggle, Richardson articulates a strategy for converting the secular theology of nationalism into a countertheology of liberation.

Clarissa, in other words, represents a threat, and in the late eighteenth and early nineteenth centuries the domestic literary tradition responded by developing enhanced strategies for discipline that sought to keep the sovereignty of the modern subject more firmly ensconced within the national whole. Having played a role in shaping the modern British individual, domestic literature likewise participated in the struggle to contain it. Later domestic authors such as Edgeworth, Austen, and Hannah More innovated new omniscient narrative techniques that probed more deeply into the minds of their characters and, crucially, allowed these authors to make the minutiae of self-governance the explicit object of their stories. *Clarissa*'s heroine uses the "God within her" as the basis for rebellion, and the solution proposed by later domestic authors is to subject this space of interiority to a newly methodical mode of discipline that ultimately derives, as I argue in the next chapter, from Britain's experience managing kidnapped African slaves on New World plantations (853). Turning to the colonial fiction of Edgeworth, the following chapter highlights both the centrality of slavery to domestic literature's construction of a newly disciplined individual as well as the instability that will continue to haunt it, both within England and beyond it.

The embodiment of God on earth, Clarissa inhabits the subjectivity of a rebel hero as well as, it must be said, a potential terrorist, and what one finds in domestic literature is the imposition of limits. These are limits, however, that I argue expand rather than restrict the modern subject's potential for political transformation. In the domestic fiction of Edgeworth, the individual meets the collective, and the result is a holy war with rules: in the name of God, those who hoard must be abolished and those who share made equally ennobled. *Omnia sunt communia*, Jerusalem descends.

4

The Other Side of Discipline

Marriage, Slavery, and the Ambivalent Politics of Maria Edgeworth's Domestic Subject

Edgeworth and the Politics of Domestic Fiction

Domestic literature was one of the most popular forms of writing in long eighteenth-century Britain, and what it offered a society experiencing a period of unprecedented economic growth and cultural change was a crucial countervailing force of stability and self-possession: a modern national self.[1] Domestic authors constructed a new kind of hero, young men and women, who, like the patriot, poet, and king before them, exemplified a mode of being both in this fallen world and at the same time safely beyond it. The idea of domesticity as an oppositional space set apart from commerce functions in these stories as a tool for reformulating familiar neoclassical values for an unfamiliar modern age. Within this effort, slavery was also essential, since, like domesticity, it pointed both backward and forward and thus provided domestic authors with another means of speaking to a modernizing present in the language of the past. At once quintessentially ancient and modern, slavery assumed in this period an important double meaning, constituted both by its long-standing figurative function in neoclassical rhetoric as a sign of moral dispossession and by its inescapable material presence in the eighteenth century as an increasingly central economic fact.[2] Be it Pope's declaration in his Horatian satires that "I am no slave," Clarissa's contention that "my mind is not that of a slave," or Edgeworth's assertion in her domestic novel

Belinda (1801) that the fashion-obsessed Lady Delacour is "a slave to the world," English-speaking authors of the eighteenth century formulate a modern idea of the British subject as individuated, domestic, and free only by first imagining the figure of the slave who was not ("Epilogue to the Satires II" 206; III; 41).

In this chapter, I begin with the Irish author Maria Edgeworth's short story "The Grateful Negro," which is set on Jamaican slave plantations, in order to show the centrality of slavery to the construction of a modern British subject whose essential political volatility Edgeworth herself demonstrates in her great anticolonial domestic Irish novel *The Absentee*, the focus of this chapter's latter half. By moving from the English setting of Richardson's *Clarissa* to the colonial context of early nineteenth-century Jamaica and Ireland, this chapter aims to underline the fact that a modern model of the British nation and subject is not simply made in England and then disseminated elsewhere. What is apparent, from the Catholic Alexander Pope's many depictions of himself as the "last of Britons" to the Scottish James Thomson's declaration in "Rule Britannia" (1740) that "Britons never will be slaves," is that the idea of England as Britain—that is, as a nation destined by God for cosmopolitan expansion—is a product in no small part of authors and events lying far outside England's eighteenth-century Anglican establishment ("Epilogue to the Satires II" 250; 6).

To appreciate the particular role that domestic fiction plays in this process, however, one must reject the still-dominant narrative that eighteenth-century Britain witnessed a transition from one *distinct* historical period to another. This view has long authorized academics to pretend that the events, figures, and facts that constituted eighteenth-century life in a single temporal frame can be divided between those that belong to a feudal past and those that anticipate a bourgeoning modern future. One challenge to this narrative has come from historians and literary scholars who argue that it was the "feudal" experience of managing slaves on agricultural plantations rather than the "modern" phenomenon of technological innovation that prompted British manufacturers to begin centralizing their work forces in the eighteenth century.[3] Britain became the world's preeminent slave-trading colonial power in this period, shipping roughly 3.4 million enslaved persons from Africa to the Americas and overseeing a dramatic expansion in the size and profits of agricultural plantations, particularly in the West Indies and American colonies.[4] In revisionist scholarship, this process appears as both feudal and modern, and what I would like to add to this picture is that the distinctive individualism of literature from this period, long hailed as one of the great hallmarks of British modernity, is also indebted to the at once forward- and backward-looking experience of the slave trade. While employers in the metropole may have gleaned the financial benefits of close supervision and discipline from Britain's increasingly profitable sugar plantations, English-speaking authors drew something from slavery as well—namely, an extreme representation of commercial society and the ensuing need to imagine how one can participate in it without being wholly owned.[5] This is all to say that Paul Gilroy's argument in *The Black Atlantic* (1993) that "slavery was integral to western civilization" applies in a specific and largely overlooked way to the humanist individualism evident in eighteenth-century British writing (xi).

Edgeworth writes "The Grateful Negro" and *The Absentee* in the aftermath of the global political unrest of the 1790s, and the particularly relevant events of the Haitian Revolution (1791–1804) and the 1798 Irish Rebellion. In both "The Grateful Negro" and *The Absentee*, Edgeworth offers Britain's rulers the same political lesson: social stability can be achieved only if a new kind of political obedience is instilled among the British body politic, and this in turn requires those who hold power to begin wielding it in a more enlightened manner. Whether it is the rational "benevolence" of the ideal plantation owner in "The Grateful Negro" or the "influence and example of a great resident Irish proprietor" in *The Absentee*, both stories center on the idea that the essentially feudal and paternalist power of landowners and employers can be used a tool of modernization (49; 198). Rather than opposing feudalism to mercantilism or paternalism to Enlightenment, Edgeworth argues for using the former to produce the latter with the assumption that the production of a hegemonic political subject—a subject who wills his or her own subjection as if it were freedom—is possible only through the democratization of paternalist power.

Like other domestic novelists, Edgeworth privileges the process of preparing for marriage in her novels because organizing one's subjectivity around the sacredness it signifies entails assuming paternalist responsibility for one's self. Although centered on the expectation of marriage, domestic novels pay little attention to marriage itself and instead focus on cultivating subjects capable of internalizing the sacred nationalism it embodies. To be ready for marriage in a domestic novel is to achieve both the self-governance needed to act as a hegemonic national subject and the judgment required to identify those worthy of a similar transformation. From Pamela and Clarissa to Fanny and Colambre, domestic protagonists learn to judge those who can be converted and incorporated into the sacred national fold from those inhuman creatures to be castigated as monsters, animals, and demons. For every Mr. B and Mr. Belford, there is a Lovelace and Mary Crawford.

However anachronistic such a conception of political subjecthood might appear, it in fact anticipates the late twentieth-century flourishing of revisionist accounts, by everyone from Marxists to feminists, of the modern individual as a product of extrapolitical forces. While my interpretation owes much to Nancy Armstrong's *Desire and Domestic Fiction* (1987) for first making the connection between this revisionist theory and domestic writing, I also depart significantly from Armstrong on a few key issues. First, Armstrong never fully escapes the sway of Whiggish historical orthodoxy in presuming that the modern British subject is secular and thus distinct from an earlier moment of history, an assumption that flies in the face of the political theology that this book traces. And, second, Armstrong, following Foucault's work in the early to mid-1970s, interprets the emergence of modernity in the Manichean terms of a moral transition. Throughout her writing, from *Desire and Domestic Fiction* to *How Novels Think* (2005), Armstrong depicts the individual cultivated by British novels as an unambiguously negative phenomenon, merely a descent into further oppression.[6] What Armstrong misses, and Foucault recognizes only at the end of his career, is that history is not a matter of moral arcs, but rather of dialectical transformation in which every new form of control is simultaneously a new tool for emancipation. This chapter makes much of the simple but easily overlooked fact that a power that operates through "hegemony" can never be absolute, because it depends upon the will of its subjects.

In a 1982 seminar titled "Technologies of the Self," Foucault briefly describes his own turn to such thinking, explaining that "perhaps I've insisted too much on domination and power . . . [and] am now more and more interested in the interaction between oneself and others in the technologies of individual domination, the history of how an individual acts upon himself, in the technology of the self" (19). Foucault elaborates that "technologies of the self . . . permit individuals to effect by their own means or with the help of others a certain number of operations on their own bodies and souls, thoughts, conduct, and way of being so as to transform themselves in order to attain a certain state of happiness, purity, wisdom, perfection, or immortality" (18). In the latter two volumes of *History of Sexuality* published in the year of his death in 1984, as well as in a series of lectures, notes, and essays from the late 1970s and early 1980s, Foucault paradoxically locates an alternative to disciplinary power within the practice of discipline itself. Foucault ends his career studying a tenet that is as central to neoclassical republicanism as it is to the domestic novel: that "self-control" is a precondition for "freedom" (*Use of Pleasure* 80).

Foucault's turn to a positive notion of "individual freedom" occurs almost entirely in the context of discussions of Ancient Greece and Rome, which leaves open the question as to how such freedom can be exercised many centuries later by Anglo-European subjects whose agency, as Foucault himself repeatedly demonstrates, is so often used a tool of domination (*Use of Pleasure* 79). Early nineteenth-century domestic fiction occupies a key transitional moment in the constitution of the modern disciplinary subject, and what Edgeworth, like few others, offers is an articulation of the emancipatory potential of self-governance before its meaning is codified as the exclusive attribute of a normatively white imperial nation, a racial model that develops in the nineteenth century and solidifies in the twentieth. Against readings of Edgeworth that would place her work within this later model of race, I contend that there is no stable notion of race or blackness in Edgeworth's writing, and that this is important because it means that the form of subjectivity that Edgeworth develops is not inherently racist, that it need not be unequivocally dismissed, and that, to the contrary, there is something worth recovering within it.

Frantz Fanon's call in *The Wretched of the Earth* (1961) "to create a new man," a new idea of humanity beyond the parameters of "this Europe which never stops talking of man yet massacres him at every one of its street corners, at every corner of the world," continues to reverberate throughout the humanities as a central pressing task (239, 235). In two important responses to Fanon's call—Sylvia Wynter's "Unsettling the Coloniality of Being/Power/Truth/Freedom" (2003) and Alexander Weheliye's *Habeas Viscus* (2014)—there is an attempt to define humanity as, in the words of Wynter, "the human species itself/ourselves," or, in Weheliye's terms, "the liminal space . . . of habeas viscus or the flesh" (260; 135). Although my argument in this book draws in several key respects from the work of Wynter and Weheliye, I part ways from their efforts to locate an alternative concept of the human in what amounts to an ahistorical space of biology, a strategy advocated by many recent theorists of humanism and biopolitics from Hortense Spillers to Roberto Esposito. Against this tendency, I would like to insist that one can construct a political alternative only by grappling with the past and using its ideas and forces to constitute something other than the racist present.

History, in other words, is something that must be surmounted rather than escaped, and returning to the fiction of Edgeworth is an opportunity to recover a part of the humanist tradition that is frequently lost in present-day theoretical discussions: that the capacity for self-governance only becomes inherently European in ideology, and that it certainly was not so for eighteenth-century humanists such as Edgeworth who took the human as an uncertain and potentially universal entity. For Edgeworth, humanity was that form of life endowed with political potential, and by political Edgeworth meant the domestic art of self-mastery. Edgeworth's fiction was a didactic effort to revitalize neoclassical republicanism within her early nineteenth-century present, an endeavor that resonates with Miguel Vatter's recent call, in *The Republic of the Living* (2015), for repeating the same gesture within our own. Despite himself lapsing into ahistorical biology by positing "species life" as the basis for a new humanism, Vatter importantly emphasizes the relevance of the republican tradition to postindustrial capitalist societies in which the bureaucratic management of life increasingly displaces actual politics (7). Speaking very much in the language of Pope and Edgeworth, Vatter hails republicanism as a solution to our current state of affairs because it "stands for the irreducibility of politics to government; it teaches that more politics may be necessary if we are going to be governed less" (6).

Wynter articulates the conclusion of many contemporary scholars in interpreting the birth of civic humanism from the Renaissance to the eighteenth century as a moment when Christian Europeans stopped "seeing themselves as one religious genre of the human [among many]" and came "to overrepresent their conception of the human as the human, thereby coming to invent, label, and institutionalize the indigenous peoples of the Americas as well as the transported enslaved Black Africans as the physical referent of the projected irrational/subrational Human Other to its civic-humanist, rational self conception" (281–82). What Edgeworth's fiction suggests is that such arguments in a sense take Eurocentrism on its own terms. In the light of racial models developed over the course of the nineteenth and twentieth centuries, such arguments presume that republican definitions of humanity are reducible to Europe, and what they therefore miss are all those moments when characters from elsewhere exercise a self-mastery and a politics that are neither white nor Western.

Slave Modernity and "The Grateful Negro"

Slavery was neither an anachronistic mode of production nor a peripheral topic in long eighteenth-century Britain. Instead, slavery was essential to the development of an Atlantic economy and a new culture of individualism, both of which transformed British society in this period. Edgeworth's decision to set a domestic tale on Jamaican slave plantations in her 1804 short story "The Grateful Negro" should therefore be read not as an aberration from domestic literary convention, but as a clarifying articulation of the integral connection between domestic narratives and slavery. From 1700 to 1800, the number of African slaves on the British colony of Jamaica increased from 45,000 to 328,000, and it is here, in a sugar colony where slaves outnumbered whites by twelve to one, that Edgeworth perfects her theory of domestic power (Higman 61).[7]

Edgeworth seizes upon the relationship between plantation owners and slaves as an opportunity to fuse paternal authority to a modern factory-like mode of disciplinary power, a synthesis at the heart of the domestic literary tradition. The final product of this synthesis in "The Grateful Negro" is Edgeworth's Caesar, a worker who, although a slave, is nevertheless in possession of "his work" and "his cottage" (53, 59). Caesar, in other words, is simultaneously a slave and not a slave at all. With a protagonist who bears the same slave name and hails from the same tribe, the "Koromantyns," Edgeworth's story represents a deliberate rewriting of Aphra Behn's early novel *Oroonoko* (1688). Edgeworth's suggestion is that the addition of an enlightened slave master could have transformed Behn's hero from a tragic leader of rebellions into a happy domestic subject. Edgeworth portrays Caesar's master, Edwards, as this ideal authority figure, one who combines Burkean paternalism, Kantian enlightenment, and Smithian theories of free labor in order to exercise a form of management that is at once feudal and enlightened. By suggesting that the Enlightenment was not altogether opposed to slavery, and in some sense derived from it, I do not mean to imply a wholesale rejection of the Enlightenment project, and this is because a profound ambivalence structures the enlightened subject cultivated by work such as Edgeworth's. The narrative of "The Grateful Negro" builds its dramatic force from an imminent "conspiracy" involving almost all of the slaves on the island of Jamaica, and the only obstacle standing in its way is the will of Edwards's newly enlightened subject, Caesar (53). The great ambivalence of this solution, which has been entirely ignored by Edgeworth criticism, is that Caesar could have decided otherwise and that everything Edwards did to foster his sense of self-possession could have been used to further empower his revolt. Self-governance is not only the hegemonic condition of the disciplinary subject, but also the inevitable basis for this subject's emancipatory overcoming, and in domestic fiction one finds both sides of this equation.

Although he articulates an unambiguously negative interpretation of discipline's function in Edgeworth's story and the plantation life it depicts, George Boulukos's "Maria Edgeworth's 'Grateful Negro' and the Sentimental Argument for Slavery" (1999) is an essential resource for understanding Edgeworth's text because of its crucial insight that "The Grateful Negro" cannot be comprehended according to the familiar rubric in which abolitionists are identified with a modern "bourgeois ideology" and planters with an outdated feudalist one (24). As Boulukos writes, many in the eighteenth and early nineteenth centuries viewed slavery "as one type of labor on a continuum with serfdom and wage labor" (13). An "endless flow of pamphlets" and literary tracts, such as "The Grateful Negro," depict planters in this period as potentially modernizing agents associated, as Boulukos explains, with "such 'bourgeois' forces as free-labor psychology, technological innovation, and market expansion."[8] What I would add is that planters played a similar role to domestic fiction itself since they accomplished in deed what domestic authors called for in principle—namely, the fusion of, in Boulukos's words, "plantation discipline" with the "internalized incentives to work of contracted wage labor," a synthesis of paternalism and Smithian economics that should be familiar to readers of Edgeworth (24).

Edgeworth's aim in "The Grateful Negro" is not to eliminate slavery but, rather, to rationalize it and thereby make it produce what it in historical fact did: a new disciplinary art of governance and a corresponding subjectivity characterized by the internalization of the employer's authority and interests. Edgeworth opens her story by distinguishing between two modes of slave owning, one irrational and anachronistic and the other virtuous and forward-thinking: "In the island of Jamaica, there lived two planters; whose methods of managing their slaves were as different as possible" (49). The two planters are Mr. Edwards, who employs free-market labor theories in managing his slaves, and Mr. Jeffries, a "thoughtless" neighboring planter who remains aloof from the management of his estate and dissolute in his own domestic economy (49). Whereas Jeffries's slaves are managed according to the irrational forces of either the malice of their overseer or the financial needs of their profligate owner—"impulses of the moment," as it were—Edwards's slaves are subjected to the abstract and predictable principle of efficiency itself (Edgeworth, *Ennui* 248).[9]

Echoing the lessons of Adam Smith's *The Wealth of Nations* (1776), Edwards assigns his "negroes ... reasonable and fixed daily tasks," after which they "were permitted to employ their time for their own advantage," or "to employ themselves longer for their master" in return for "regular wages." Edgeworth's ideal hegemonic mode of labor management crystallizes in the self-reflexive verb phrase "to employ themselves," which she uses to describe the "extra work" of Edwards's slaves. As Edgeworth's narrator reports, the offer of "regular wages ... operated most powerfully upon the slaves," who illustrated that "those who are animated by hope can perform what would seem impossibilities, to those who are under the depressing influence of fear" (50). According to Edgeworth's paternalist narrative, slavery, if rationally managed, becomes voluntary, which is to say that it becomes wage labor.[10] Published as part of Edgeworth's *Popular Tales* (1804), "The Grateful Negro" is written, in the words of the *Edinburgh Review*'s influential assessment, for "the great and respectable multitude of English tradesman, yeoman, and manufacturers" (Jeffrey 330). It is to this class that Edgeworth promotes the Smithian argument that workers directed by their own self-interest are more productive than those managed by external force. Where Edgeworth departs from Smith is in her Burkean insistence on the social necessity of politics, and, in particular, the politics of paternalist care as practiced by both the state and the home.

"The Grateful Negro" turns on the relationship of Edwards and Caesar. It opens with Caesar distraught at the prospect of being sold by Jeffries and forever separated from his fiancé, and with Edwards fortuitously hearing and responding to "his cry of distress." Edgeworth's narrator contextualizes Caesar's plight by explaining that he was "the best negro in Jeffries' possession," for "such had been his industry and exertion, that notwithstanding the severe tasks imposed by Durant, the overseer, Caesar found means to cultivate his provision-ground to a degree of perfection no where else seen on this estate" (50). After learning from

Durant that Caesar must be sold to pay off Jeffries's creditors, Edwards asks to whom and at what price and then pleads, "And must he leave this cottage which he has built, and these bananas which he has planted?" (51). Rather than drawing attention to Clara, who is "weeping bitterly" by Caesar's side, Edwards prioritizes the injustice of separating a slave from the cottage he has built and the land he has cultivated because together these add up to a home, and, for Edgeworth, the home is not merely, as in Smith, a site for the necessary maintenance and reproduction of a labor force; instead, the home is the embodiment of neoclassical self-possession, which acts as the essential guarantee of social order (51). This is why Edgeworth's narrator names Caesar "the best negro in Jeffries' possession," based not on the labor he performs in the sugar fields, of which there is no mention, but rather on the "industry and exertion" that he devotes to his house (50).

For Edgeworth, the point of efficient plantation management is producing both greater profits and more disciplined domestic subjects. Without the latter, Edgeworth's fiction suggests that the economic prosperity generated by the former will be for naught, since the underlying fabric of society will be forever menaced by the threat of social unrest. By faithfully and rationally exercising his paternal responsibilities, Edwards transforms Caesar from a rebellious subject in league with an imminent slave rebellion led by his "particular friend" and countryman Hector into a politically docile and efficient individual bound to his master by "the principle of gratitude" (54, 58). The irrational neglect, on the other hand, practiced by Jeffries "exacerbated the slaves under his dominion," inspiring them to lead a "conspiracy ... [that] extended to all the negroes in the island of Jamaica"—except those on Edwards's plantation—"to extirpate every white man, woman, and child in the island" (53). With such a conspiracy, Edgeworth clearly alludes to the infamous massacres of whites in the slave uprisings of the Haitian Revolution, as well as on a more distant register to the mass killings of Protestants and Catholics in the 1798 Irish Rebellion. Such an uprising is thwarted in "The Grateful Negro" only because Caesar alerts Edwards to the danger, allowing him to save from destruction every plantation on the island but Jeffries's. Through this narrative, Edgeworth makes a historically significant yet ultimately false argument that employers can avoid revolutionary uprisings by embracing their politically essential duty to exercise rational paternalist care.

What should not be forgotten in the midst of excavating Edgeworth's argument in "The Grateful Negro" is that this argument and the "grateful" protagonist who embodies it are fantasies that directly contradict historical experience in the colonial West Indies. In one of the early revolts that marked the beginning of the Haitian Revolution, African descendants in and around the key northern colonial trading city of Le Cap developed a plot that, in the words of C. L. R. James's *Black Jacobins* (1938), "aimed at exterminating the whites and taking the colony for themselves." Following a procession of steps that closely mirrors Hector's strategy in "The Grateful Negro," the plan was for slaves on the outskirts of Le Cap to set fire to their plantations, at which point "the slaves in town would massacre the whites and the slaves on the plains would complete the destruction" (86). The revolt failed to capture Le Cap, but it succeeded in burning one-half of the fertile sugar-producing region that surrounded it. And, as James emphasizes, the revolt was led by slaves on the Gallifet plantation, whose reputation for benevolent management inspired the proverb "happy as the Negroes of Gallifet" (87).

In the words of James, this was a "phenomenon noticed in all revolutions," the best-treated and most-educated workers, whether they were West Indies slaves, Luddite weavers, or Irish tenants, tended to be the ones to lead the way (87). James observes that one planter in the town of Port-Margot "had taught his black foreman to read and write, had made him free, had left him in his will 10,000 francs, had given to the foreman's mother land on which she had made a coffee plantation," and that this foreman nevertheless went on to lead a rebellion "on the plantations of his master and his own mother, set them on fire, and joined the revolution, which gave him a high command" (89). All of this is to say that had Edgeworth's tale been fully drawn from history, Caesar not only would have remained involved in Hector's conspiracy, but in fact would have been further immersed in it, perhaps supplanting Hector as its leader, as a result of the power he accumulated as a slave on a relatively lax plantation with access to tools such as internalized discipline and "sharp knives" ("The Grateful Negro" 58).

Edgeworth's Domestic Enlightenment

What Marilyn Butler's authoritative biography of Edgeworth, *A Literary Life* (1972), makes clear is that the many allusions to Enlightenment thought in Edgeworth's fiction are neither the product of chance nor of an underlying collective unconscious. After being educated at two North Midlands girl schools, where she learned "the routine accomplishments of the better-taught upper-class women of the period," Edgeworth moved to

Ireland at the age of fourteen to be educated by her father, Richard Lovell Edgeworth, an Enlightenment enthusiast who "extend[ed] her education far beyond what was common for a woman" (Butler 55, 36). Richard had spent "fifteen years in the English Midlands in the bright morning of the industrial revolution" and had been immersed in mechanical experiments and theoretical discussions as a member of the Lunar Society of Birmingham (77). Richard was at the center of what has been termed the "Midlands Enlightenment," and he ensured that Maria knew the political economy of Smith as well as the aesthetic, political, and moral philosophies of John Locke, Bernard Mandeville, David Hume, Jean-Jacques Rousseau, Voltaire, and Edmund Burke, to name only a few of the thinkers mentioned in Richard and Maria's coauthored works.

Throughout her short stories, novels, and two coauthored books of pedagogy, *Practical Education* (1798) and *Essays on Professional Education* (1809), Edgeworth celebrates what Kant names in his seminal 1784 article "What Is Enlightenment?" as the essence of enlightened practice: "To use one's own understanding without guidance from another" (54–5). Whether Edgeworth read Kant is not known and seems unlikely, but what is nevertheless clear is that Edgeworth's enlightened philosophy aligns closely with Kant's, given its emphasis on the freedom of moral self-governance and the necessity of cosmopolitan politics.[11] In a particularly Kantian moment from Edgeworth's oeuvre, the heroine of *Belinda* hears a story of human folly from her tutor in courtship and worldly affairs—"the fashionable Lady Delacour"—and suddenly "saw things in a new light; and for the first time in her life she reasoned for herself upon what she saw and felt" (6, 69). As Edgeworth's narrator elaborates, "When the understanding is suddenly roused and forced to exert itself, what a multitude of deductions it makes in a short time" (69).[12]

Where Edgeworth fundamentally departs from Kant is in insisting that paternalist authority plays an essential and positive role in fostering enlightenment, rather than a merely a negative one, as Kant suggests. Despite frequently opposing such thinking as "fanaticism," Kant nevertheless cannot help but posit the Enlightenment as a supersensible principle of reality itself, a part of "a hidden plan of nature," and if political leaders only stay out of the way, then "enlightenment is almost inevitable" (*Critique of Judgment* 351; "Idea for a Universal History" 50; "What Is Enlightenment?" 55). In his third and final critique, the *Critique of Judgment* (1790), Kant in truth successfully bridges the gap between the human mind and the manifold world of things only by presupposing a common end, "a *cosmopolitan* whole," representing the world's final purpose, whose realization is arranged by "a deeply hidden and perhaps intentional endeavor of the supreme wisdom" (320). In *Belinda*, Edgeworth pointedly satirizes such idealist thinking through the story of Clarence Hervey and his attempt to turn an orphaned girl into a perfect, purely innocent wife. The handsome and impressionable young Clarence was inspired by "the works of Rousseau" to embark upon the "romantic project of educating a wife for himself ... [who is] secluded from all intercourse with the world" (362, 370). Clarence keeps his child of nature in a state of "perfect innocence," forbidding her from learning to write or from speaking to anyone but himself, her widowed tutor Mrs. Ormond, and an elderly clergyman who visits every Sunday (381, 370). By privileging nature over culture in his paternal care, Clarence succeeds in producing a subject who is, in the words of Edgeworth's narrator, "ignorant and indolent, ... [with] few ideas, and no wish to extend her knowledge" (379).

Edgeworth's satire of idealism and in particular Rousseau resembles Burke's many and varied attacks over the course of his career on the idea that an undisciplined humanity exists in a state of admirable innocence. Undoubtedly an influence on Edgeworth, Burke's insistence on the need for governments to actively manage and shape their populations stems from the assumption that a natural humanity is, as he states in his *Reflections on the Revolution in France* (1790), "an unsocial, uncivil, [and] unconnected chaos of elementary particles" (97). In works such as the *Reflections*, Burke reverses the terms of Jacobin ideology by arguing that "the restraints on men, as well as their liberties, are to be reckoned among their rights" (60). For Burke, nature provides no rights, only the fearful prospect of violence; political constitutions alone, "settled upon some compact, tacit or expressed," are what bring rights and liberty into existence (*Appeal* 118).

While Edgeworth certainly draws from Burke and writes positively of him on several occasions, describing him as an exemplary statesmen in *Essays on Professional Education*, Edgeworth, like Austen and indeed the domestic genre as a whole, parts from Burke in using her fiction to democratize the process of moral regulation, depicting it as a practice that subjects can and should perform upon themselves. Writing in the aftermath of the controversy sparked by his *Reflections*, Burke stridently contends, in the pamphlet *An Appeal from the New to the Old Whigs* (1791), that "the people are the natural control on authority," which they themselves ought never to exercise since, according to Burke, only "the natural aristocracy ... bred in a place of estimation" is capable of the self-regulation necessary for the practice of politics (120, 129). In opposition to such elitism, Edgeworth maintains the optimistic position that "the people"—workers, servants, slaves, and women—are capable of much more than the brute, prepolitical role Burke assigns them.

Edgeworth's notion of enlightenment is at once orthodox and innovative. She draws from Burke's paternalist and one might say antienlightenment philosophy, but she does so to pursue the Kantian end of popularizing self-discipline and the moral action it makes possible. While critics such as Mitzi Myers and Clíona Ó Gallchoir have sought to separate Edgeworth from the Enlightenment by arguing that she constructs a kind of feminist alternative, the truth is that Edgeworth develops a fairly canonical enlightened philosophy, and, in "The Grateful Negro," it is one that fashions Caesar as a kind of Kantian hero. In stark contrast to Myer's image of Edgeworth as an author devoted to the politics of "survival and saving" rather than "blood sacrifice," Edgeworth, like Behn in *Oroonoko*, celebrates her African hero for his willingness to sacrifice not only himself, but also his wife and the domesticity she embodies, to the principle of moral virtue (375). The enlightened Caesar rejects all forms of enthusiasm except the enthusiasm of Kantian morality itself, and it is in the name of this higher principle that he is willing to sacrifice everything.

In a crucial moment in Caesar's transformation from rebel to loyal subject, Edwards offers Caesar a knife so that he can better prune his domestic plot, explaining, "I am not one of those masters who are afraid to trust their negroes with sharp knives" (58). Caesar experiences a profound change in response:

> Caesar received the knife without uttering a syllable; but no sooner was Mr. Edwards out of sight, than he knelt down, and, in a transport of gratitude, swore that, with his knife, he would stab himself to the heart, sooner than betray his master! The principle of gratitude conquered every other sensation. The mind of Caesar was not insensible to the charms of freedom: he knew the negro conspirators had so taken their measures that there was the greatest probability of their success. His heart beat high at the idea of recovering his liberty; but he was not to be seduced from his duty, not even by his delightful hope. (58–59)

A tension between self-possession and self-abandonment structures this passage, and that is because, in giving Caesar a knife, Edwards endows him with the capacity to construct a sense of self-possession that is paradoxically grounded in self-sacrifice. Edwards's gift enables Caesar both to more efficiently manage his symbolically rich garden and to exercise the "deprivation" that Kant posits at the center of moral law. A knife, in this latter sense, gives Caesar the possibility of liberty and of achieving that even higher state described by Kant in the *Critique of Judgement* as the sublimity of moral law, whose "might actually reveals itself aesthetically only through sacrifice" (131).

At once uplifted and humbled, Caesar stands as an enlightened hero who choses the supremacy of abstract principles over "the charms of freedom." The first definition of "charms" in the *OED* is "the chanting or recitation of a verse supposed to possess magic power or occult influence," and it is thus by resisting the superstitious semblance of freedom promised by mass revolt that Caesar comes to experience the only true form of freedom according to Kant, the ability to make and follow universal laws for one's self. Caesar obeys the categorical imperative that Kant defines in *Groundwork of the Metaphysics of Morals* (1785) as acting only "*in such a way that I could also will that my maxim should become a universal law*" (15). As a result of his Kantian fidelity, Caesar achieves the condition Kant celebrates as the "sovereign" and uniquely human state of the freely governed (41). In following Kant's categorical imperative, Caesar also demonstrates one of its key consequences: a refusal to treat the life of others—in this case, Edwards—as a means of achieving one's own ends, since to do so would be to introduce a utilitarianism that could not be applied universally. Kant explains that "all rational beings stand under the *law* that each of them is to treat himself and all others *never merely as means* but always ... *as ends in themselves*," as subjects not of a "market price," but of a "dignity" (41, 42). The human capacity to make laws endows one with both freedom and restraint because it places every lawgiver within a community of similarly endowed subjects.

Although it has not been read as such by critics, "The Grateful Negro" is an enlightened tale that takes the degradation of slavery as an exemplary setting for testing a character's commitment to acting upon moral principle rather than self-interest. Edgeworth challenges the integrity of Caesar's capacity for moral action by confronting him with the successive temptations of his loyalty to a rebellion led by his friend and countryman Hector, his related yearning for liberty, and, finally, his domestic love for Clara. Like Kant, Edgeworth takes freedom, which for her is domestically grounded self-possession, as a heightened form of subjection entailing sacrifice, and, in the case of "The Grateful Negro," sacrifice of the family itself. When Hector learns of Caesar's new loyalties, he devises a plan to force him to chose between his devotion to Clara and "the principle of gratitude" (60). On orders from Hector, a sorceress allied to the rebel conspiracy lures Clara into her cottage, sedates her, and then tells Caesar that "she lies in the sleep of death," to be saved only by his renewed loyalty to the rebel cause, emphasizing that "Victory! Wealth! Freedom! and Revenge! will be theirs!" Edgeworth's narrator explains that the "conflict in his [Caesar's] mind was violent; but his sense of gratitude and duty would not be shaken by hope, fear, or ambition: nor could it be vanquished by love" (61). As Caesar states in an earlier exchange with Hector, "There is one for whose sake all must be spared," and Caesar proves himself enthusiastically bound to this antiutilitarian principle of moral action, so much so that he is willing to sacrifice the domestic relationship that made him capable of such action in the first place (60).

Utilitarianism was a key competing philosophy of modernity in this period, and against its central presumption that morality can be calculated—according to the Benthamite dictum of the greatest amount of good for the greatest number—Kant offers a moral philosophy of absolutism, one begging for a liberation that Kant denies but never truly escapes. Instead, it remains a stubborn source of tension for Kant as well as for the many British domestic authors, like Edgeworth, who follow in his wake. The tension is that, to be an enlightened self-governing subject, one cannot have a master outside of one's self, no matter what limitations Kant attempts to impose from the categorical imperative to his repressive notion of private reason.[13] Viewed from the perspective of enlightened autonomy, Caesar's decision to abstain from rebellion represents a betrayal of the subjectivity he bears, one that mirrors the conjugal surrender of the many domestic heroines who forsake self-governance for the patriarchal authority of a husband.[14] Caesar resembles every domestic protagonist but Clarissa in that he is capable of formulating and following laws for himself yet refuses to insist that his capacity for moral autonomy receive a material foundation. From this perspective, Boulukos is right to contend that "The Grateful Negro" is in the end an argument for the continuation of slavery. Boulukos is wrong, however, to attribute this argument to racism and to assert that Edgeworth's story is structured by a "belief in a gap between 'blacks' and 'whites' that is, for practical purposes, unbridgeable" (22). In fact, Edgeworth's treatment of Caesar serves as a kind of model that she alters in works such as *The*

Absentee only by starting with protagonists who are less perfect. Caesar in a sense belongs to an earlier moment of domestic fiction, exemplified by the novels of Richardson and Burney, in which protagonists begin their stories as already-constituted domestic subjects whose task is to protect their virtue in the midst of adversity. The heroes and heroines of early nineteenth-century domestic novels, on the other hand, start as flawed individuals who must be colonized, or, more precisely, must learn to colonize themselves in order properly to cultivate and internalize the at once domestic and national virtue of marriage.

For Edgeworth's readers, humanity was understood as a single species composed of a hierarchy of cultures from the rational to the savage, and many of the poorer Irish communities depicted in Edgeworth's fiction were understood as less advanced than well-known African societies, including Caesar's "Koromantyns," a colonial West Indies term for slaves taken from the Akan people of present-day Ghana. Though it flies in the face of contemporary Anglo-European conceptions of race, the Irish were understood as "Negroid" in eighteenth- and nineteenth-century Britain. This was a moment when, as the sociologist Zine Magubane writes, there were "hundreds of monographs and articles, published in both Britain and the United States, that used craniology to establish the racial inferiority and Negroid ancestry of the Irish Celt" (831n3). To say this is not to minimize the horror of chattel slavery for African-descended people, which was incomparable to anything that happened in Ireland in this period or after; it is rather to make an acknowledgement that both accurately reflects the eighteenth-century archive and, even more important, allows one to see the hope within it.

The Marriage Plot and Its Monsters

The Absentee represents not a break with but an elaboration of the subject-building project at the heart of "The Grateful Negro," one that uses an enlightened marriage plot as a tool for cultivating subjects like Caesar. Edgeworth's novel opens in the fashionable world of London and then follows its protagonist through his journey into Ireland, his frantic return to England, and finally his culminating journey back to his native Ireland. The story's most pressing question is whether its hero, the young Anglo-Irish Protestant Lord Colambre, can make the right decision in marriage and, in the process, return his "Absentee" family, the Clonbronys, from their fashionable exile in London to their long-neglected Irish estates. The enlightened heart of Edgeworth's novel is Colambre's educational journey through Ireland, where he learns the critical judgment necessary both to evaluate correctly the Irish people and choose the one bride who will cement his bond with them. The primary conflict in *The Absentee*'s opening pages is between Colambre's commitment to the idea that, as he states, "marriage is sacred," and his parents' countervailing attempts to commodify it, a tension that structures the story to follow (18). Colambre in fact only visits Ireland in an effort to "to make all farther doubt impossible" regarding his intentions with the English heiress Miss Broadhurst, whom his parents urge him to marry since, as his mother states, "if you don't . . . we can't live in Lon'on another winter" (56, 18).

Set against the backdrop of the 1798 Rebellion, *The Absentee* raises the optimistic expectation that the marriage of Colambre to Grace Nugent, a woman steeped in Irish Catholic lore, will symbolically complete the 1801 Union of Great Britain and Ireland. To save his family and, by extension, the colonial cause in Ireland, Colambre must see past prejudice and recognize that Grace Nugent exemplifies the kind of self-governing subjectivity that marks one as both truly British and a fitting partner in marriage. In terms, however, of this cosmopolitan promise, *The Absentee* is a profound failure. Colambre succeeds in transforming himself into an enlightened subject of marriage and, as a result, becomes capable of choosing the correct bride and cultivating the right kind of subjects. And yet the first subject Colambre produces after himself, a once-drunken Irish Catholic carriage driver named Larry Brady, uses his newly instilled capacity for discipline to disrupt rather than obey. Through a carefully staged conclusion, Larry fundamentally undoes not only *The Absentee*'s redemptive marriage plot, but also the imperial national theology that underpins it.

To understand the nationalism that underlies the romantic narrative of *The Absentee* and of domestic novels more generally, it is helpful to recall the specific meaning of marriage in sixteenth- through nineteenth-century England. In his study of the rituals surrounding three key events in the life of early modern England—*Birth, Marriage, and Death* (1998)—David Cressy singles out marriage as unique in that it was a preeminently "cultural event" that unlike birth and death "is susceptible to planning and choice" (298). Countering Lawrence Stone's seminal thesis that marriage only became "companionate" and consensual in the eighteenth century, Cressy contends that "the ideal of companionate marriage ... was enshrined in the prayer book [BCP] from its inception" in 1549, and that "individual consent was the *sine qua non*" of English marriage from at least this period (297, 256). Marriage was a moment of individual choice and political subjection, or, in other words, hegemony, a ritual in which young men and women publicly devoted themselves to the intertwined power of the English Church and state.

As a matter of both individualizing consent and incorporation into a broader public, the marriage ceremony represented a ritualized enactment of precisely that conjunction between nationalism and individualism that Foucault describes in the late seminar "The Political Technology of Individuals" (1982–84) as the "main characteristic of our [modern Western] political rationality." In the words of Foucault, this rationality is marked by the fact that "the integration of individuals in a community or in a totality results from a constant correlation between an increasing individualization and the reinforcement of this totality" (162). National incorporation through marriage is the reason why, as Cressy explains, early modern "husbands and wives inhabited a different moral universe from that of bachelors and maids" (288). Married subjects were expected to assume paternalist responsibility for regulating their own behavior as well as the "conduct of the their partners and dependents" (288).

Marriage was an important act of nation-building for post-Reformation England, a moment when a subject was proclaimed truly a part of the whole, and, because of this, changing its meaning entailed changing the terms of national belonging itself. By largely ignoring the marriage ceremony, as well as the life of the married couple, and instead focusing almost entirely on the kind of subject one can cultivate in anticipation of marriage, domestic novels thus altered the definition not only of marriage, but of the nation as well. Just as Dryden shifted the source of the king's authority from Church ritual to royal blood in "Astraea Redux" and "To His Sacred Majesty," domestic authors transferred the locus of marriage's significance from a sacrament to a subjectivity, and, in the process, they helped engender a new vision of the nation as a community sacralized by the subjectivity of its constituents rather than the monopoly claims of the English Church.

Domestic authors participated in the creation of a secular theology that would be essential for the globalization of Britain, since it centered on the deeply ecumenical and hence expansive idea that the nation was neither a geographical entity nor a race, but a particular mode of being. Whether it is Caesar, Colambre, or Austen's Elinor Dashwood, domestic protagonists exemplify a capacity for "self-command" that becomes a defining characteristic of what it means to be both British and Western (*Sense and Sensibility* 246). And though one might expect the theological dimension of marriage to remain relatively subtle in the domestic novel, given its turn away from sacrament, Edgeworth, for her part, makes its presence painfully clear in *The Absentee* by depicting all those who obstruct the development of her protagonist as literally demonic, and no character is represented in quite the same irremediable light as "Mr. Mordicai, the famous London coachmaker" (9).

For Edgeworth, the Jewish merchant who refuses to put anything above profit resembles the unenlightened slave insofar as both figures embody the threat of pure commodification, and yet there is a crucial difference. Whereas Edgeworth attributes the frenzied behavior of someone like Hector to the failures of his master, she resorts to the more essentializing language of racial anthropology to explain the same conduct in Mordicai. Within Edgeworth's system, the "Jew" stands as a darker, more irretrievably inhuman character than any other, than either the Koromantyn or the Irish. Although Edgeworth renounces her anti-Semitism following an exchange of letters in 1815 with the concerned Jewish American reader Rachel Mordicai and the ensuing publication of *Harrington* (1817), a novel explicitly opposed to anti-Semitism, Edgeworth's demonic portraits of Jews in *The Absentee*, as well as in other works, are far from a superficial attribute of her thought.[15]

In a particularly dramatic scene early in *The Absentee*, Edgeworth foreshadows what awaits Colambre's family, should they continue to live beyond their means in London, with the tale of the Berryls, a landed English family whose heir Colambre befriended at Cambridge and whose finances are cast into doubt when the patriarch falls suddenly ill, and creditors, most prominent among them Mordicai, begin to press for payment. While "absenteeism" was understood throughout the eighteenth and early nineteenth centuries as a term for landed Irish families living abroad, Edgeworth uses the story of the Berryls to argue that the physical and moral dispossession of absenteeism is a problem common to English, Irish, and indeed elites anywhere in the world who shirk their paternalist responsibilities (153). Just as Lady Clonbrony's "vain ambition to vie with superior rank and fortune" in London alienates her husband from "his tenantry, his duties, his country, [and] his home," Lady Berryl's "passion for living in London and at watering places ... had made her husband an ABSENTEE—an absentee from his home, his affairs, his duties, and his estate" (44). In both cases, Mordicai appears in the midst of a family crisis as the embodiment of pure credit, of an absenteeism without a home.

Edgeworth uses the deathbed scene of Sir John Berryl to stage a theatrical encounter between a grieving family and the rapacious creditor Mordicai, who is interpellated as both a "monster" and a slave for refusing to recognize the superiority of domestic value. As a result of their "ignorance and extravagance," the Berryls had accumulated a sizeable debt to Mordicai that "swelled afterwards to an amazing amount by interest, and interest upon interest" (43). "Conscious that the charges in his account were exorbitant, and that they would never be allowed if examined by a court of justice, . . . Mordicai was impatient to obtain payment whilst Sir John yet lived, or at least to obtain legal security for the whole sum from the heir," and he consequently orders his bailiff to illegally break into the Berryl home, where he confronts "Lady Berryl and Mr. Berryl's sisters, in an agony of grief," declaring, "It's all useless, . . . these tricks upon creditors won't do with me; I'm used to these scenes; I'm not made of such stuff as you think" (42–43). Anticipating the Berryls' response, Mordicai proclaims, "Leave a gentleman in peace in his last moments—No! he ought nought, nor sha'n't die in peace, if he don't pay his debts" (43). Mordicai privileges economic value above all else, including domestic affection and even human life, and, as a result, he can only interpret Sir John's request for peace and the "agony of grief" displayed by his family in the economic terms of "tricks" intended to further the Berryl family's financial advantage.

Edgeworth's point in this scene is that privileging economic value above the family leads Mordicai not only into a state of personal dispossession—he is "livid with malice" and clearly not capable of self-governance—but also to misinterpret genuine emotion as a theatrical performance (42). Since all of this occurs shortly after Lady Clonbrony engages in a Restoration theater–style plot to attach her son to the heiress Ms. Broadhurst by staging "easy, intimate" moments between the two, it seems that Mordicai's extreme dramatization of the link between unbridled commerce and theatrical morals is meant as a critique of the Clonbrony family as well (37). However, what separates the Clonbronys, the Berryls, and again even outright rebellious characters such as Hector from the likes of Mordicai is that only Mordicai appears intrinsically opposed to the domestic art of self-governance.

The morning after *The Absentee*'s opening scene in a London playhouse, Colambre visits Mordicai's workshop on behalf of Mr. Berryl, who is awaiting word from Mordicai as to whether he would honor his pledge to be "answerable" for all repairs for a carriage Mr. Berryl had purchased three months earlier (9). In narrating the exchange between Colambre and Mordicai, Edgeworth uses the language of racial anthropology to construct the Jew as perhaps the quintessential figure of otherness, a portrait that is without parallel in her oeuvre:

> [Colambre] began a statement of his friend's grievances, and an appeal to common justice and conscience, which he, unknowing the nature of the man whom he had to deal, imagined must be irresistible. Mr. Mordicai stood without moving a muscle of his dark wooden face—indeed, in his face there appeared to be no muscles, or none which could move; so that, though he had what are generally called handsome features, there was, altogether, something unnatural and shocking in his countenance. When, at last, his eyes turned and his lips opened, this seemed to be done by machinery, and not by the will of a living creature, or from the impulse of a rational soul. (10)

When confronted with appeals to "common justice and conscience," Mordicai's "countenance" appears "unnatural" and "shocking" because it fails to exhibit the sympathetic response that Colambre expects from a person endowed with a human soul. Mordicai's face has the "dark" and "wooden" quality of the static, the dead, and the inanimate, so when "his eyes turned and his lips opened" he appears to be moved by a force from outside of life. What makes Mordicai truly terrifying is that he signifies not the possibility of degeneracy in which lower forms of life appear as higher ones, but, rather, that life itself may be counterfeited.

Edgeworth clarifies Mordicai's inhuman status by noting that his movements "seemed to be done by machinery, and not the will of a living creature, or from the impulse of a rational soul." Defined by Johnson as either "complicated workmanship" or "that part which the deities, angels, or demons act in a poem," "machinery" underlines the at once commercial and demonic quality of a character animated by profit alone (1.444). The problem with Mordicai is not that he appears to be without spouse or child, a status he shares with Edgeworth as well as Austen; it is that he refuses to become a subject of marriage by internalizing the incarnational nationalism it embodies. Mordicai rejects the novelistic and conjugal opportunity "to live in God's holy ordinance" as the subject of God's new "true religion," and this is why Edgeworth casts him as the prince of darkness (*Book of Common Prayer* 136, 238).

Although Mordicai represents the most inhuman of *The Absentee*'s characters, he is—and for this reason, actually—far from the gravest threat Colambre faces in Edgeworth's story. Until *The Absentee*'s conclusion, it is the young English widow and libertine fortune hunter Lady Isabel who poses the most serious danger to the fulfillment of the novel's redemptive promise. By mimicking the role of a virtuous young woman dedicated to the sacredness of marriage and the nation, Isabel stands as a danger worse than Colambre's parents or the "monster" Mordicai himself, for only Isabel uses the appearance of sacrality as a tool for worldly gain (43). Whereas Colambre immediately recognizes Mordicai as a man "who looked . . . not the least like a gentleman" and with similar ease sees his parents' attempts to profit from his marriage as an affront to honor, Colambre is truly deceived by Isabel's "acting" and mistakes her theatrical performance for a subjective interiority rich in "sensibility" and "delicate penetration" (9, 77). Isabel and her mother, the witty socialite Lady Dashfort, pose a generic and epistemological threat to Colambre's negotiation of the courtship process and the larger redemption of both England and Ireland. Edgeworth casts Isabel and Lady Dashfort as characters from the world of Restoration theater, and, as is the convention for domestic novels, the protagonist who seeks to go beyond the theatrical morals and dispossessed subjectivities of British literature's Restoration past must engage in a struggle of intense self-cultivation.

Shortly after arriving in Ireland, Colambre fittingly first encounters Isabel and Lady Dashfort at a Dublin playhouse, "where their appearance instantly made that *sensation*, which is usually created by the entrance of persons of the first notoriety in the fashionable world." Colambre himself is transfixed; he twice determines to visit the nearby box of Sir James Brooke, one of his rational mentors in Ireland, who happens to be at the playhouse that night, but finds that "he could move no farther" than the door for he is engrossed by the spectacle of a "mother's masculine boldness [that] heightened, by contrast, the charms of the daughter's soft sentimentality" (77). Colambre concludes that "no young woman, could have such art," and plans to tell Brooke that "he had been unwarrantably severe" in his earlier warning that Isabel and her mother were capable of "incalculable mischief" (73). Colambre visits Brooke the next morning to deliver his message, but is thwarted since Brooke "this day received orders for his regiment to march to quarters in a distant part of Ireland," and "his head was full of arms, and ammunition, and knapsacks, and billets, and routes" (73, 77–78). Colambre refrains from voicing his concern, with the implication that he now believes it to be trifling in comparison to Brooke's new orders to suppress one of the many intermittent revolts that shook post-Union Ireland.[16]

And yet, as Brooke—and, by extension, Edgeworth—makes clear, Colambre is wrong. Brooke's final comment before leaving for combat is another warning to Colambre: "To beware of counterfeits" and to remember that *"Deeds not words,* is my motto ... [for] we can judge better by the conduct of people towards others than by their manner towards ourselves" (78). Brooke urges Colambre to evaluate people in a manner conducive to Kant's insistence that enlightened judgment occurs only when one resists the "tyranny" of the senses and the "despotism of desires" in order to view the objects of experience from the disinterested perspective of universal reason (*Critique of Judgment* 321, 319). For Kant, humanity has a utopian cosmopolitan future, but it depends on subjects acting like Caesar and connecting the objects of their experience to the moral realm of reason.[17] In *The Absentee,* Edgeworth sketches a Kant-like narrative of cosmopolitan redemption that hinges, like Kant's, on the integrity of human judgment, and this precisely is what Isabel and Lady Dashfort put into doubt.

Lady Dashfort's strategy is to offend Colambre with anti-Irish comments that "drew him out in defense of his beloved country, and gave him opportunities of appearing to advantage; this he could not help feeling, especially when lady Isabel was present." Edgeworth's narrator elaborates that "Lady Dashfort had dealt long enough with human nature to know, that to make any man pleased with her, she should begin by making him pleased with himself" (79). Isabel thus becomes a reflection of Colambre's own self-image, or what Freud terms his "ego-ideal," and his desire for her in turn reflects Freud's observation that "in many forms of love-choice, ... the object serves as a substitute for some unattained ego ideal of our own" (56–57). Edgeworth underlines the severity of Colambre's error with the irony of its consequences: Colambre's narcissistic infatuation with the image of the Irish patriot causes him to fall victim to Lady Dashfort's plot to make him a permanent absentee.

Colambre succeeds in unmasking Isabel and Lady Dashfort's ruse as a result of both the rational education provided by his cosmopolitan mentors, Sir James Brooke and Count O'Halloran, as well as the knowledge fortuitously disclosed to him by chance, an emphasis reflecting Edgeworth's empiricist leanings. In the words of Edgeworth's narrator, "A slight accident" occurs in the library of an Irish gentry home, when

Colambre, "who was sitting in one of the recesses reading," overhears Isabel telling one of the family's daughters that an unnamed man "was never a favourite of mine; I always detested him; I only flirted with him to plague his wife" (98). Colambre becomes capable of following Brooke's lesson that "we can judge better by the conduct of people toward others than by their manner towards ourselves" only by happening to hear Isabel speak when she does not believe him present (78).

The effect is immediate: "The face, the whole figure of lady Isabel, at this moment, appeared to lord Colambre suddenly metamorphosed; instead of the soft, gentle, amiable female, all sweet charity and tender sympathy; formed to love and to be loved, he beheld one possessed and convulsed by an evil spirit—her beauty, if beauty it could be called, the beauty of a fiend" (98). Once able to perceive Isabel without regard to himself, Colambre judges her as analogous to Mordicai, a being animated by something other than human forces. Just as Mordicai's movements "seemed to be done by machinery," Isabel's embodiment of those "softer virtues" ascribed to beauty by Burke appears to be the work of a "fiend" (*On the Sublime and Beautiful* 145). Within the terms of domestic literature, Isabel stands alongside characters such as the alluring Mary Crawford of Austen's *Mansfield Park* (1814) as a moral, theological, and, above all else, political problem. Isabel mimics the virtue of being a good subject of marriage—that is, one who chooses subjection. And, as a result, she ultimately represents a kind of living profanation, a false member of the elect, and Colambre accordingly can fulfill Edgeworth's marriage plot only by expelling her from the ranks of the chosen in favor of the one woman who most deserves to join them.

Adopted by the Clonbrony family at an early age and raised as Colambre's orphaned cousin, Grace Nugent appears in *The Absentee*'s first few pages as the embodiment of both self-governance and Catholic Ireland, and much of the drama in the story to follow centers on Colambre's struggle to authenticate her virtue. Having returned from his studies at Cambridge to meet his family in London in the opening scenes of the novel, Colambre is shocked to learn of the debts his family has been incurring, and he becomes even more alarmed when he hears his mother planning an extravagant London gala. At this point, however, Grace intervenes, saying "everything he [Colambre] wished to have said," but could not do so "knowing that he should say too much if he said any thing" at all. In response to Grace's performance, Colambre "leaned on the table, and fixed his eyes upon her [Grace]—years ago he had seen his cousin—last night he had thought her handsome, pleasing, graceful—but now he saw a new person, or he saw her in a new light. He marked the superior intelligence ... [and] the address, temper, and patience, with which she at last accomplished her purpose, and prevented lady Clonbrony from doing any thing preposterously absurd, or exorbitantly extravagant" (15). Colambre, in other words, begins *The Absentee* in love with Grace, but that love is deferred initially by his mother's dislike for such an arrangement and then more seriously by Lady Dashfort, who, in the midst of Colambre's survey of Ireland, informs him of the rumor that Grace is the product of an illegitimate union between an Irish Catholic woman and a stranger abroad.

Lady Dashfort's story that Grace's mother "conducted herself ill" is enough to put Grace's entire character into doubt, since it implies that she was shaped in her earliest moments by a woman unable to exercise the self-restraint necessary to be a faithful subject of marriage (88). And because Grace appears in *The Absentee* as a representative of Catholic Ireland—one who refuses to change the name "Nugent" to something less clearly Irish while in London, as Lady Clonbrony implores her to do—her possible illegitimacy is a question of Ireland's integrity as well.[18] Through the assistance of Count O'Halloran, Colambre is in the end able to legitimize Grace's birth, and in doing so, he authenticates not only her capacity for reason and self-restraint, but all of Ireland's. With this cosmopolitan marriage plot, Edgeworth makes a political argument, urging Britain's imperial leaders to adopt an enlightened approach to colonialism, one that understands national belonging to depend not on any specific faith, rite, or race, but instead upon a particular practice of the self. Edgeworth implores these leaders to understand Britain as potentially global, and had she ended her novel here, with the impending promise of Grace and Colambre's union, she would have written a fairly conventional domestic story.

Larry's Rebellion and the Utopia of the Sovereign

Until thirty years ago, Edgeworth had been read as an unambiguous apologist for British colonialism, whose fiction, in the influential verdict of Tom Dunne, centered on "reshaping ... every aspect of Irish life and society along English lines" (quoted in Gallchoir 95). The expectation of Colambre's marriage to Grace at the end of *The Absentee* was interpreted from this perspective as an "imperial union" signifying the subsumption of Irish culture by British colonial power (Corbett 886). Over the past two decades, however, critics such as Marilyn Butler and Murray Pittock have rejected such interpretations in favor of an "Irish reading" of *The Absentee* and of Edgeworth's work as a whole. While persuasive in demonstrating that *The Absentee* is by no means unequivocally imperialist, these revisionist critics have continued to miss what makes *The Absentee* a truly singular moment in the domestic novel tradition.

As Butler, Heidi Van de Veire, and Kim Walker show in their coauthored introduction to the authoritative Pickering edition of *The Absentee* (1999), critics have now convincingly established that the marriage of characters bearing the names Colambre and Grace Nugent would have been interpreted by Edgeworth's readers—at least by those with some knowledge of Ireland—as heralding not the culmination of a Protestant Ascendancy in Ireland, but, rather, the return of its elite Catholic predecessors. The Nugents, after all, were an actual well-known and once-powerful Catholic family from County Longford in the Irish Midlands, where they had owned an estate that included both a Coolamber manor and a Nugent castle until Catholic penal laws steadily deprived them of both over the course of the seventeenth and eighteenth centuries (Veire, Walker, and Butler xxvii). Once influential and now dispossessed, the Nugents symbolized the plight of Ireland's previously dominant class of Catholic landowning elites in this period, an era that saw Catholic land ownership decline from roughly 59 to 5 percent.[19] Having had connections to James II as well as Catholic armies on the Continent, the Nugents were by the time of *The Absentee* "synonymous with latter-day recusancy," and Edgeworth would have known their history well since she herself grew up in landowning circles in their same county of Longford (6n8).

Given all this, it seems clear that, with the marriage of Grace and Colambre, Edgeworth indeed intends to depict not only the reunification of a lost estate and the return of a single Irish Catholic family to power, but also the broader revival of the class this family represented. Such a reading only finds further justification in the fact that Edgeworth stages *The Absentee*'s conclusion on an estate named Clonbrony, since "Clonbroney" was the site where British forces decisively ended the 1798 Irish Rebellion, meaning that Edgeworth situates the restoration of the Nugents on land associated with control of Ireland as a whole (Veire, Walker, and Butler xxvii). Edgeworth's overarching message in *The Absentee* thus appears to be that, in the words of Pittock, "native Catholic Ireland is not just a zone of peasant subjection: it has its own ruling class, and they are dispossessed" (180). According to such an interpretation, *The Absentee* belongs alongside other national novels, such as Lady Morgan's *The Wild Irish Girl* (1806) and Walter Scott's *Waverly* (1814), insofar as it articulates a nostalgic, anticolonial sympathy for a fallen native elite.[20] While attributing this kind of sentiment to *The Absentee* works for the marriage of Colambre and Grace, it fails as an explanation for Edgeworth's novel in its entirety, since it is precisely this brand of anticolonial elitism that Edgeworth ultimately challenges in *The Absentee* by concluding the story with a newly disciplined Irish peasant who uses his modernized self to resist rather than obey colonial British authorities.

The Absentee's final narrative voice is neither Scott's nor Morgan's. It is not from the past, and it does not presume that some are chosen to rule, while others are "by nature slaves."[21] Instead, it is the innovative and forward-looking voice of the Clonbrony tenant Larry Brady, who concludes Edgeworth's novel with a letter that purports merely to inform his brother in London of the Clonbrony family's happy return, but that in fact subtly predicts their imminent destruction. Although he couches his letter in the language of feudal dependence, imploring his brother to return home to participate in the festivities and "great gladness" of tenants celebrating the fact that "the master's come home," Larry's description of one of these celebrations, a raucous bonfire that he organized, makes a series of allusions to Gaelic mythology, Christian apocalypticism, and radical republicanism that together send a very different message to his brother: return home to celebrate not Colambre and family, but God, whose impending arrival promises "fire and brimstone" for all masters, whether they English or Irish (200; Revelation 21:8). *The Absentee*, in other words, ends with a call for a left-wing holy war.

Switching from the polite third-person narration used up to this point in the story to the epistolary first-person voice of Larry, Edgeworth ends her novel by challenging both English and Irish readings of *The Absentee*. Edgeworth utters what remains present but unsaid in the novels of Austen: that the heroic largely female protagonists of domestic fiction, with their magisterial capacities for "self-command," are in need of no masters. According to Butler's biography, it was Edgeworth's father who suggested that she conclude *The Absentee* with Larry's letter, an idea that Richard presumably drew from a fictional epistolary exchange carried on by both pro- and anti-Union activists in the years preceding the 1801 Union. Written between a London-based Irish chairman named Darby

Tracy and his friends in Ireland, these letters attempt to depict the Union from the perspective of the Irish commoner, and what both sides of the argument presume is that, for such a person, politics is a matter of choosing which ruling elite will act most benevolently on his or her behalf.[22]

Edgeworth herself promotes this rigidly elitist brand of paternalism in coauthored works with her father such as *Castle Rackrent* and *Essays on Professional Education*. Writing together, Maria and Richard Edgeworth suggest that only "persons of education and leisure" are capable of leading "the progress of improvement" in England as well as in its colonies (*Essays on Professional Education* 269, 270). One can assume that Richard proposed ending *The Absentee* with a servant's letter with the idea that it would unequivocally confirm the novel's overall argument that political stability is best achieved through the cultivation of enlightened self-governing subjects. Edgeworth herself, in the final sentence of *The Absentee*'s third-person narration, reinforces this expectation in assuring her readers that the Irish people are "peculiarly subject to the influence and example of a great resident Irish proprietor" (199).

While it is easy to overlook Larry and Colambre's relationship in the midst of *The Absentee*'s romantic narrative, their bond is essential to understanding the unraveling of Edgeworth's novel. Colambre had hired Larry as his driver during his initial tour of his family's Irish estates, and from him he learned that his father's corrupt agents had displaced Larry and his family from their farm, forcing his brother Pat Brady to emigrate to London, where he labored in Mordicai's carriage workshop while Larry and his father endured an impoverished life in Ireland. Larry's degradation included excessive drinking, which, as he explains to Colambre, he "took to ... only when I had lost hope." Colambre responds by promising to "do my best to send your landlord to you soon," and instructs Larry that "in the mean time, ... keep away from the sign of the Horse-shoe—a man of your sense to drink and make an idiot and a brute of yourself!" (137). Colambre's final act before leaving his family's Irish estates for London and his first upon returning to his tenants is to hold Larry to his pledge. As Larry reports, Colambre "remembered and noticed me the minute he lit at our inn, and condescended to beckon me out of the yard to him, and axed me—'Friend Larry,' says he, 'did you keep your promise?,'" to which Larry replies, "My lord, I surely did" (201). The fulfillment of Larry's oath anticipates the marriage of Grace and Colambre, which, as Larry states in the penultimate sentence of *The Absentee*, "may be sooner than is expected" (203). If one follows the English reading of Edgeworth, then Larry's transformation into a sober, self-governing individual signifies the imminent imposition of Colambre's patriarchal colonial authority upon Grace and the Irish people she signifies. From this perspective, Larry's transformation reflects the elitist paternalism evident on all sides of the Darby Tracy letter war; he is a product ultimately of Colambre's actions rather than his own.

Such an interpretation, however, cannot explain why Larry would violate the orders of his newly appointed and symbolically named estate manager "Mr. Burke" in celebrating the return of his ruling family with an unruly bonfire that disrupts the denouement of Edgeworth's marriage plot with memories of the 1798 Rebellion. In an earlier article, "Never Getting Home" (2011), I answer the question of why the seemingly docile Larry revolts by arguing that the Freudian "logic of the uncanny" haunts Edgeworth's novel, transforming what first appear to be sources of imperial stability into dangerously foreign threats (Jackson 505). I now contend that revisionist archival scholarship by historians such as David Miller, Jim Smyth, and Ian McBride offers a more specific and persuasive explanation: that Larry's transformation into a self-governing subject need not be understood as a purely imperial phenomenon because it can be read as a reflection of the disciplinary individualism cultivated by both Catholic and Protestant rebels in the 1798 Rebellion. Larry blends Colambre's colonial paternalism with the republicanism of Irish Presbyterian and Catholic radicals, a three-way synthesis whose possibility upends not only the conventional reading that 1798 was ruined by a division between secular, Western-oriented Presbyterian rebels and their unenlightened Catholic allies, but also, and more fundamentally, the very possibility of distinguishing a supposedly secular West from all its allegedly fundamentalist others.

The real source of revolutionary hope at the end of *The Absentee* is not, as I have previously argued, the "irrational crowd," but rather the self-governing individual (526). Larry's portrait of the "men, women, and children . . . shouting and dancing like mad" around his illicit bonfire clearly invokes notorious and widely circulated images of the 1798 Rebellion as the work of a "popish multitude" animated by "savage cruelty" (Musgrave 118, 74). Yet Edgeworth depicts this crowd through the self-disciplined voice of Larry, a narrative frame that raises the possibility of interpreting in a new way both *The Absentee* and the 1798 Rebellion. Rather than being the product of involuntary collective passions, Edgeworth suggests that the infamous mobs of 1798 may instead have been the effect of conscious political choices made by individuals who were neither Western nor other, and who therefore put the entire edifice of British identity construction into question. The true terror of Edgeworth's conclusion for the managers of imperial Britain may be that the Irish had too much rather than too little reason.

For most of the twentieth century, canonical accounts of 1798 by both Irish sympathizers and skeptics represented the model of the self-disciplined individual as an essentially foreign phenomenon to "native" Catholic Ireland, a reading that reinforced the idea of this individual as an exclusively Western entity. For enthusiasts such as Thomas Pakenham, Catholic Ireland gave rise in 1798 to an "army of country people" whose disorder was synonymous with cultural alterity and resistance, whereas for historians such as R. B. McDowell, the "sectarian rioting" of the Rebellion darkly foreshadowed the troubles to come (221, 347). The two major organizations behind the 1798 Rebellion were the United Irishmen, started by Presbyterian radicals from Northern Ireland, and the Defenders, a secret Catholic society formed in the Irish Midlands. The United Irish joined forces with the Defenders in 1795, and together they planned a national revolution that was to begin with an uprising in Dublin on the night of May 23, 1798. Although government spies were able to thwart this initial action in Dublin, uprisings nevertheless occurred throughout May and June in both predominantly Catholic counties in the South as well as in largely Presbyterian ones to the North. According to the canonical twentieth-century interpretation of 1798, the initial arrest of United Irish leaders in Dublin, in the words of McDowell, "deprived the movement of its supreme command," allowing it to be overrun by what McDowell and many others have depicted as "armed crowds" of Catholic peasants, who, in the absence of their rational Western leaders, committed sectarian massacres such as the murder of hundreds of Protestant captives in the Wexford town of New Ross (347, 355).

While revisionist historians have maintained the same general outline of events in their accounts of 1798, they have dramatically altered the interpretative framework through which the Rebellion is understood. The old opposition between the modern, secular United Irish and the premodern, fundamentalist Defenders has been replaced by a more nuanced and, one might say, postsecular understanding of these groups. What new archival research shows is that neither the Ulster Presbyterians who made up the ranks of the United Irish nor the Catholics who constituted the Defenders were secular, and that both were at the same time nevertheless modern. McBride's *Scripture Politics* (1998) exemplifies this work by convincingly reinterpreting the United Irish in particular as a simultaneously republican and apocalyptic organization that drew special inspiration from the French Revolution because it viewed "the dismantling of the Roman Catholic Church in France ... as a vital step towards the destruction of the Roman Antichrist" (12). And, far from disavowing Gaelic Ireland, as historians like McDowell have argued, the United Irish took what the revisionist Luke Gibbons describes as the "apocalyptic emblem of the harp" as their group insignia, part of a broader effort, in the words of Pittock, to "hybridize" their Presbyterian-inflected republicanism with Irish Gaelic culture (236; 108).

As a landless worker from the predominantly Catholic region of the Irish Midlands, Larry would have been identified by Edgeworth's readers as more of a Defender than a United Irishman, and it is thus of great significance to interpreting *The Absentee*'s conclusion that the once-dominant image of the Defenders as a premodern peasant organization has been dismissed, and, in its place, the group is now understood as a product of Ireland's mid- to late eighteenth-century transformation into an increasingly commercial, literate, and populated country. As one of the historians responsible for this shift, Jim Smyth, writes, "It is no longer in doubt ... [that] the Defenders originated in an area of intense commercialization, north County Armagh," part of Ulster's "Linen triangle," a region characterized by "proto-industrialization," "population density," and religious conflict (7–8). The Defenders' membership, in the words of Smyth, reflected "the social diversity of a commercializing society" and included "canal workers, publicans, schoolmasters, blacksmiths, and pedlars as well as small tenant farmers and agricultural laborers" (9).

Against this backdrop, it is time to take more seriously the Defenders' own representations of themselves as members of a disciplined organization committed to the republican principle of individual self-governance. In a membership oath included in the appendix to Richard Musgrave's *Memoirs of Different Rebellions in Ireland* (1802)—a fiercely Protestant but extremely influential account of 1798—the Defenders introduce themselves as a community of individuals who, of their "own free will," agree to live "under subjection ... in all things lawful, and not otherwise" (220). The oath elaborates that "all persons entering must be under all rules and regulations" and then enumerates a list that includes, "There is no person to come to the monthly meeting drunk; or if they do, to pay six-pence, and to be excluded for three months" (221). Other rules ask members to submit any acts of resistance to the authority of a central committee, refrain from violence toward one another, and keep the identity of the group a secret. To become a Defender, in other words, one had to pledge one's self capable of practicing the same enlightened art of self-governance cultivated by domestic novels.

The presence of republican rhetoric within Defender literature suggests that Larry's renunciation of whisky prior to Colambre's return should not be read as the result of colonial Anglo power alone. In an ironic reversal entirely characteristic of *The Absentee*, what at first glance seems to symbolize the stabilization of the British colonial project in fact indicates the very opposite. Although Larry's sobriety might strike many readers as an unambiguous sign of colonial subjection, his letter forcefully articulates the counter-possibility that his newly honed skill at self-regulation marks his conversion into a Defender committed to the political-theological struggle to begin God's new republican millennium in Ireland. From this perspective, Edgeworth's decision to stage *The Absentee*'s conclusion in Clonbrony has the effect of adding a broader political significance not to the Nugent family's return, but to their tenants' impending rebellion against them.

Edgeworth establishes Larry as a figure for 1798 by having him describe his bonfire with the same cryptic blend of Christian apocalypticism, Gaelic mythology, and revolutionary class politics that revisionist historians have located at the center of both United Irish and Defender thought.

> He (that is, old Nick and St Dennis) would have been burnt that night—I *mane*, in *effigy*, through the town of Clonbrony, but that the new man, Mr. Burke, came down that day too soon to stop it, and said, "it was not becoming to trample on the fallen," or something that way, that put an end to it; and though it was a great disappointment to many, and to me in particular, I could not but like the jantleman the better for it any how.... Well, when I was disappointed of the *effigy*, I comforted myself by making a bonfire of old Nick's big rick of duty turf, which, by great luck, was out in the road.... And such another blaze! I wished you'd seed it—and all the men, women, and children, in the town and country, far and near, gathered round it shouting and dancing like mad!—and it was light as day quite across the bog....
> And I heard after, they seen it from all parts of the three counties, and

they thought it was St John's Eve in a mistake—or couldn't make out what it was; but all took it in good part, for a good sign, and were in great joy. (200)

Larry's claim to "like the jantleman [Burke] better" for an order that he violates resembles the playful duplicity in Defender assertions of loyalty to the British, such as the pledge contained within their membership oath that "we are bound to his majesty King George III, and his successors to the crown, *so for this present year 1789,* we promise faithfully the same obedience, and *also while we live the subject to the same government.*"[23] Like the Defenders, Larry undermines his light-hearted assertions of allegiance with allusions to a coming revolution.

When Colambre learns earlier in the novel that his family's corrupt agents are two brothers named "Old Nick" and "St. Dennis," it appears that Edgeworth is engaging in a bit of Francophobic humor by suggesting that Old Nick, a pseudonym for Satan, is next of kin to the first bishop and patron saint of France, St. Dennis. The point behind this joke is that the post-Union rulers of Ireland are akin to the French ancien régime, and that they therefore must reform or risk incurring the same fate as their French counterparts. However, the significance of these names, like so many names in *The Absentee,* changes by the end of the novel. "Old Nick" and "St. Dennis" resurface in Larry's letter not as a moderate plea for reform couched in the language of Francophobia, but rather as markers of the at once apocalyptic and Jacobin nature of Larry's rebellion as well as the broader legacy of 1798 that it represents.

By having Larry metaphorically burn a character named for a central figure in France's ancien régime, St. Dennis, Edgeworth clearly intends to raise the specter of Jacobin executions, which were widely depicted in the 1790s Anglophone press and would have been fresh in the mind of her early nineteenth-century readers. With "Old Nick," on the other hand, Edgeworth endows the Jacobin terror invoked by "St. Dennis" with broader theological significance, suggesting that Larry's enemies are Satanic and his struggle against them holy. Edgeworth elaborates on the scriptural underpinning of Larry's action by noting that people "from all parts of the three counties" mistook Larry's fire for "St John's Eve" (200). Unlike most Saints' Days, the Feast Day of St. John commemorates a birth rather than a death, and the especially generative birth of John in particular, which is said to anticipate the arrival of God himself in Christ. Also known as Midsummer's Eve, the night before St. John's is still celebrated in rural Ireland with bonfires, a practice cited by the eighteenth- and early nineteenth-century antiquarian scholar Francis Plowden as evidence that the Irish are derived from the ancient Phoenicians, whose legacy persists, according to Plowden, as the "original national character" and "innate genius" of the Irish people (2).[24] Given the well-known Christian and Gaelic significance of "St. John's Eve," as well as the Jacobin undertones of executing French bishops, it seems safe to assume that Edgeworth knowingly couches Larry's fire in the synthetic vocabulary that characterized the rhetoric of 1798 rebels, whose political catechisms, in the words of Smyth, "packed an explosive blend of biblical, Jacobite, Jacobin, and masonic symbolism" (9).

Edgeworth completes the association of Larry's bonfire with the 1798 Rebellion by having him substitute "a big rick of duty turf" for the traditional figurative form of an effigy, a decision that underlines the centrality of both novelty and economics within Larry's revolt. After Burke explicitly forbids burning effigies, Larry uses his newly sober mind to innovate, replacing the figurative images that would have been the norm for such celebrations with an effigy of far greater political significance (200). "Duty turf" was a feudal practice of forcing tenants to sow grass as a means of paying their rent, which continued well into the eighteenth century, and, by burning it in place of figurative effigies, Larry signals that the target of his at once political and theological rebellion is not simply the personal corruption of two particular agents; it is the broader phenomenon of inequality itself.[25] With his synthetic bonfire, Larry enacts the natality embodied by the simultaneously pagan and Christian event of Midsummer/St. John's Eve, but in doing so he takes this annual reiteration of Scripture's promise a step further. Larry does not simply announce that God will return; instead, he hearkens the arrival with a ritual identifying post-Union Ireland as the beginning of a new age, the start of humanity's at once Christic and socialist redemption. Like the Defenders and United Irish before him, Larry blends Christian, Gaelic, and republican rhetoric in order to create a protosocialist vision of something new.

As a symbolic eradication of corruption that is mistaken for St. John's Eve, Larry's blaze invokes the divine fire prophesized by John the Apostle in the book of Revelation. John predicts that the fulfillment of God's covenant and his return to "his people" will entail a "day of judgment" in which believers will be freed from death, pain, and alienation, while the "fearful, and unbelieving, and the abominable, and murderers, and whoremongers, and sorcerers, and idolaters, and all liars shall have their part in the lake which burneth with fire and brimstone" (21:3, 8). When the "holy city, new Jerusalem" descends "from God out of heaven," that portion of humanity written into the "book of life" will come to live with the sovereignty of their creator (21:2, 20:12). For the chosen, "there shall be no more death, neither sorrow, nor crying, neither shall there be any more pain" (20:12, 21:4). The redeemed will live beyond alienation, and Larry's great innovation is to make the elimination of the feudal practice of "duty work," or paying one's rent through labor, a sign not simply of feudalism's end, but of humanity's ascent to this hallowed position.

Although Edgeworth at different points in her career restricts the meaning of "duty work" to a particular historical moment and mode of power, describing it as a "feudal custom" in *Castle Rackrent*, the truth is that Edgeworth's celebration of feudalism's end in the guise of Larry's fire asserts a republican politics of self-governance that supersedes feudalist, capitalist, and patriarchal economies alike (59). Larry's ritual is a scripturally sanctioned punishment of the idolatry behind systems of exploitation—that is, systems in which sovereignty is hoarded rather than shared. *The Absentee*'s final fire is a critique, then, not only of British colonial power in Ireland but also of the 1798 Rebellion itself, insofar as it excluded women from their place at the table of the human. The struggle of the United Irish to create a "free republic on the broad basis of liberty and equality," in the words of its leader Wolfe Tone, was predicated on the exclusion of women from what would become an exclusively male public sphere (66). From the perspective of *The Absentee*'s unruly conclusion, the United Irish worked to replace one form of idolatry with another, substituting a vision of men as the arbiters of God's new Israel for the earlier assertion of Britain as God's chosen vehicle for salvation.

While Clíona Ó Gallchoir's *Edgeworth: Women, Ireland, and Nation* (2005) importantly demonstrates Edgeworth's politics to be something other than the patriarchal republicanism of both the United Irish and the later Irish nationalist movement, it fails to state clearly what Edgeworth's alternative politics are (7). Edgeworth's fiction is not simply a statement on the unsettled nature of human identity, as Gallchoir suggests; it is more specifically an argument for what I would call a domestic republicanism, and, in *The Absentee*, this domestic republicanism assumes an apocalyptic and socialist dimension. In *The Absentee*, Edgeworth turns the domestic art of self-governance into a viable revolutionary philosophy, one that invokes the law of God to sever the subject of the marriage plot from the imperial order it was meant to buttress. Though Edgeworth is by no means consistent in advocating such politics elsewhere in her work, in *The Absentee*, at least, she endorses a particular kind of demystification that rejects anti-Semitic and sexist tropes in favor of identifying the rich as humanity's simultaneously political and theological enemy. The final figure of evil in *The Absentee* is neither the demonic Jewish merchant nor the duplicitous coquette—it is the elite, those who exploit and hoard, whatever race, gender, religion, or nationality they may be. *The Absentee*'s ultimate enemy is anyone who separates humanity from its sovereign right to ascend, to live as it were in "the holy city, new Jerusalem, coming down from God out of heaven, prepared as a bride adorned for her husband" (Rev. 21:2).

Larry stands in the final pages of *The Absentee* as a dual subject, the product of both an imperial British marriage plot and a "Negroid" Irish republican movement. Larry can occupy this seemingly impossible position because he is in the final instance a subject of neither England nor Ireland, but of that utopian state of sovereign fulfillment that is scriptural Jerusalem. Larry's newfound capacity for self-governance, his power "[to] no longer make a brute of himself," belongs to a historical process of political theology whose point of completion is synonymous with human equality and God's return (137). The incarnation of a transcendent God in Christ is the beginning of sovereignty's modern form, its political profanation, and, in *The Absentee*'s unruly conclusion, Larry dramatizes what the fulfillment of this process entails. A socialist Jerusalem is sovereignty perfected, and Edgeworth's suggestion is that imperial Britain unknowingly hearkens its arrival.

The real dénouement of *The Absentee* is Larry's bonfire rather than the marriage of Grace and Colambre, because it is only there that Edgeworth articulates the means through which one can resolve the animating conflicts of her novel and, more expansively, of British modernity itself. In Larry's ritual, Edgeworth spells out how to harmonize what the conjugal dénouement of Grace and Colambre merely represses. Couched in allusions to the "fire and brimstone" of the book of Revelation and with a burning symbol of human inequality at its center, Larry's rebellion is an argument that narrative resolution will be found only through the eradication of exploitation in all its forms. Larry's action articulates a universalism that overwhelms every particularism, whether it is the English, the Irish, or even the scriptural notion of the chosen.

Although he invokes scriptural images of God's angry "day of judgement," Larry's event calls for a moment of reckoning that is predicated upon the universalization of the subject doing the punishing (Rev. 21:3). In Edgeworth's revised Christian vision, divine justice entails not the punishment of all those sinners identified in the book of Revelation— "the fearful, and unbelieving, and the abominable, and murderers, and whoremongers, and sorcerers, and idolaters, and all liars"—but more precisely the annihilation of exploitation itself (21:8). While such annihilation undoubtedly implies violence toward those who would insist upon the idolatry of exploitation, Edgeworth's revisions to Scripture are important because they leave us with a new image of the apocalypse as in essence a universal elevation of humanity rather than a bloody parceling out of the chosen from the damned.

The Sovereign End of the Modern British Subject

Edgeworth's message by the end of *The Absentee* is that Larry and all the other enlightened self-governing subjects of her story carry a subjectivity that demands social transformation. Despite her many attempts to deny it, Edgeworth's commitment to domestic self-governance, like Austen's, ultimately entails a radical abolitionism whose consequences extend well beyond either the home, the plantation, or the self. Edgeworth, in a sense, moves in the final pages of *The Absentee* from the Kantian ethics that govern much of her work to a Hegel-like insistence that something more is at stake, that the question is not whether an action can be made universal, but, rather, whether it leads to freedom, to that state described by Hegel as "the unity of different independent self-consciousnesses which, in their opposition, enjoy perfect freedom and independence: 'I' that is 'We' and 'We' that is 'I'" (110).²⁶ Shifting from the universality of the categorical imperative to the universality of freedom, *The Absentee's* conclusion dramatizes the consequences of fashioning a national self in opposition to slavery and other forms of capitalist dispossession.

The Absentee's narrative is driven by the expectation that its denouement will mark the redemption of the British imperial project as a whole, and, in a way, Edgeworth's story delivers, since it indeed ends by depicting the imminent perfection of Britain, only it is a perfection that promises to undo the nation. With *The Absentee's* conclusion, Edgeworth exposes a crucial contradiction within Britain and Anglo-American modernity more broadly—namely, that the sovereignty they claim can find its point of worldly resolution only once made universal. From the day it began to drape itself in the borrowed majesty of God, the modern Anglo-American State sealed its fate: a socialist society of the equally sovereign is its highest possibility that it can deny but never escape. This is the modernity that we have yet to make.

EPILOGUE
An Immanent Language of Change

The task of literary criticism is not simply to understand how works reflect and shape their own times, but also how they might affect our own. Scholars sell art and literature short if they do anything less: art and literature are some of the most enduring and powerful objects of a human world, which is to say that they are objects of politics both past and present, and understanding them means answering the essential questions of how they lived before and how we ought to make them live again now. Art and literature are alive, and it is high time for scholars to stop treating them as if they were dead. In this spirit, *We Are Kings* turns to the literature of early imperial Britain in order to better understand both what it has accomplished and what it can become.

The expanding print culture of eighteenth-century Britain is a moment of cultural ascendancy for literature, and what literary authors accomplish in this period is nothing less than the perfecting of a longstanding political faith, one that would inform the self-presentation of British and American empires for centuries to come. Even today, when British and American leaders talk of the nation, they do so in terms that eighteenth-century British literature helped establish. The city on a hill and the sovereign individual remain at the center of modern Anglo-American political thought, and the literature that accompanied Britain's rise to imperial prominence played a key role in putting them there. *We Are Kings* returns to the imaginative universe of these works in order to ask from within them, "What next?" From Dryden's panegyrics to Charles II to Edgeworth's prose celebrations of disciplined Akan slaves and Irish peasants, this book traces the democratization of sovereignty in literature, and what it ultimately shows is that this democratization provides a basis for a distinct Anglo-American brand of socialism, one grounded in liberation theology and predicated upon rather than opposed to the figure of the modern individual.

The contemporary African American reverend and noted civil rights activist William Barber is someone who exemplifies the possibility of such politics today. When Barber speaks of his moral movement for equality in America, he articulates the same political vision expressed by Larry Brady's apocalyptic bonfire: it is a collectivism grounded in the right of individuals and an equality demanded by God. As Barber states,

> We gather here declaring it's time for a moral uprising all across America. We are in the same moral tradition of the prophets of Israel, who challenged kings and rulers to stop legislating evil. We are in the same moral tradition of Jesus, whose evangelical work was not being against gay people, but being against poverty. We are in the same moral tradition of the Apache and other indigenous spiritual people, who taught us to care and not destroy and poison the air, water and the land. We are in the same moral tradition of the abolitionists, who knew, if slavery was legal, it was still immoral, and it had to be challenged. ("50 Years")

From his "Moral Monday" marches on the North Carolina statehouse in 2013 to his ongoing national revival of Martin Luther King's "Poor People's Campaign," Barber everywhere emphasizes that he stands as one of "God's messengers" tasked by Jeremiah 22 with an obligation to challenge any power that is hoarded rather than shared—that is, power that is bolstered by racist redistricting laws, cuts to social welfare programs, and handouts to those who already have too much. Like Lady Huntingdon, who explains to her skeptical interlocutor that the *"true Church . . .* belongs not to this world," Dr. Barber reminds those in positions of authority that "they do not have the power to override God," and that "they do not [therefore] have the power to override our moral dissent" ("Now Is the Time"). This is the battle cry under which Barber and his companions have engaged in acts of civil disobedience around the country, occupying statehouses and the halls of Congress and being arrested sometimes in the hundreds as a result, knowing, however, that they answer to a law greater than that which they oppose.

America is the wealthiest country in human history, and yet 140 million of its citizens live in poverty and 250,000 people die every year of that condition, and the situation is only getting worse.[1] In the face of this crisis, Barber invokes, like Larry before him, visions of a reckoning to come:

> Oh Lord, I'm ready to have a bible conversation, because Jesus said, "The spirit of the Lord is upon me, for he has anointed me to preach good news to the poor." In Greek, that's *ptōchos*, it means those who've been made poor by the economic unjust systems in this world. That's what he said at the beginning of his life, and at the end of his life he said, "I'm going to judge every nation, America, Afghanistan, Egypt, South America. I'm going to judge every nation." ("Forward Together")

Barber is out for justice, and his movement has the capacity to unite the vast majority of Americans around the conviction that we are not free until we are equal. Barber's movement represents a profound threat to the American status quo because it challenges modern America on its own terms, at its foundation, at that point where it brushes up against its imperial predecessor in claiming to wield a power whose very transcendence guarantees that it cannot ever be entirely owned. Paradoxical as it may seem, Barber is building a movement for racial, economic, and social equality in the name of sovereignty.

Given that scholars of the humanities are in the business of rhetoric, it is unfortunate that we have become so reticent in formulating the moral, legal, and/or historical justifications for emancipatory change. Too much of the academy has taken to either ignoring politics altogether or imagining that political solutions can lie only in purified spaces beyond the messiness of the present and the history that made it. Though hardly a model for uniting scholarship with politics, Quentin Skinner's observation on this point is apt: "What is possible to do in politics is generally limited by what it is possible to legitimize" (105). It is not enough to simply say that change will happen or assume that it should, and this is part of what makes Barber's movement so powerful: it is rooted in the ideology of empire and yet argues for something entirely different. Barber preaches an immanent language of change, and, in this book, I have sought to follow his example.

We Are Kings turns to eighteenth-century British literature for insight, and what it finds is that at the origins of Anglo-American modernity stands a body politic subsumed by the ennobling authority of God, and, furthermore, that upon this foundation subjects can speak in the sacred language of a sovereignty that demands to be shared. To be enfranchised within Anglo-American modernity is to have a responsibility, a task to face, and that is finding in the bloody history of a Godly racist nationalist tradition some basis for hope. The democratization of sovereignty is one such site because it gives us the right to declare, from the interiority of the Anglo-American nation, from the very heart of its nationalism, that we have a right to a society of the equally sovereign, a society in which every person is king.

NOTES

Introduction

1. See Hunter's *Before Novels* (1990), Armstrong's *Desire and Domestic Fiction* (1987), and McKeon's *The Origins of the English Novel* (1987).
2. See Hunter's *The Reluctant Pilgrim* (1966), Starr's *Defoe and Casuistry* (1971), Damrosch's *God's Plot and Man's Stories* (1985), and During's "The Novel's Mysticism" (2011).
3. See also Damrosch 3, 17.
4. On the connection between early fiction and wonder, see Kareem's *The Invention of Wonder* (2014).
5. For an example of recent revisionist scholarship on Marx, see Roberts's *Marx's Inferno* (2015), a book that convincingly demonstrates the presence of a republican political argument in Marx's great and seemingly most economist of works, *Capital: Volume I* (1867).
6. On Marx's messianism, see Agamben's *The Time That Remains*, 29–33.
7. As an introduction to the idea of cultural capital, see Bourdieu's "The Forms of Capital" (1986).
8. Before Felski, it was Edward Said, who, in *The World, the Text, and the Critic* (1983), excoriated American literary critics for retreating into "another world altogether" from the one inhabited by "the reader of a daily newspaper" (25). Said elaborates that in the American academy of his time 'Marxism' has become "principally an academic, not a political, commitment" (29).
9. For an anticipation of this argument, see Gallagher's "Embracing the Absolute" (1998), in which Gallagher shows how seventeenth-century female authors, such as Mary Cavendish, fashion a new individual after the example of the king.
10. The same could be said of many antisecular interpretations of the early novel, such as Hunter's *The Reluctant Pilgrim* and Damrosch's *God's Plot and Man's Stories*.
11. See Taylor's *A Secular Age* (2007), and Pfau's *Minding the Modern* (2013).
12. Such politicization has its historical precursors, of course. For a discussion of the anti-imperialist, protosocialist theology of early Christians, see Stolze's *Becoming Marxist* (2019) 36–74, and Hardt and Negri's *Empire* (2000) 21, 205–18.

13. My use of the word "capitalism" here, rather than "mercantilism" or "commercialism," is deliberate and draws on Hopkins and Cain's observation "that modern British history is bound up with the evolution of several separate but interacting forms of capitalist enterprise—agricultural, commercial, and financial, as well as industrial" (42). As Hopkins and Cain contend, critics who argue that the eighteenth century pre-dates capitalism because it pre-dates industrialism overlook the complexity of British capitalism itself and, in particular, those financial and commercial services that have been integral to it ever since the 1688 Revolution. In other words, the United Kingdom's postindustrial service economy has been present in many respects since capitalism's preindustrial origins.
14. See Hilton's *A Mad, Bad, and Dangerous People?* (2006), 353–55.
15. For a historical account of these points of continuity between the British and American Empires, see Go, *Patterns of Empire* (2011). As Go notes, "the discourse of British exceptionalism reveals that the Americans did not so much invent a novel conception of expansion and empire as they did appropriate and rearticulate the idioms and ideology of their former imperial master" (52).
16. Wedding parties have been a frequent target of US drone strikes. On July 6, 2008, to cite one example from the Bush administration, forty-seven civilians, including thirty-nine women and children, were killed in eastern Afghanistan. See BBC, July 11, 2008, http://news.bbc.co.uk/2/hi/south_asia/7501538.stm. For more on drones, and particularly how they lend themselves to the Manichaeism evident in Obama's speech, see Chamayou's *Drone Theory* (2013).
17. Clinton, "Remarks" (2003).
18. Blair, "Speech to the US Congress" (2003).
19. On the idea of political theology in left-wing post–Vatican II thought, see Metz's "Religion and Society in the Light of a Political Theology" (1968).
20. See Kahn's *The Future of Illusion* (2014); Hammill's *The Mosaic Constitution* (2012); and Lupton's *Citizen-Saints* (2005), which is, I should note, an exception to this tendency.
21. Agamben does recognize a shift beginning in the Middle Ages in which the *oikonomia* of biopolitical governance steadily subsumes the glory of monarchical sovereignty. As he explains, "To have completely integrated Glory with *oikonomia* in the acclamative form of consensus . . . is the specific task carried out by contemporary democracies and their *government by consent*." See *The Kingdom and the Glory* (2011), xii.
22. In *Homo Sacer* and then more extensively in *The Use of Bodies*, Agamben calls for, as he states in the latter, "a politics beyond every figure of the relation" (272).

23. See *Technologies of the Self* (1988), *The Use of Pleasure: Volume 2 of The History of Sexuality* (1985), and *The Care of the Self: Volume 3 of The History of Sexuality* (1986).
24. For similar pleas, see the work of the political philosopher Peter Hallward, particularly his *Absolutely Postcolonial* (2001).
25. The gap has been on the rise since the early 2000s. On this, see www.pewsocialtrends.org/2016/06/27/1-demographic-trends-and-economic-well-being, and Oliver and Shapiro, *Black Wealth/White Wealth* (2006).

1. Dryden's Political Theology and the Making of a Modern Subject

1. See Dowling's *The Epistolary Moment* (1991) for an example of the former and Zwicker's *Dryden's Political Poetry* (1972) for the latter.
2. For a summary of the changes in the 1690s, see Hoppit's *Land of Liberty?* (2000), 329, 333, 127.
3. For a recent illuminating account of the politics driving Dryden's theatrical work, see Chua's *Ravishment of Reason* (2017).
4. For more on this, see William's *Milton's Leveller God* (2017).
5. For a summary of the vogue for political arithmetic in the 1690s, see Hoppit, *Land of Liberty?* (2000) 190–91.
6. Derrida's critique of the epistemological "construction of Foucault's project" in *Madness and Civilization* (1961) as potentially "totalitarian" is relevant to this discussion. See Derrida's *Writing and Difference* (1967), 57.
7. For an example of this, see Coppe's pamphlet "A Fiery Flying Roll" (1649), in which he declares, "That excellent Majesty, which dwels in the Writer of this Roule, hath reconciled ALL THINGS to himselfe" (86). For Ranters such as Coppe, God was present in everything from authors to candlesticks.
8. Dryden's eroticized retelling of the star of Bethlehem narrative expresses the corporeal power of the king to inspire obedience in his subjects, an uncanny ability that contemporary authors such as Aphra Behn and Thomas Hobbes also ascribed to the monarch. See Thompson's "Hobbesian Obligation and the Durability of Romance in Aphra Behn's *Love-Letters*" for an astute analysis of this phenomenon.
9. For examples, see Matthew 2:2, 8, 11.
10. In Winn's biography of Dryden, he notes that Dryden and Davenant shared "a vision of the poet as the herald of fame, . . . as the laureate of heaven, whose 'Art toward God' would place him in the line of sacred poets descended from King David" (76).
11. For Visconsi, Dryden uses the "messiness of representation" to demonstrate the "ethical ambiguities" that accompany any act of judgment, which

Visconsi defines, following Kant, as the attempt to apply universal ideas to particular instances (34).
12. See Hill's *The World Turned Upside Down* (1972), 279–80.
13. The first quote is from the autobiography of the Presbyterian preacher Henry Newcome, and the second is from the anonymously published pamphlet *The Armies Vindication of This Last Change* (1659).
14. Late medievalists used the pagan and Christian myth of the self-begotten and triumphantly individualistic phoenix that would burn itself and its nest in order to produce an offspring as a symbol for the paradoxical nature of the dynastic king. After the execution of Charles in 1649, royalists minted a medallion that displayed a phoenix rising from its burning nest (Kantorowicz 413).
15. See the OED entry for "goodness" and in particular the example listed under the second definition from the *Book of Common Prayer:* "Pr. for all Conditions of Men, We commend to thy fatherly goodness all those who are any ways afflicted."
16. From Pierre Charron, *Of Wisdom* (1601), and quoted by Hooker and Swedenburg in *The Works of John Dryden, Volume I* (1956), 239.
17. For further discussion of the popular myth in the seventeenth century that England descended from Troy, see Visconsi's *Lines of Equity* (2008), 62.
18. See Derrida, "La différance" (1968). In the political language of his day, Derrida explains that "iit is the dominance of being that différance comes to solicit" (60). Derrida elaborates that the forces of différance "foment the subversion of every kingdom," which make them "obviously menacing and infallibly dreaded by everything in us that desires a kingdom [royaume]" (60).
19. The neologism *différance* derives from *différer*, a verb that signifies both an economic sense of deferral and an antieconomic sense of alterity. Derrida posits *différance* at the origin in order to both disrupt the possibility of an origin and hold open the possibility of its fulfillment in a time to come (41–44).
20. Dryden's association of rebels with the turbulent sea also alludes to Virgil's analogy of the raging sea with the "rabble" in book 1 of the *Aeneid*, a scene that Dryden later translated for his 1697 collection *The Works of Virgil*.
21. For a description of the 1675–76 Native-American revolt, see Pestana's *Protestant Empire* (2009), 132.
22. For more on this point, see Makdisi's *Making England Western* (2014).
23. To name one major example of such criticism, Dipesh Chakrabarty draws attention to the experience of twentieth-century India where "peasants" rather than proletarians called on "the agency of gods, spirits, and other supernatural beings" to help them institute what was a nevertheless modern political sphere. See *Provincializing Europe* (2000), 12–13.

24. A related but equally incomplete interpretation is Zwicker's argument that the decline of Dryden's commitment to sacred history is a reflection of the new arbitrary status of language in the late seventeenth century. See *Politics and Language in Dryden's Poetry* (1984), 33.
25. It was rumored but never confirmed that Lord Rochester orchestrated this attack.
26. Johnson defines "rout" as a "a clamorous multitude; a rabble; a tumultuous crowd." See his *Dictionary, Vol. II* (1756), 15. Though he refused the title of king, Cromwell made the position of Lord Protector hereditary, and, in Dryden's vision, the nondynastic nature of Cromwell's rule only renders the sovereignty he physically manifests, in his "mien" and "count'nance," all the more miraculous; it must descend from "Heav'n alone" (71, 73, 21).
27. Dryden's 1685 translation of Horace's second epode opens: "How happy in his low degree/ How rich in humble poverty, is he / Who leads a quiet country life; / Discharg'd of business, void of strife, / And from the griping scrivener free!" (135). With the verb "bless'd," Dryden alludes to Psalm 1: "Blessed is he who does not walk in the counsel of the wicked or stand in the way of sinners or sit in the seat of mockers."
28. Winn suggests that Dryden's celebration of the second son of his uncle is also in part an expression of his hostility to his firstborn, Sir Robert Driden (504).
29. Winn notes on a more practical level that Dryden had received "a turkey hen with Eggs, and a good young Goose, besides a very kind letter" from his cousin in the spring of 1699, the period in which he started writing this epistle (503).
30. This is particularly striking given that, as Hoppit explains, "the hard work of country government had for some decades increasingly been borne by Justices of the Peace, who also provided a vital link between the county on one side and the parish and the borough on the other" (466).
31. Hoppit notes "the increasing significance of the professions in towns—especially doctors and lawyers, but also of bankers, surveyors, clerics, and military men" (423).
32. Christopher Hill summarizes this view in *Century of Revolution* in the following terms: "Dryden and Waller perfected the rhymed couplet, whose studied antitheses and balanced rhetoric reflected the greater stability towards which society was moving.... Their flowing numbers contrast markedly, both in form and content, with the earlier 'metaphysical' lyric of internal conflict" (252).
33. The new mode of security seems to appear earlier in England than in France, which is perhaps in part due to the 1688 revolutionaries' rejection, in the words of Pincus, of the "modern, bureaucratic absolutist state model developed by Louis XIV" (8). The modern state that these revolutionaries

helped create tended to focus on managing the flows of commerce and life rather than attempting to more directly govern them through a centralized, bureaucratic power.
34. Hoppit explains that the "dramatic urbanization of English society in the seventeenth century rested fairly and squarely on the explosive growth of London," which went from a population of about 200,000 to around 490,000 over the course of the century (420).
35. See Numbers 25:1–13 (King James Version).
36. Dryden does something similar in another late work, "Eleonora" (1692), which concludes its remembrance of the Countess of Abingdon with, "Thy Reliques (such thy Works of Mercy are) / Have, in this Poem, been my Holy care. / As Earth thy Body keep, thy Soul the sky, / So shall this Verse preserve thy Memory; / For thou shalt make it live, because it sings of thee" (373–76).

2. The Domestic Novel's First Heroine

1. I am continuing to use the King James Bible, but will make passing references to the Catholic Douay-Rheims Bible, since Pope would have likely known both. The Douay-Rheims circulated in England in the late sixteenth and early seventeenth centuries both illegally as well as in Protestant publications, which reprinted it in an effort to demonstrate its shortcomings. On the little we know of the Catholic religious instruction that Pope received in school, see Mack's *Alexander Pope*, 50. For an account of the Catholic Bible in English, see Walsham's "Unclasping the Book?" (2003).
2. The 1635 Douay-Rheims reads "Arise, be illuminated Jerusalem: because thy light is risen and the glory of our Lord is risen upon thee" (521).
3. The Douay-Rheims offers the more poetic "In that day the bud of the Lord shal be in magnificence, and glorie, and the fruit of the earth high, and exultation to them, that shal befaued of Israel," for "thy people . . . for ever shal inherite the land" (450, 522).
4. For more on this conflict, see Kramnick's *Bolingbroke and His Circle* (1968).
5. Hoppit notes that government spending in the decade before 1688 "was usually about £ 1.7m a year" and then rose to £ 4.9m annually during the Nine Years War and then to £ 7.8m with the War of Spanish Succession (124). The debt that made such spending possible was attained through "heightened parliamentary taxation" in the form of higher duties on consumer goods and, even more important, increases in land and assessed taxes (4). For more on the national debt, see Kramnick's *Bolingbroke and His Circle*, 43.
6. For an example, see Hoppit, 225, 208. To his credit, Hoppit questions the idea that such statistics mark the rise of secularism, asserting that "it was

not so much that God, Christ, or the Church were less significant by 1727, rather that there was more uncertainty as to just what their significance was" (241).
7. For Kant's discussion of cosmopolitanism, see "Idea for a Universal History with a Cosmopolitan Purpose" and "Perpetual Peace" (1795).
8. In the third volume of this series, *The Kingdom and the Glory* (*Homo Sacer II 2*), Agamben notes that for Foucault "racism becomes the apparatus through which sovereign power is reinserted into biopower" (76). The rest of his work, while dealing with precisely this conjunction, nevertheless fails to address the specific problem of race.
9. The latter function became particularly important as the Royal Navy expanded to meet Britain's growing imperial needs over the course of the seventeenth and eighteenth century. The years following 1688 were a period of particularly rapid growth. As Hill notes, by 1713 the "number of ships had risen by over forty per cent since 1688; tonnage by over sixty per cent" (*Century of Revolution* 276).
10. Windsor Castle was England's "most expensive secular building project in the entire Middle Ages" (39). See Brindle and Kerr, *Windsor Revealed* (1997).
11. For more on the ironic heroism favored by Pope and his Tory Augustan peers, see Noggle's *The Skeptical Sublime* (2001).
12. This insight is indebted to Deutsch's interpretation of Pope's "fitful" exemplarity in this epistle. See "Bolingbroke's Laugh" (1995).
13. Dryden's publication of *The Works of Virgil*, done in collaboration with the publisher Jacob Tonson, was a major moment in British book history since it was the first time a work printed by subscription—that is, with the support of subscribers—achieved financial success. As Dryden's editors William Frost and Vinton Dearing note, the success of a publishing method based on the support of readers was a "watershed in the economic liberation of authorship from the exclusive reliance on the stage, on patronage, or on politics" (848).

3. "Beyond What the Crown Itself Can Confer"

1. Like the many critics who have followed him, Richardson assumes that the true value of his heroine's religious practice lies in the hereafter and thus misses the "reward" that she achieves in the here and now (1498). See the novel's postscript, 1495–99.
2. See Damrosch's *God's Plot and Man's Stories* (1985), 213–62, and, for another example, Hill's "Clarissa Harlowe and Her Times" (1955).
3. On the previously overlooked regularity of marriage in the eighteenth century, see Cressy, *Birth, Marriage, and Death* (1997) 317, and Probert,

Marriage, Law, and Practice in the Long Eighteenth Century (2009) 1–2, 53–54. For a study of marriage's function in eighteenth-century literature that insightfully builds on this recent historical work, see O'Connell's *The Origins of the English Marriage Plot* (2019).

4. For an article that anticipates this interpretation, see Henseley's "Thomas Edwards and the Dialectics of Clarissa's Death Scene" (1992). Though he does not frame the novel in terms of nationalism or political theology, Hensley insightfully argues that both spiritual and secular readings of *Clarissa* "are built into its structure," forming a kind of irresolvable dialectic (142).
5. With its emphasis on language, Clarissa's monasticism prefigures the late Heidegger as well. In the *Letter on Humanism* (1949), Heidegger represents language rather than death as the central means through which humanity fulfills its role as the "shepherd [*Hirt*] of Being" (221). In thought, a person allows his or herself to be "claimed by Being" in order to "say the truth of Being," thus fulfilling humanity's highest task, which is not to think, but more precisely to bring "the unspoken word of Being to language" (194, 239).
6. In the late seventeenth and eighteenth centuries, there was, as Ruth Perry contends, "a change in the definition of what constituted the primary kin group ... [that] involved a movement from an axis of kinship based on consanguinal ties or blood lineage to an axis based on conjugal and affinal ties of the married couple." See *Novel Relations*, 2. Revisionist historians such as Joanne Bailey and David Turner have challenged the idea that such a transition took place, and while their critiques are convincing on the level of sociology, they fail to account for the very real shift that occurs in literature of this period, where the nuclear family unit undeniably receives increasing attention.
7. Pamela's first letter to her parents opens with "I Have great Trouble, and some Comfort, to acquaint you with" (11).
8. See Rahmani's *Blank Subjects* (2014) for an exploration of how the novelistic subject, from Edgeworth to Sebald, is in essence an orphan.
9. Luther's injunction is a reformulation of Paul's *Epistle to the Galatians* 2:19.
10. See Langford's *Polite and Commercial People* (1989), 257–59.
11. In the words of one London-based evangelist, "We have Churchmen, Presbyterians, Scottish and English, Lutherans, Calvinists, Independents, Baptists, Quakers, Papists, Jews, Arians, and Arminians" (quoted in Langford, *Polite and Commercial People*, 245).
12. Wesley offers an earlier formulation of the same idea in *Justification by Faith* (1738), wherein he states, "*Justification*; which, taken in the largest sense, implies, A Deliverance from Guilt and Punishment" (13).
13. Wesley also differed from Whitefield, Lady Huntingdon, and the Church of England itself in his denial of predestination, a position he dramatically

announced in *Free Grace* (1740), a sermon he preached to Whitefield's congregation while the latter was in America.
14. Wesley himself insisted that even the perfected are subjected to "infirmities" and "temptation." As Wesley states, "none are perfectly freed till their spirits return to God." See *A Plain Account of Christian Perfection*, 4.
15. Rosenthal makes the important observation that "for a narrative so ostensibly concerned with the next world, we get a lot of material details about this one" (151).
16. On the development of a popular consumer society in the early eighteenth century, see McKendrick et al.'s *The Birth of a Consumer Society* (1982).
17. McKendrick notes that "most authorities place the turning point in the reign of George I [1714–1727] and see the culmination of fashion frenzy early in the reign of George II [1727–1760]," following which, the mark of a gentleman increasingly became a matter of fabric and tailoring (54).
18. This is the same sense in which Alain Badiou speaks of the "Christ-event" in Paul as a moment of "pure excess" that "establishes the authority of a new subjective path over future eras" (57, 63). For Badiou as well as Paul and Luther, Christ exemplifies the possibility of bodies becoming the subjects of eternal and universal truth. This helps explain why Slavoj Žižek cites religion as the missing yet essential fifth category of truth in Badiou's thought. See Badiou's *Saint Paul* (1997) and Žižek's *The Ticklish Subject* (1997), 144.
19. This paradox—law finding its foundation in lawlessness—inspires Derrida to argue that all law is grounded in the "mystical" authority of its own proclamations and the willingness of its subjects to "believe" in them ("The Force of Law" 242, 240).
20. Huntingdon expresses these thoughts in a letter to a student considering the ministry.

4. The Other Side of Discipline

1. For a table detailing the growth of real GDP per head from 1270 to 1870, see Broadberry et al.'s *British Economic Growth* (2015), 204. The eighteenth century was a period of steady, continuous growth, which, at this point in history, was unprecedented. On the popularity of domestic literature and in particular its female authors in this era, see Mellor's *Mothers of the Nation* (2000), 3–4.
2. This double meaning was also present in the thought of Greek and Roman antiquity. See duBois's excellent *Slaves and Other Objects* (2003).
3. See Hilton's *A Mad, Bad, and Dangerous People?*, 10; Boulukos's "Maria Edgeworth's 'Grateful Negro' and the Sentimental Argument for Slavery" (1999), 23–24; and Brion Davis's *The Problem of Slavery in the Age of Revolution* (1975), 457–58.

4. See Richardson's "The British Empire and the Atlantic Slave Trade" (1998).
5. The historical consensus is now that, contrary to the arguments of C. L. R. James and Erik Williams in the 1930s and 1940s, British slave plantations were in fact highly profitable until the point of slavery's abolition in 1833. See Davis (1975), 59 and Hilton (2006), 186.
6. See Armstrong, *How Novels Think* (2005), 25.
7. Slavery as a whole exploded over the course of the eighteenth century. It is estimated that 60 percent of the over 10 million Africans forced into the European slave trade were transported between 1721 and 1820. See Curtin's *The Atlantic Slave Trade* (1969), 265; and Ward et al.'s *The Cambridge World History of Slavery: Volume 3* (2011), 432.
8. As David Brion Davis notes, a central preoccupation of abolitionists was imagining how plantation discipline could be extended to the poor and working classes. Various proposals for reform put forth by abolitionists, such as Bentham's panoptic prison and 'Houses of Industry,' were thus ironically, in the words of Davis, "a virtual caricature of the planter ideal" (456). See Davis 302–6, 358–68.
9. The hero of Edgeworth's Irish novel *Ennui* (1809) must learn to act "from rational motive, which alone can be permanent in its operation," as opposed to the irrational "impulse of the moment" (248).
10. Boulukos makes a similar point, arguing that Edgeworth "envisions slavery . . . reformed in the image of wage labor" (13).
11. See my article "Never Getting Home" (2011) for more on Edgeworth's Kantian cosmopolitanism.
12. For more on this aspect of Edgeworth, see Butler's *The War of Ideas* (1975) 273–74.
13. In "What Is Enlightenment?" Kant famously distinguishes between the necessary freedom of public reason wherein someone acting as scholar addresses "the entire *reading public*," and "the private use of reason" one exercises in "a *civil* post or office," which rightfully "may quite often be very narrowly restricted" (55).
14. For a different take on the ambivalence of domestic heroines, see Thompson's *Ingenuous Subjection* (2005).
15. For another example, see *Belinda*, 445–47.
16. See S. J. Connolly in *A New History of Ireland: Volume V*, 17.
17. See *Critique of Judgment*, 318–24, as well as Kant's "Idea for a Universal History with a Cosmopolitan Purpose" (1784) and "Perpetual Peace" (1795).
18. Lady Clonbrony explains early in the story that Grace "would have *got on* much better [in the London marriage market], if, when she first appeared in Lon'on, she had taken my advice, and wrote herself on her cards miss

de Nogent, which would have taken off the prejudice against the *Iricism* of Nugent" (16).
19. The majority of the decline occurred during the Cromwellian War in Ireland. See Connolly's *Religion, Law, and Power* (1992), 13.
20. In *The Wild Irish Girl*, Morgan exemplifies such nostalgia by praising traditional Ireland's "ancient Milesian government . . . [in which] the people were divided into classes;–the *Literati* holding the next rank to royalty itself, and the *Beataghs* [keepers of open houses] the fourth, so that as in China the state was so regulated, that every one knew his place from the prince to the peasant" (181).
21. Behn's nostalgic African hero utters these lines regarding his fellow slaves after they fail to stay loyal to his rebellion (69).
22. For examples, see "A Letter from Darby Tracy" (1799) 8–9, "The Answer of Denis Feagan" (1799) 8–9, and "A Letter from Murtagh Feagan" (1800), 4–5.
23. Musgrave includes the oath in the lengthy appendix to his *Memoirs*, 221.
24. As Plowden elaborates, "To this day the Irish peasants are in the annual habit of lighting upon certain hills, on the eve of Midsummer, what they still call *Bal's fire*, though fully as ignorant, that *Bel* was the god of their Phoenician ancestors" (8).
25. On the persistence of this custom into the eighteenth century, see Cullen in *A New History of Ireland: Volume IV*, 168.
26. For Hegel's critique of Kant's categorical imperative as ultimately a "fear of the truth," see *Phenomenology of the Spirit* (1807), 49.

Epilogue

1. I am using Barber's own expanded definition of poverty as anyone living in a state of economic hardship. For more on this, see Barber's *Forward Together* (2014) and "We Need a Moral Breakthrough" (2017).

BIBLIOGRAPHY

Adorno, Theodor, and Max Horkheimer. *Dialectic of Enlightenment.* Translated by Edmund Jephcott. Stanford, CA: Stanford University Press, 2002.

Agamben, Giorgio. *Homo Sacer.* Translated by Daniel Heller-Roazen. Stanford, CA: Stanford University Press, 1998.

———. *The Kingdom and the Glory.* Translated by Lorenzo Chiesa and Matteo Mandarini. Stanford, CA: Stanford University Press, 2011.

———. *The Time That Remains.* Translated by Patricia Dailey. Stanford, CA: Stanford University Press, 2005.

———. *The Use of Bodies.* Translated by Adam Kotsko. Stanford, CA: Stanford University Press, 2016.

Althusser, Louis. "Ideology and Ideological State Apparatuses." In *Lenin and Philosophy and Other Essays,* translated by Ben Brewster. New York: New Left Books, 1970.

Andrews, John Hardwood, Ann Buckley, Francis John Byrne, James Patrick Carney, Nancy Margaret Edwards, Thomas Mowbray Charles-Edwards, Marie Therese Flanegan et al. *A New History of Ireland: Volume IV, Eighteenth-Century Ireland, 1691–1800.* Edited by T. W. Moody and W. E. Vaughan. Oxford: Clarendon, 1986.

Anidjar, Gil. *Semites.* Stanford, CA: Stanford University Press, 2008.

The Answer of Denis Feagan, Breeches-Maker, at Edenderry, to the Letter of Darby Tracy. Dublin: James Moore, 1799.

Armstrong, Nancy. *Desire and Domestic Fiction.* Oxford: Oxford University Press, 1987.

———. *How Novels Think.* New York: Columbia University Press, 2005.

———, and Leonard Tennenhouse. *The Imaginary Puritan.* Berkeley: University of California Press, 1992.

Asad, Talal. *Formations of the Secular.* Stanford, CA: Stanford University Press, 2003.

Audra, E., and Aubrey Williams. "Introduction." In *The Twickenham Edition of the Poems of Alexander Pope: Volume 1.* New Haven, CT: Yale University Press, 1961.

Austen, Jane. *Sense and Sensibility.* New York: Penguin Books, 2003.

Badiou, Alain. *Saint Paul.* Translated by Ray Brassier. Stanford, CA: Stanford University Press, 2003.

Balibar, Etienne. "Citizen Subject." In *Who Comes After the Subject?,* edited by Eduardo Cadava, Peter Connor, and Jean-Luc Nancy. New York: Routledge: 1991.

Barber, William. "50 Years After MLK's Poor People's Campaign." *Democracy Now*, June 25, 2018. https://www.democracynow.org/2018/6/25/50_years_after_mlk_s_poor.

———. "Forward Together, Not One Step Back." University of California, Berkeley, April 14, 2019. https://news.berkeley.edu/2019/04/14/berkeley-talks-transcript-rev-dr-william-j-barber-ii/.

———. "Now Is the Time for Prophetic Moral Action." *Common Dreams*, July 17, 2017. https://www.commondreams.org/views/2017/07/17/now-time-prophetic-moral-action.

———. "We Need a Moral Breakthrough." Seventy-Fourth Union for Reform Judaism, December 6, 2017. https://urj.org/blog/2017/12/06/we-need-moral-breakthrough-rev-dr-william-j-barber-iis-remarks-urj-biennial-2017.

Bataille, Georges. *Accursed Share: Volume III, Sovereignty*. Translated by Robert Hurley. New York: Zone Books, 1991.

Behn, Aphra. *Oroonoko: or, The Royal Slave*. New York: Penguin Books, 2014.

Blair, Tony. "Speech to the US Congress." US Congress, July 17, 2003, Washington, DC, http://news.bbc.co.uk/2/hi/uk_news/politics/3076253.stm.

Book of Common Prayer. London: Wright & W. Gill, 1770.

Boulukos, George. "Maria Edgeworth's 'Grateful Negro' and the Sentimental Argument for Slavery." *Eighteenth-Century Life* 23, no. 1 (1999).

Bourdieu, Pierre. "The Forms of Capital." In *Handbook of Theory and Research for the Sociology of Education*. New York: Greenwood, 1986.

Boyarin, Daniel, and Jonathan Boyarin. "Diaspora: The Generation and Ground of Jewish Identity." *Critical Inquiry* 19, no. 4 (1993).

Brindle, Steven, and Brian Kerr. *Windsor Revealed: New Light on the History of the Castle*. London: English Heritage, 1997.

Brown, Bill, ed. *Things*. Chicago: University of Chicago Press, 2004.

Brown, Laura. *Alexander Pope*. London: Blackwell, 1985.

———. "Dryden and the Imperial Imagination." In *The Cambridge Companion to Dryden*, edited by Steven Zwicker. Cambridge: Cambridge University Press, 2004.

———. *Ends of Empire*. Ithaca, NY: Cornell University Press, 1993.

Burke, Edmund. *An Appeal from the New to Old Whigs*. London: J. Dodsley, 1791.

———. *A Philosophical Enquiry into the Origin of Our Ideas of the Sublime and Beautiful*. New York: Penguin Classics, 1999.

———. *Reflections on the Revolution in France*. Oxford: Oxford University Press, 2009.

Burney, Frances. *Evelina*. New York: W. W. Norton, 1998.

Bush, George. "9/11 Address to the Nation." *American Rhetoric*, September 11, 2001, Washington, DC, www.americanrhetoric.com/speeches/gwbush911addresstothenation.htm.

Butler, Marilyn. *Jane Austen and the War of Ideas*. Oxford: Clarendon, 2002.
———. *Maria Edgeworth: A Literary Biography*. Oxford: Clarendon, 1972.
———, Heidi Van de Veire, and Kim Walker. "Introductory Note." In *The Novels and Selected Works of Maria Edgeworth*, vol. 5. London: Pickering & Chatto, 1999.
Cain, P. J., and A. G. Hopkins. *British Imperialism: 1688–2000*. London: Routledge, 2000.
Casarino, Cesare. *Modernity at Sea: Melville, Conrad, and Marx*. Minneapolis: University of Minnesota Press, 2002.
Castle, Terry. *Clarissa's Ciphers*. Ithaca, NY: Cornell University Press, 1982.
Chakrabarty, Dipesh. *Provincializing Europe*. Princeton, NJ: Princeton University Press, 2000.
Chamayou, Grégoire. *Drone Theory*. Translated by Janet Lloyd. London: Penguin Books, 2015.
Chapin, Chester. "Alexander Pope: Erasmian Catholic." *Eighteenth-Century Studies* 6, no. 4 (1973).
Charron, Pierre. *Of Wisdom*. Translated by George Stanhope. London: M. Gillyflower, 1697.
Chua, Brandon. *Ravishment of Reason: Governance and the Heroic Idioms of the Late Stuart Stage, 1660–1690*. Lewisburg, PA: Bucknell University Press, 2014.
Clark, J. C. D. *English Society: 1660–1832*. Cambridge: Cambridge University Press, 2000.
Cleland, John. *Fanny Hill*. New York: Penguin Books, 1985.
Clinton, Hillary. "Remarks." Council on Foreign Relations, December 15, 2003, New York, www.cfr.org/iraq/remarks-senator-hillary-rodham-clinton-transcript/p6600.
Colley, Linda. *Britons: Forging the Nation 1707–1837*. New Haven, CT: Yale University Press, 1992.
Connolly, S. J. "Aftermath and Adjustment." In *A New History of Ireland: Volume V, Ireland Under the Union, 1801–1870*, edited by W. E. Vaughan. Oxford: Clarendon, 1989.
———. *Religion, Law, and Power: The Making of Protestant Ireland*. Oxford: Clarendon, 1992.
Coppe, Abiezer. "A Fiery Flying Roll." In *A Collection of Ranter Writings from the Seventeenth Century*. London: Junction Books, 1983.
Corbett, Mary Jean. "Public Affections and Familial Politics: Burke, Edgeworth, and the 'Common Naturalization' of Great Britain." *English Literary History* 61, no. 4 (1994).
Cressy, David. *Birth, Marriage, and Death: Ritual, Religion, and the Life Cycle in Tudor and Stuart England*. Oxford: Oxford University Press, 1997.
Cromwell, Oliver. *The Writings and Speeches of Oliver Cromwell: Vol. IV*. Oxford: Oxford University Press, 1989.

Crossley, Aaron, and Seymour, Hobart. *The Life and Times of Selina, Countess of Huntingdon*. London: William Edward Painter, 1839.

Cunnington, C. W., and P. Cunnington. *A Dictionary of English Costume: 900–1900*. London: Faber & Faber, 1960.

Curtin, Phillip D. *The Atlantic Slave Trade: A Census*. Madison: University of Wisconsin Press, 1969.

Damrosch, Leopold. *God's Plot and Man's Stories: Studies in the Fictional Imagination from Milton to Fielding*. Chicago: University of Chicago Press, 1985.

Davis Brion, David. *The Problem of Slavery in the Age of Revolution, 1770–1823*. Oxford: Oxford University Press, 1999.

Dearing, Vincent. "Commentary." In *The Works of John Dryden, Volume VII*. Berkeley: University of California Press, 2000.

Denham, John. "Cooper's Hill." In *Broadview Anthology of Seventeenth-Century Verse and Prose*, edited by Alan Rudrum, Joseph Black, and Holly Faith Nelson. Peterborough, ON: Broadview, 2001.

Derrida, Jacques. "La différance." In *Théorie d'Ensemble*. Paris: Éditions du Seuil, 1968.

———. "The Force of Law." In *Acts of Religion*, translated by Mary Quaintance and Gil Anidjar. New York: Routledge, 2002.

———. *Of Grammatology*. Translated by Gayatri Spivak. Baltimore: Johns Hopkins University Press, 1997.

———. *Writing and Difference*. Translated by Alan Bass. Chicago: University of Chicago Press, 1980.

———. *Specters of Marx*. Translated by Peggy Kamuf. New York: Routledge, 2006.

Deutsch, Helen. "Bolingbroke's Laugh: Alexander Pope's Epistle to Bolingbroke and the Rhetoric of Embodied Exemplarity." *Studies in the Literary Imagination* 38, no. 1 (1995).

———. *Resemblance and Disgrace*. Cambridge, MA: Harvard University Press, 1996.

Dowling, William. *The Epistolary Moment*. Princeton, NJ: Princeton University Press, 1991.

Dryden, John. "Absalom and Achitophel." In *The Works of John Dryden, Volume II*, edited by H. T. Swedenburg. Berkeley: University of California Press, 1972.

———. "Astraea Redux." In *The Works of John Dryden, Volume I*, edited by H. T. Swedenburg and Edward N. Hooker. Berkeley: University of California Press, 1956.

———. "Of Dramatick Poesie." In *The Works of John Dryden, Volume XVII*, edited by Samuel Holt Monk and A. E. Wallace Maurer. Berkeley: University of California Press, 1971.

———. "Eleonora." In *The Works of John Dryden, Volume III*, edited by Earl Miner and Vincent A. Dearing. Berkeley: University of California Press, 1969.

———. "The First Book of the Aeneis." In *The Works of Virgil: Volume the Second*. London: Jacob Tonson, 1721.

———. "The Georgics Book II." In *The Works of Virgil, Volume the Second*. London: Jacob Tonson, 1721.

———. "Heroic Stanzas." In *The Works of John Dryden, Volume I*, edited by Edward N. Hooker and H. T. Swedenburg. Berkeley: University of California Press, 1956.

———. "Horace's Second Epode." In *Sylvae*. London: Jacob Tonson, 1685.

———. "To His Sacred Majesty." In *The Works of John Dryden, Volume I*, edited by H. T. Swedenburg. Berkeley: University of California Press, 1956.

———. "Mac Flecknoe." In *The Works of John Dryden, Volume II*, edited by H. T. Swedenburg. Berkeley: University of California Press, 1972.

———. "To My Honour'd Kinsman." In *The Works of John Dryden, Volume VII*, edited by Earl Miner and Vincent A. Dearing. Berkeley: University of California Press, 2000.

———. "Ode to Anne Killigrew." In *The Works of John Dryden, Volume III*, edited by Earl Miner and Vincent A. Dearing. Berkeley: University of California Press, 1969.

DuBois, Page. *Slaves and Other Objects*. Chicago: University of Chicago Press, 2003.

Dunne, Tom. "Edgworthstown in Fact and Fiction, 1760–1840." In *Longford: Essays in County History*, edited by Raymond Gillespie and Gerard Moran. Dublin: Lilliput, 1989.

During, Simon. "The Novel's Mysticism." Paper presented at *Is the Novel Secular?*, Stanford Center for the Study of the Novel, April 29–30, 2011, http://academia.edu/764252/Is_the_novel_secular_2011_.

Eaves, T. C., and Ben Kimpel. *Samuel Richardson: A Biography*. Oxford: Clarendon, 1971.

Edgeworth, Maria. *The Absentee*. Vol. 5 of *The Novels and Selected Works of Maria Edgeworth*. Edited by Heidi Van de Veire, Kim Walker, and Marilyn Butler. London: Pickering & Chatto, 1999.

———. *Belinda*. Oxford: Oxford University Press, 1994.

———. *Castle Rackrent*. Vol. 1 of *The Novels and Selected Works of Maria Edgeworth*. Edited by Jane Desmarais, Tim McLoughlin, and Marilyn Butler. London: Pickering & Chatto, 1999.

———. *Ennui*. Vol. 1 of *The Novels and Selected Works of Maria Edgeworth*. Edited by Jane Desmarais, Tim McLoughlin, and Marilyn Butler. London: Pickering & Chatto, 1999.

———. "The Grateful Negro." In *The Novels and Selected Works of Maria Edgeworth*, part 2, vol. 12, edited by Elizabeth Eger, Clíona Ó Gallchoir, and Marilyn Butler. London: Pickering & Chatto, 2003.

Edgeworth, Richard, and Maria. *Essays on Professional Education*. London: J. Johnson, 1809.
Engels, Friedrich, and Karl Marx. "The Manifesto of the Communist Party." In *The Marx-Engels Reader*, edited by Robert C. Tucker. London: W. W. Norton, 1978.
Epicurus. "Letter to Menoeceus." In *Letters, Principal Doctrines, and Vatican Sayings*, translated by Russell M. Greer. New York: Macmillan, 1964.
Erskine-Hill, Howard. "Pope and Slavery." In *Alexander Pope: World and Word*. Oxford: Oxford University Press, 1998.
Fanon, Frantz. *The Wretched of the Earth*. Translated by Richard Philcox. New York: Grove, 2004.
Felski, Rita. *The Limits of Critique*. Chicago: University of Chicago Press, 2015.
Fletcher, Phineas. "The Locusts, or Apollyonists." In *The Poetical Works of Giles Fletcher and Phineas Fletcher: Volume I*. Cambridge: Cambridge University Press, 1908.
Foucault, Michel. *The Care of the Self: Volume 3 of The History of Sexuality*. Translated by Robert Hurley. New York: Pantheon Books, 1986.
———. *Discipline and Punish*. Translated by Alan Sheridan. New York: Vintage Books, 1995.
———. *The History of Sexuality: An Introduction, Volume I*. Translated by Robert Hurley. New York: Vintage Books, 1990.
———. *Security, Territory, Population*. New York: Palgrave Macmillan, 2007.
———. *Society Must Be Defended*. Translated by David Macey. New York: Picador, 2003.
———. *Technologies of the Self: A Seminar with Michel Foucault*. London: Tavistock, 1988.
———. *The Use of Pleasure: Volume 2 of The History of Sexuality*. Translated by Robert Hurley. New York: Vintage Books, 1985.
Freud, Sigmund. *Group Psychology and the Analysis of the Ego*. Edited by James Strachey. New York: W. W. Norton, 1990.
Gallagher, Catherine. "Embracing the Absolute: The Politics of the Female Subject in Seventeenth-Century England." *Genders* 1, no. 2 (1988).
Gallchoir, Clíona Ó. *Edgeworth: Women, Enlightenment, and Nation*. Dublin: University College Dublin Press, 2005.
Gibbons, Luke. "Republicanism and Radical Memory." In *Revolution, Counter-Revolution, and Union*, edited by Jim Smyth. Cambridge: Cambridge University Press, 2000.
Gilroy, Paul. *The Black Atlantic*. Cambridge, MA: Harvard University Press, 1993.
Go, Julian. *Patterns of Empire: The British and American Empires, 1688 to the Present*. Cambridge: Cambridge University Press, 2011.

Goodman, Amy. "'This Flag Comes Down Today': Bree Newsome Scales SC Capitol Flagpole, Takes Down Confederate Flag." Democracy Now, July 3, 2015, www.democracynow.org/2015/7/3/this_flag_comes_down_today_bree.
Gourgouris, Stathis. *Lessons in Secular Criticism*. New York: Fordham University Press, 2013.
Hallward, Peter. *Absolutely Postcolonial*. Manchester: Manchester University Press, 2001.
Hammill, Graham. *The Mosaic Constitution*. Chicago: University of Chicago Press, 2012.
Hammond, Paul. *Dryden and the Traces of Classical Rome*. Oxford: Oxford University Press, 1999.
Hardt, Michael, and Antonio Negri. *Empire*. Cambridge, MA: Harvard University Press, 2000.
Hegel, G. W. F. *Phenomenology of the Spirit*. Translated by A. V. Miller. Oxford: Oxford University Press, 1977.
Heidegger, Martin. *Being and Time*. Translated by Joan Stambaugh. Albany: State University of New York Press, 1996.
———. "Letter on Humanism." In *Basic Writings*, edited by David Farrell Krell. New York: Harper & Row, 1977.
Henseley, David. "Thomas Edwards and the Dialectics of Clarissa's Death Scene." *Eighteenth-Century Life* 16, no. 3 (1992).
Hill, Christopher. *The Century of Revolution: 1603–1714*. London: Routledge, 2001.
———. "Clarissa Harlowe and Her Times." *Essays in Criticism* 5, no. 4 (1955).
———. *The World Turned Upside Down: Radical Ideas during the English Revolution*. New York: Penguin Books, 1991.
Hilton, Boyd. *A Mad, Bad, and Dangerous People? England 1783–1846*. Oxford: Oxford University Press, 2006.
Higman, B. W. *Slave Population and Economy in Jamaica, 1807–1834*. Barbados: University of West Indies Press, 1995.
Hooker, Edward N., and H. T. Swedenburg. "Commentary." In *The Works of John Dryden, Volume I*. Berkeley: University of California Press, 1956.
Hoppit, Julian. *Land of Liberty? England 1689–1727*. Oxford: Oxford University Press, 2000.
Horace. *The Complete Odes and Epodes*. Translated by David West. Oxford: Oxford University Press, 2008.
———. *The Odes*. Translated by John Hollander. Edited by J. D. McClatchy. Princeton, NJ: Princeton University Press, 2002.
Hunt, Alan. *Governing Morals: A Social History in Moral Regulation*. Cambridge: Cambridge University Press, 1999.
Hunter, Paul J. *Before Novels*. New York: W. W. Norton, 1990.

———. "Binarism and the Anglophone Couplet." *Modern Language Quarterly* 61, no. 1 (2000).

———. *The Reluctant Pilgrim: Defoe's Emblematic Method and Quest for Form in Robinson Crusoe*. Baltimore: Johns Hopkins University Press, 1966.

Ingrassia, Catherine. *Authorship, Commerce, and Gender in Early Eighteenth-Century England*. Cambridge: Cambridge University Press, 1998.

Jackson, Spencer. "Never Getting Home: The Unfulfilled Promise of Maria Edgeworth's Irish Tales." *Studies in Romanticism* 50, no. 3 (2011).

James, C. L. R. *The Black Jacobins: Toussaint L'Ouverture and the San Domingo Revolution*. New York: Vintage Books, 1989.

Jeffrey, Francis. "Miss Edgeworth's Popular Tales." In *The Edinburgh Review: or Critical Journal, April 1804 . . . July 1804, Volume 4*. Edinburgh: D. Willison, 1804.

Jonson, Ben. "To Penshurst." In *The Complete Poems*, edited by George Parfitt. New York: Penguin Classics, 1988.

Johnson, Samuel. *A Dictionary of the English Language, Vol. I*. London: W. Strahan, 1755.

———. *Dictionary, Vol. II*. London: J. Knapton, 1756.

———. *The Lives of the English Poets, in Two Volumes: Vol. II*. London: J. F. Dove, 1826.

———. *The Lives of the English Poets, in Two Volumes: Vol. I*. Leipzig: Berhnard Tauchnitz, 1858.

Kahn, Victoria. *The Future of Illusion: Political Theology and Early Modern Texts*. Chicago: University of Chicago Press, 2014.

Kant, Immanuel. *Critique of Judgment*. Translated by Werner S. Pluhar. Indianapolis: Hackett, 1987.

———. *Groundwork of the Metaphysics of Morals*. Translated by Mary Gregor. Cambridge: Cambridge University Press, 1997.

———. "Idea for a Universal History with a Cosmopolitan Purpose." In *Kant's Political Writings*, translated by H. B. Nisbet. Cambridge: Cambridge University Press, 1970.

———. "Perpetual Peace: A Philosophical Sketch." In *Kant's Political Writings*, translated by H. B. Nisbet. Cambridge: Cambridge University Press, 1970.

———. "What Is Enlightenment?" In *Kant's Political Writings*, translated H. B. Nisbet. Cambridge: Cambridge University Press, 1970.

Kantorowicz, Ernst. *The King's Two Bodies*. Princeton, NJ: Princeton University Press, 1997.

Kareem, Sarah. *The Invention of Wonder*. Oxford: Oxford University Press, 2014.

King, Martin Luther, Jr. "Letter from Birmingham Jail." In *Why We Can't Wait*. Boston: Beacon, 2011.

Kramnick, Isaac. *Bolingbroke and His Circle*. Cambridge, MA: Harvard University Press, 1968.

Langford, Paul. *A Polite and Commercial People: England, 1727–1783*. Oxford: Clarendon, 1989.
Laqueur, Thomas. *Making Sex*. Cambridge, MA: Harvard University Press, 1990.
"A Letter from Darby Tracy, Chairman, in London, to Mr. Denis Feagan, Breeches-Maker, at Edenderry." Dublin: W. Folds, 1799.
"A Letter from Murtagh Feagan, Cousin German to Denis Feagan, of Edenderry, in Answer to Darby Tracy." Dublin: J. Stockdale, 1800.
Lukács, Georg. *The Theory of the Novel*. Translated by Anna Bostock. Boston: MIT Press, 1971.
Lupton, Julia Reinhard. *Citizen-Saints: Shakespeare and Political Theology*. Chicago: University of Chicago Press, 2005.
Luther, Martin. *A Treatise Touching the Libertie of a Christian* [*A Treatise on Christian Liberty*]. Translated by James Bell. London: Printed by Thomas Harper for William Sheares, 1636.
Maynard Mack. *Alexander Pope, A Life*. New York: W. W. Norton, 1986.
Macpherson, Sandra. *Harm's Way: Tragic Responsibility and the Novel Form*. Baltimore: Johns Hopkins University Press, 2010.
Magubane, Zine. "Which Bodies Matter? Feminism, Poststructuralism, and the Curious Theoretical Odyssey of the 'Hottentot Venus.'" *Gender and Society* 22, no. 6 (2001).
Makdisi, Saree. *Making England Western*. Chicago: University of Chicago Press, 2014.
Marvell, Andrew. "Upon Appleton House." In *The Complete Poems*, edited by Elizabeth Story Donno. New York: Penguin Classics, 2005.
Marx, Karl. *Capital: Volume 1*. Translated by Ben Fowkes. London: Penguin Classics, 1990.
———. "Contribution to the Critique of Hegel's Philosophy of Right: Introduction" [1844]. In *The Marx-Engels Reader*, edited by Robert C. Tucker. London: W. W. Norton, 1978.
———. "On the Jewish Question" [1844]. In *The Marx-Engels Reader*, edited by Robert C. Tucker. London: W. W. Norton, 1978.
Mapletoft, John. *A Sermon Preach'd at the Church of St. Mary le Bow, to the Societies for Reformation of Manners, January the 1st. 1700*. London: B. Aylmer, 1700.
McBride, Ian. *Scripture Politics: Ulster Presbyterians and Irish Radicalism in the Late Eighteenth Century*. Oxford: Oxford University Press, 1998.
McDowell, R. B. "The Age of the United Irishmen: Revolution and the Union 1794–1800." In *A New History of Ireland: Volume IV, Eighteenth-Century Ireland 1691–1800*, edited by T. W. Moody and W. E. Vaughan. Oxford: Clarendon, 1986.
McKendrick, Neil, John Brewer, and J. H. Plumb. *The Birth of Consumer Society*. London: Europa, 1982.

McKeon, Michael. *The Origins of the English Novel*. Baltimore: Johns Hopkins University Press, 2002.

———. "The Politics of Pastoral Retreat: Dryden's Poem to His Cousin." In *Enchanted Ground: Reimagining John Dryden*, edited by Jayne Lewis and Maximillian Novak. Toronto: University of Toronto Press, 2004.

Meillassoux, Quentin. *After Finitude*. Translated by Ray Brassier. London: Continuum, 2008.

Mellor, Anne. *Mothers of the Nation*. Bloomington: University of Indiana Press, 2000.

Metz, Johannes B. "Religion and Society in the Light of a Political Theology." *Harvard Theological Review* 61, no. 4 (1968).

Milton, John. *Milton: Political Writings*. Cambridge: Cambridge University Press, 1991.

Morgan, Lady. *The Wild Irish Girl*. Oxford: Oxford University Press, 1999.

Morgan, Phillip D. "Slavery in the British Caribbean." In *The Cambridge World History of Slavery: Volume 3*. New York: Cambridge University Press, 2011.

Musgrave, Richard. *Memoirs of the Rebellions in Ireland: Vol. II*. Dublin: John Marchbank, 1802.

Myers, Mitzi. "Gender, History, and Edgeworth's Rebellion Narratives." *Nineteenth-Century Contexts* 19, no. 4 (1996).

Noggle, James. *The Skeptical Sublime: Aesthetic Ideology in Pope and the Tory Satirists*. Oxford: Oxford University Press, 2001.

Obama, Barack. "Remarks by the President." National Defense University, May 23, 2013, Washington, DC, www.whitehouse.gov/the-press-office/2013/05/23/remarks-president-national-defense-university.

O'Connell, Lisa. *The Origins of the English Marriage Plot*. Cambridge: Cambridge University Press, 2019.

Oliver, Melvin, and Thomas Shapiro. *Black Wealth/White Wealth*. New York: Routledge, 2006.

"On Views of Race and Inequality, Blacks and Whites Are Worlds Apart." Pew Research Center, June 27, 2016, www.pewsocialtrends.org/2016/06/27/1-demographic-trends-and-economic-well-being.

Pakenham, Thomas. *The Year of Liberty: The Story of the Great Irish Rebellion of 1798*. London: Granada, 1972.

Perry, Ruth. *Novel Relations*. Cambridge: Cambridge University Press, 2004.

Pestana, Carla. *Protestant Empire: Religion and the Making of the British Atlantic*. Philadelphia: University of Pennsylvania Press, 2009.

Pfau, Thomas. *Minding the Modern*. Notre Dame, IN: Notre Dame University Press, 2013.

Pincus, Steven. *1688: The First Modern Revolution*. New Haven, CT: Yale University Press, 2009.

Pittock, Murray. *Scottish and Irish Romanticism*. Oxford: Oxford University Press, 2008.
Plowden, Edmund. *The Commentaries, or Reports of Edmund Plowden, in Two Parts*. London: S. Brooke, 1816.
Plowden, Francis. *An Historical Review of Ireland*. 2 vols. London: C. Rowarth, 1803.
Pocock, J. G. A. *Machiavellian Moment: Florentine Political Thought and the Atlantic Republican Tradition*. Princeton, NJ: Princeton University Press, 1975.
Pope, Alexander. "Epilogue to the Satires, Dialogue I." In *The Twickenham Edition of the Poems of Alexander Pope: Volume IV*, edited by John Butt. New Haven, CT: Yale University Press, 1953.
———. "Epilogue to the Satires, Dialogue II." In *The Twickenham Edition of the Poems of Alexander Pope: Volume IV*, edited by John Butt. New Haven, CT: Yale University Press, 1953.
———. "The First Epistle of the First Book of Horace. To Lord Bolingbroke." In *The Twickenham Edition of the Poems of Alexander Pope: Volume IV*, edited by John Butt. New Haven, CT: Yale University Press, 1953.
———. "The First Satire of the Second Book of Horace" [1733]. In *The Twickenham Edition of the Poems of Alexander Pope: Volume IV*, edited by John Butt. New Haven, CT: Yale University Press, 1953.
———. "Messiah." In *The Twickenham Edition of the Poems of Alexander Pope: Volume 1*, edited by E. Audra and Aubrey Williams. New Haven, CT: Yale University Press, 1961.
———. "The Rape of the Lock." In *The Twickenham Edition of the Poems of Alexander Pope: Volume II*, edited by Geoffrey Tillotson. New Haven, CT: Yale University Press, 1940.
———. "Sober Advice from Horace" [1734]. In *The Twickenham Edition of the Poems of Alexander Pope: Volume IV*, edited by Norman Ault and John Butt. New Haven, CT: Yale University Press, 1953.
———. "Spring." In *The Twickenham Edition of the Poems of Alexander Pope: Volume 1*, edited by E. Audra and Aubrey Williams. New Haven, CT: Yale University Press, 1961.
———. "Universal Prayer." In *The Twickenham Edition of the Poems of Alexander Pope: Volume VI*, edited by Norman Ault and John Butt. New Haven, CT: Yale University Press, 1964.
———. "Windsor Forest." In *The Twickenham Edition of the Poems of Alexander Pope: Volume 1*, edited by E. Audra and Aubrey Williams. New Haven, CT: Yale University Press, 1961.
Pope Clement XI. "Universal Prayer." *Holy Cross Hymn Book*. Notre Dame, IN: Notre Dame University Press, 1904.
Porter, Roy. *London: A Social History*. Cambridge, MA: Harvard University Press, 1995.

Probert, Julia. *Marriage, Law, and Practice in the Long Eighteenth Century*. Cambridge: Cambridge University Press, 2009.

Rahmani, Sina. "Blank Subjects: Orphanhood and the Rise of the British Novel." PhD diss., University of California, Los Angeles, 2014. https://escholarship.org/content/qt95q2007s/qt95q2007s.pdf.

Richardson, David. "The British Empire and the Atlantic Slave Trade, 1660–1807." In *The Oxford History of the British Empire: Volume II*. Oxford: Oxford University Press, 1998.

Richardson, Samuel. *Clarissa*. New York: Penguin Books, 1985.

———. *The History of Sir Charles Grandison*. Oxford: Oxford University Press, 1972.

———. *Pamela*. Oxford: Oxford University Press, 2001.

Roach, Joseph. *Cities of the Dead*. New York: Columbia University Press, 1996.

———. *It*. Ann Arbor: University of Michigan Press, 2007.

Robert, William Clare. *Marx's Inferno: The Political Theory of Capital*. Princeton, NJ: Princeton University Press, 2016.

Roberts, Justin. *Slavery and the Enlightenment in the British Atlantic*. Cambridge: Cambridge University Press, 2013.

Rogers, Pat. *The Symbolic Design of Windsor-Forest*. Newark: University of Delaware Press, 2004.

Roper, Alan. *Dryden's Poetic Kingdoms*. London: Routledge & Kegan Paul, 1965.

Rosenthal, Laura. *Infamous Commerce: Prostitution in Eighteenth-Century British Literature and Culture*. Ithaca, NY: Cornell University Press, 2006.

Russell, John Fuller. *The Life of Dr. Johnson*. London: James Burnes, 1847.

Said, Edward. *The World, the Text, and the Critic*. Cambridge, MA: Harvard University Press, 1983.

———. *Orientalism*. New York: Vintage Books, 2003.

Salisbury, John of. *Policraticus*. Translated by Cary J. Nederman. Cambridge: Cambridge University Press, 1990.

Schmitt, Carl. *Political Theology*. Translated by George Schwab. Chicago: University of Chicago Press, 2006.

Skinner, Quentin. *Liberty Before Liberalism*. Cambridge: Cambridge University Press, 1998.

Smith, Adam. *The Wealth of Nations: Books 1–3*. New York: Penguin Books, 1982.

Smith, Nigel. "*Paradise Lost* from Civil War to Restoration." In *The Cambridge Companion to Writing of the English Revolution*, edited by N. H. Keeble. Cambridge: Cambridge University Press, 2001.

Smyth, Jim. "Introduction." In *Revolution, Counter-Revolution, and Union*, edited by Jim Smyth. Cambridge: Cambridge University Press, 2000.

Soni, Vivasvan. *Mourning Happiness: Narrative and the Politics of Modernity*. Ithaca, NY: Cornell University Press, 2010.

Starr, G. A. *Defoe and Casuistry*. Princeton, NJ: Princeton University Press, 1971.
Stoler, Ann. *Race and the Education of Desire*. Durham, NC: Duke University Press, 1995.
Stolze, Ted. *Becoming Marxist: Studies in Philosophy, Struggle, and Endurance*. Boston: Brill, 2019.
Taylor, Charles. *A Secular Age*. Cambridge, MA: Harvard University Press, 2007.
The Thirty-Nine Articles and the Constitution and Canons of the Church of England. London: John Baskett, 1739.
Thompson, Helen. "Hobbesian Obligation and the Durability of Romance in Aphra Behn's *Love-Letters*." In *Women's Writing in Britain, 1660–1830*, edited by J. Batchelor and C. Kaplan. London: Palgrave Macmillan, 2005.
———. *Ingenuous Subjection*. Philadelphia: University of Pennsylvania Press, 2005.
Thomson, James. "Rule Britannia." In *Norton Anthology of English Literature: Volume C*. New York: W. W. Norton, 2006.
Tone, Wolfe. *Writings of Theobald Wolfe Tone, 1763–98*. Oxford: Oxford University Press, 2002.
Trump, Donald. "Inaugural Address," January 24, 2017, Washington, DC, www.whitehouse.gov/inaugural-address.
"US 'Killed 47 Afghan Civilians.'" BBC, July 11, 2008, http://news.bbc.co.uk/2/hi/south_asia/7501538.stm.
Vatter, Miguel. *The Republic of the Living: Biopolitics and the Critique of Civil Society*. New York: Fordham University Press, 2015.
Virgil. *Georgics*. Translated by James Rhoades. London: Kegan Paul, Trench, Trübner, 1891.
Visconsi, Elliott. *Lines of Equity: Literature and the Origins of Law in Later Stuart England*. Ithaca, NY: Cornell University Press, 2008.
Wahrman, Dror. *The Making of the Modern Self*. New Haven, CT: Yale University Press, 2004.
Walsham, Alexandra. "Unclasping the Book? Post-Reformation English Catholicism and the Vernacular Bible." *Journal of British Studies* 42 (April 2003): 141–66.
Wasserman, Earl. "Nature Moralized: The Divine Analogy in the Eighteenth Century." *ELH* 20, no. 1 (1953).
Watt, Ian. *The Rise of the Novel*. Berkeley: University of California Press, 1957.
Weber, Max. *The Protestant Ethic and the Spirit of Capitalism*. Translated by Talcott Parsons. New York: Charles Scribner's Sons, 1976.
Weheliye, Alexander. *Habeas Viscus: Racializing Assemblages, Biopolitics, and Black Feminist Theories of the Human*. Durham, NC: Duke University Press, 2014.

Wesley, John. *An Earnest Appeal to Men of Reason and Religion.* London: G. Whitefield, 1796.

———. *A Plain Account of Christian Perfection.* New York: James & John Harper, 1821.

———. "Free Grace." In *The Works of John Wesley, Vol. VII.* Grand Rapids, MI: Zondervan, 1872.

———. *Justification by Faith.* London: John Hutton, 1738.

———. "On God's Vineyard." In *The Works of John Wesley, Vol. VII.* Grand Rapids, MI: Zondervan, 1872.

Whitefield, George. *A Letter to John Wesley.* London: W. Strahan, 1741.

Williams, David. *Milton's Leveller God.* Montreal: McGill-Queen's University Press, 2017.

Winn, James. *John Dryden and His World.* New Haven, CT: Yale University Press, 1987.

Woodhouse, John. *A Sermon Preach'd at Salters-Hall to the Societies for Reformation of Manners, May 31, 1697.* London: John Lawrence, 1697.

Woodward, Josiah. *An Account of the Rise and Progress of the Religious Societies in the City of London.* London: Printed by J. D., 1698.

Wynter, Sylvia. "Unsettling the Coloniality of Being/Power/Truth/Freedom." *CR: The New Centennial Review* 3, no. 3 (2003).

Zwicker, Steven. *Dryden's Political Poetry.* Providence: Brown University Press, 1972.

———. *Politics and Language in Dryden's Poetry.* Princeton, NJ: Princeton University Press, 1984.

INDEX

Abingdon, Countess of, 188n36
absenteeism of landed Irish families, 159–60
absolutism, 30, 39, 60, 97–98, 155
Adam (biblical), 54–55, 57
Adorno, Theodor: *Dialectic of Enlightenment* (with Horkheimer), 6–8
Aeneas, 40
Agamben, Giorgio, 4, 15, 22–23, 86, 110, 184n21; *Homo Sacer*, 15–17, 31, 33–34, 53, 57, 86, 184n22, 189n8; *The Use of Bodies*, 184n22
Agricola, Johanna, 133
alienation, 100, 124, 174–75
Althusser, Louis, 118, 137
Anidjar, Gil, 4
Anne (queen), 71, 76
anticolonialism, 19, 141, 167
antinomianism, 110, 122, 130–34
anti-Semitism, 159, 176
Armies Vindication of This Last Change, The (anonymous 1659), 186n13
Armstrong, Nancy, 3, 11–12; *Desire and Domestic Fiction*, 143; *How Novels Think*, 143; *The Imaginary Puritan* (with Tennenhouse), 112–14, 116, 118
Asad, Talal, 4
Audra, E., 87
Austen, Jane, 2, 10, 138, 152, 161, 167, 177; *Mansfield Park*, 109, 164; *Sense and Sensibility*, 158–59
authorial self, 96, 98–104, 105
authority: in Dryden's works, 33, 36, 40–41, 43–45, 55–56, 63–65; in Edgeworth's works, 152, 172; modern subjects endowed with, 16; patriarchal, 125, 155; in Richardson's works, 108, 117, 122, 127, 133–35; secularized, 20–21; theological foundation of, 19–20, 180; transcendence of, 20

Badiou, Alain, 191n18
Bailey, Joanne, 190n6
Balibar, Étienne, 135
Bank of England, 81
Barber, William, 180–81, 193n1
Barthes, Roland, 137
Bataille, Georges: *The Accursed Share*, volume 3, 16–18, 21
Behn, Aphra, 185n8, 193n21; *Oroonoko*, 146, 153
Bentham, Jeremy, 192n8
biblical citations. *See* scriptural citations
biopolitics: Dryden's works and, 31–34, 53, 55, 57; Edgeworth's works and, 145; justice and, 33; Pope's works and, 86, 88; sovereignty and, 15–16
Blair, Tony, 13
Bolingbroke, Henry St. John, 10, 28
Book of Common Prayer, 109
Boulukos, George, 192n10; "Maria Edgeworth's 'Grateful Negro' and the Sentimental Argument for Slavery," 147, 155
Brown, Bill, 117
Brown, Laura, 29, 43, 47; *Alexander Pope*, 82, 83, 88
Burke, Edmund, 146, 148, 151, 164; *An Appeal from the New to Old Whigs*, 18, 152–53; *Reflections on the Revolution in France*, 152
Burney, Frances "Fanny," 156; *Cecilia*, 69; *Evelina*, 109, 118
Bush, George W., 13

209

Butler, Marilyn: *The Absentee* introduction (Pickering edition), 166; *A Literary Life*, 150–51, 167

Cain, P. J.: *British Imperialism: 1688–2000* (with Hopkins), 10, 184n13
Calvin, John, 12, 133
capitalism: British history and, 184n13; Marxist critiques of, 5–6; nationalism and, 10, 131; religion and, 8–9, 72, 75, 127, 129–31; secularism and, 46
Carter, Nicholas, 133
Casarino, Cesare, 106
Castle, Terry: *Clarissa's Ciphers*, 136–37
Catholicism: divine sovereignty and, 8; Dryden's affiliation with, 49, 51; in Edgeworth's works, 19, 20, 157, 164–66, 169–71; Exclusion Crisis and, 27, 48, 50; individualism and, 169; Irish Rebellion (1798) and, 142, 149, 157, 169–75; political theology and, 34; Pope's affiliation with, 72–74, 100, 102, 141
Cavendish, Mary, 183n9
Chakrabarty, Dipesh, 186n23
Chapin, Chester, 104
Charles I, 16, 27, 30, 38–39, 73–74, 186n14
Charles II, 8, 27–28, 30, 35–43, 46, 48, 67, 95
Chronos (Greek god), 47
Church of England, 19, 121–22, 129, 158, 190n13; *Thirty-Nine Articles*, 12, 122, 124–25, 131–32, 134
civic humanism, 79–80, 100, 145
civil society, 4, 62
Clark, J. C. D., 9
Clement XI: *Universal Prayer* (1721), 104
Clinton, Hillary, 13
Coleridge, Samuel, 10
Colley, Linda, 9
colonialism: in Dryden's works, 44–46; in Edgeworth's works, 141, 150, 156–57, 165–69, 172, 175; in Pope's works, 79–80, 84, 104. *See also* anticolonialism
community, 52–53, 113–17, 134, 154, 158, 171

consumer society, 17, 66, 125–26, 191n16
Coppe, Abiezer, 133, 134; "A Fiery Flying Roll," 185n7
corpus mysticum, 37–38
Cressy, David: *Birth, Marriage, and Death*, 157–58
Cromwell, Oliver, 27, 39, 49–50, 134, 187n26
Cronus (Greek god), 47
Cunnington, C. W., 126
Cunnington, P., 126

Damrosch, Leo, 3, 109
Dante, 90
Davenant, William, 38, 185n10
Davis, David Brion, 192n8
Dearing, Vinton, 189n13
Defoe, Daniel: *Moll Flanders*, 107, 128
democratization, 18, 71, 128, 142, 179, 182
Denham, John: "Cooper's Hill," 59–61, 92, 96
Derrida, Jacques, 4, 44, 185n6, 191n19; "La différance," 186nn18–19; *Of Grammatology*, 113; *Specters of Marx*, 136–37
Deutsch, Helen, 3, 71, 189n12; *Resemblance and Disgrace*, 99–100
divine: in Dryden's works, 33, 37, 40–42, 47–51, 54–57, 60, 63–64, 67; in Edgeworth's works, 174; in Pope's works, 74, 95, 97, 100, 104; in Richardson's works, 120, 128, 132, 137
divine authority, 20, 27–28, 53, 58, 73, 128, 130
domesticity, 107–8, 140, 153
domination, 16, 21, 143–44
Douay-Rheims Bible, 188n1. *See also* scriptural citations
Dowling, William, 47, 52
Driden, John, 52–58
Driden, Robert, 187n28
Dryden, John, 27–68; "Absalom and Achitophel," 32, 34, 47–50; "Annus Mirabilis," 45, 47; "Astraea Redux," 28, 35–42, 44–47, 60, 61, 76, 158; authorial

identity and, 95; biopolitics of, 31–34; "Eleonora," 34, 188n36; *Georgics* (translation), 103–4; "Heroic Stanzas," 49–50; *The Hind and the Panther*, 34; "The Medall," 34, 48, 50; modernity of, 27–30; "Ode to Anne Killigrew," 34, 67; political theology of, 8, 15, 34–47; *Sylvae*, 54; "To His Sacred Majesty," 28, 35, 39–44, 60, 61, 158; "To My Honour'd Kinsman," 9, 10, 18, 19, 28, 29, 31–34, 47, 50, 52–62, 66–67, 69–70, 93, 104; Tory Augustan movement and, 2; *The Works of Virgil*, 186n20, 189n13

Dunne, Tom, 165

During, Simon, 3

Eaves, T. C. Duncan: *Samuel Richardson* (with Kimpel), 121–22

economy, 5, 66, 74, 77, 89, 93

Edgeworth, Maria, 140–78; *The Absentee*, 9, 19–21, 142, 155–78; *Belinda*, 141, 151–52; *Castle Rackrent* (with R. Edgeworth), 168, 175; *Ennui*, 192n9; *Essays on Professional Education* (with R. Edgeworth), 151, 152, 168; "The Grateful Negro," 9, 140–56; *Harrington*, 159; political theology and, 2, 8, 15; politics of domestic fiction and, 140–46; *Practical Education*, 151

Edgeworth, Richard Lovell, 151, 167; *Castle Rackrent* (with M. Edgeworth), 168, 175; *Essays on Professional Education* (with M. Edgeworth), 151, 152, 168

Edinburgh Review on Edgeworth, 148

Edward VI, 73

Elizabeth I, 73, 131

English Civil War (1642–51): in Dryden's works, 27, 32, 41, 44–45, 47–48, 60; in Pope's works, 73–74, 76; in Richardson's works, 129–30, 133

Epicurus, 103

equality, 5, 17, 20, 175, 180–81

Erasmus, 104

Esposito, Roberto, 145

Eucharist, 37

Exclusion Crisis (1678–81), 27, 48, 50

exploitation, 175–77. *See also* oppression; subjection

Fanny Hill (Cleland), 119

Fanon, Frantz: *The Wretched of the Earth*, 144

Felski, Rita: *The Limits of Critique*, 4, 6

Fielding, John, 119

Filmer, Robert, 58

Fletcher, Phineas, 12; "The Locusts," 73–75, 84

Foucault, Michel: Agamben on, 189n8; on biopolitics, 31–32; on *Clarissa*, 112, 137; *Discipline and Punish*, 11–12, 15, 21; *History of Sexuality*, 15, 31, 144; *Madness and Civilization*, 185n6; "The Political Technology of Individuals," 158; on race and power, 22–23, 86; *Security, Territory, Population*, 62; *Society Must Be Defended*, 84–87; "Technologies of the Self" (seminar), 143–44

freedom: in Dryden's works, 44–45, 54–55; in Edgeworth's works, 142, 144, 151, 153–55, 177; equality and, 181; of patriot individual, 10; political authority and, 21–22; political theology and, 109–10; in Richardson's works, 109–10, 111–12, 113; secularism and, 13; sovereignty and, 30

Freud, Sigmund, 163, 169

Frost, William, 189n13

Gallagher, Catherine: "Embracing the Absolute," 183n9

Gallchoir, Clíona Ó, 153; *Edgeworth: Women, Ireland, and Nation*, 175

Gay, John, 28

George I, 191n17

George II, 191n17

Gibbons, Luke, 171

Gilroy, Paul: *The Black Atlantic*, 142

Go, Julian: *Patterns of Empire*, 184n15

Gourgouris, Stathis: *Lessons in Secular Criticism*, 7
governance, 18, 31–32, 62, 71, 147
Granville, George, 101
Gunpowder Plot (1605), 73

Haitian Revolution (1791–1804), 142, 149–50
Hallward, Peter: *Absolutely Postcolonial*, 185n24
Hammill, Graham, 14
Hammond, Paul: *Dryden and the Traces of Classical Rome*, 43–44, 54, 71, 103
Hastings, Selina, Countess of Huntingdon, 122, 124, 130, 133–34, 190n13
Haywood, Eliza: *Fantomina*, 107
Hegel, G. W. F., 177, 193n26
Heidegger, Martin: *Being and Time*, 110–11; *Letter on Humanism*, 190n5
Henry VIII, 12
Henseley, David, 190n4
Hervey, James, 122
Hill, Christopher, 189n9; *Century of Revolution*, 38–39, 50, 79, 187n32; "Clarissa Harlowe and Her Times," 129–30; *The World Turned Upside Down*, 129
Hobbes, Thomas, 44, 84, 185n8
Homer, 96
Hooker, Edward, 36
Hopkins, A. G.: *British Imperialism: 1688–2000* (with Cain), 10, 184n13
Hoppit, Julian, 50, 51, 76, 187nn30–31, 188nn5–6, 188n34
Horace, 53–54, 57, 67, 94, 187n27
Horkheimer, Max: *Dialectic of Enlightenment* (with Adorno), 6–8
humanism: civic, 79–80, 100, 145; in Dryden's works, 32; in Edgeworth's works, 25, 142, 145; in Pope's works, 24, 71, 76, 78–82, 87–88, 92, 100, 104
Hume, David, 151
Hunt, Alan: *Governing Morals*, 63, 64
Hunter, J. Paul, 3; "Binarism and the Anglophone Couplet," 42

Huntingdon, Selina Hastings, Countess of, 122, 124, 130, 133–34, 190n13

idolatry of exploitation, 175, 177
immortality, 55, 66–67, 70, 144
individualism: in Dryden's works, 19, 65; in Edgeworth's works, 142, 146, 158, 169; Marxism and, 5; in Pope's works, 69, 71–72; in Richardson's works, 108–9
Ingrassia, Catherine, 3, 71, 100
Interregnum (1649–60), 32, 35, 39, 41, 49–50, 133
Ireland: colonial context of, 141, 157; Edgeworth's education in, 151; in Edgeworth's works, 156–57, 162, 165–66, 168, 171–73, 175–76
Irish Rebellion (1798), 142, 149, 157, 169–75

Jackson, Spencer: "Never Getting Home," 169
James, C. L. R., 192n5; *Black Jacobins*, 150
James I, 73
James II, 27, 32, 48, 50–51, 166
Jews, 159, 161, 176
John of Salisbury, 18
Johnson, Samuel, 104, 112, 161; *Lives of the English Poets*, 36
Jones, Inigo, 119
Jonson, Ben, 71; "To Penshurst," 93
Julius Caesar, 43
justice: biopolitics and, 33; in Dryden's works, 56; equality and, 181; Marx on, 5; political theology and, 41–42; religion and, 63; sovereignty and, 18

Kahn, Victoria, 14, 110; *The Future of Illusion*, 90–92
Kant, Immanuel, 146, 151–55, 177, 186n11, 193n26; *Critique of Judgment*, 151–52, 154, 163; *Groundwork of the Metaphysics of Morals*, 154; "Idea for a Universal History with a Cosmopolitan Purpose," 86; "What Is Enlightenment?," 151, 192n13

Kantorowicz, Ernst, 37, 40–42, 58, 110, 130, 132; *The King's Two Bodies*, 8–9, 12, 33, 73, 90–91
Kimpel, Ben D.: *Samuel Richardson* (with Eaves), 121–22
King James Bible, 188n1. *See also* scriptural citations
kings: as divine, 8–9, 15, 24; divine authority of, 20, 27–28, 53, 58, 73, 128, 130; dynastic, 33, 58, 130. *See also specific individuals*
kinship, 190n6
Kramnick, Jonathan, 117

Langford, Paul, 121
Laqueur, Thomas: *Making Sex*, 66
Lazzarato, Maurizio, 65
Leapor, Mary, 52
legal exceptionalism doctrine, 73
liberation theology, 14, 20, 180
liberty: in Dryden's works, 61–62; in Edgeworth's works, 152–54, 175; in Pope's works, 82; in Richardson's works, 133. *See also* freedom
Locke, John, 151
Louis XIV (France), 76, 187n33
Louis XVI (France), 16
Lucretius, 103; *De rerum natura*, 54
Lukács, Georg, 2–3, 4
Lupton, Julia Reinhard, 14
Luther, Martin, 12, 120, 121, 131–37, 190n9; *On Christian Liberty*, 132, 134–35

Machiavelli, Niccolò, 84
Mack, Maynard, 99
Macpherson, Sandra: *Harm's Way*, 116–18
Magubane, Zine, 156
Makdisi, Saree: *Making England Western*, 85
Mandeville, Bernard, 151
Mapletoft, John, 63–65
marriage: in Dryden's works, 39, 57; in Edgeworth's works, 19, 140, 142, 156–59, 162, 164, 166; function in eighteenth-century literature, 19, 189–90n3; in

Richardson's works, 19, 107–10, 112–13, 128; secularization of, 37
Marvell, Andrew, 71; "Upon Appleton House," 93
Marx, Karl, 4–7, 66, 112; *Capital*, 5, 183n5
Marxism, 4–6, 14, 112, 143, 183n8
Mary (Princess of Orange), 51
Mary II (queen), 27
Matthew (biblical), 36, 38
May, Theresa, 13
McBride, Ian, 169; *Scripture Politics*, 171
McDowell, R. B., 170, 171
McKendrick, Neil, 191n17
McKeon, Michael, 3, 28, 92; "The Politics of Pastoral Retreat," 55, 59
Meillassoux, Quentin, 117
Miller, David, 169
Milton, John, 29–30, 53; *Paradise Lost*, 94–95; *The Tenure of Kings and Magistrates*, 30
modernity: Agamben on, 15–16; Bataille on, 16–17; in Dryden's works, 28, 32, 46, 55; in Edgeworth's works, 143, 155, 178; Foucault on, 15; Marxist analysis of, 4–6; in Pope's works, 71–72, 86; racism and, 17, 23; in Richardson's works, 118–20, 125, 127–28, 130–31; secularism and, 4, 13–14, 112, 170; selfhood and, 25, 32, 66, 69, 128, 131
monasticism, 108, 112, 118–26, 135
Monmouth, James Scott, Duke of, 48, 50
Montague, Charles, 52
Mordicai, Rachel, 159
More, Hannah, 138
Morgan, Philip, 105
Morgan, Sydney: *The Wild Irish Girl*, 167, 193n20
Musgrave, Richard, 193n23; *Memoirs of Different Rebellions in Ireland*, 171–72
Myers, Mitzi, 153

national identity: in Dryden's works, 38; literature's role in, 11; in Pope's works, 77, 85, 93, 96; religion and, 9; selfhood and, 11

nationalism: capitalism and, 10,
    131; domestic novelists and, 3;
    in Edgeworth's works, 157–58,
    182; political theology and, 15; in
    Pope's works, 72, 74–75, 85–87; in
    Richardson's works, 108, 131, 138; Tory
    Augustan poets and, 3; as unifying
    faith, 3
Newcome, Henry, 186n13
Newsome, Bree, 20, 22, 30
Nine Years' War (1688–97), 81, 188n5
nostalgia, 27, 167, 193nn20–21

Oakeshot, Michael, 10
Obama, Barack, 13
oppression, 15, 17, 20, 22, 82, 143. *See also*
    colonialism; race and racism
Oxford English Dictionary (OED), 99,
    117, 154

Pakenham, Thomas, 170
Parliament: capitalism and, 5; Dryden on,
    51, 52, 59; Exclusion Crisis and, 48, 50;
    Pope on, 76, 93; popular sovereignty
    and, 30
Pascal, Blaise, 118
patriarchal authority, 125, 155
patriots: in Dryden's works, 9–10, 24, 29,
    33, 47, 50–51, 54–55, 58–63, 66–67;
    in Edgeworth's works, 140; in Pope's
    works, 69–70; in Richardson's works,
    125
perfection: of domination, 16, 23; in
    Dryden's works, 35, 43, 56, 57; in
    Edgeworth's works, 148–49, 177; in
    Pope's works, 77, 103; in Richardson's
    works, 114, 123–24, 128; spiritual, 25,
    123
Perry, Ruth, 190n6
Pfau, Thomas, 9
piety, 102, 119, 127–28
Pincus, Steven, 187n33; *1688: The First
    Modern Revolution*, 10, 50–52, 81
Pittock, Murray, 166–67, 171
Plowden, Edmund, 12, 73–75, 193n24

Plowden, Francis, 174
Pocock, J. G. A.: *The Machiavellian
    Moment*, 80–81
Pole, Reginald, 12
political authority, 21–22, 29–30, 63. *See
    also* divine authority
political theology: as analytical
    framework, 2, 4; in Dryden's works,
    28–29, 32–34, 41, 45–46, 51, 57,
    65; in Edgeworth's works, 143, 176;
    freedom and, 109–10; justice and,
    41–42; literature's role in formulating,
    21; Marx on, 4; nationalism and, 15;
    in Pope's works, 19, 72, 90–91; in
    Richardson's works, 2, 109–12, 136;
    secularism and, 12; sovereignty and,
    14–21
Pope, Alexander, 69–106; authorial
    self and, 98–104; Dryden and, 28;
    "Epilogue to the Satires II," 109–10;
    "Epistle to Bolingbroke," 100; "First
    Epistle of the First Book of Horace,"
    100; humanism and, 24, 71, 76, 78–82,
    87–88, 92, 100, 104; "Messiah," 76–77;
    as meta-author, 92–98; nationalism
    and, 78–82; political theology and,
    72–78, 90–91; "The Rape of the
    Lock," 94–95; slavery as figurative
    language for, 140–41; sovereignty
    and, 73, 75, 82–89, 90; "Spring," 102;
    Tory Augustan movement and, 2,
    9–11; *Universal Prayer*, 104; verse
    epistles of, 52; "Windsor Forest," 9, 13,
    69–106
popular sovereignty, 30
Porter, Roy, 119
Pound, Ezra, 10
predestination, 38, 131–32, 190–91n13
prostitutes, 62, 65–66, 119, 121, 125
Protestantism, 48–49, 64, 127, 149, 169,
    171

race and racism: Agamben on, 15, 86;
    authorial self and, 100; Bataille on, 17;
    in Edgeworth's works, 144, 155–56,

158, 165, 176; Foucault on, 84, 86; modernity and, 17, 23; in Pope's works, 100, 102; power and, 22–23. *See also* slavery

Reform Act (1832), 11

religion: Bataille on, 17; capitalism and, 8–9, 72, 75, 127, 129–31; in Dryden's works, 32, 36, 52; in Edgeworth's works, 176; freedom and, 13; justice and, 63; liberation theology and, 14, 20, 180; national identity and, 9; in Pope's works, 82; in Richardson's works, 110, 121–22; sovereignty and, 17. *See also* Catholicism; political theology; Protestantism

Revolution of 1688, 50–51, 76, 184n13

Richardson, Samuel, 107–39; *Clarissa*, 9, 11, 19–21, 30, 69–70, 107–39, 140; *The History of Sir Charles Grandison*, 118; *Pamela*, 107, 113–14, 118; political theology of, 2, 109–12, 136

Roach, Joseph, 67; *Cities of the Dead*, 83, 88

Robert, William Clare: *Marx's Inferno*, 183n5

Rochester, John Wilmot, Earl of, 52, 187n25

Rogers, Pat, 81, 87–88; *The Symbolic Design of Windsor-Forest*, 76

Roper, Alan: *Dryden's Poetic Kingdoms*, 58

Rosenthal, Laura, 112, 125, 128, 191n15; *Infamous Commerce*, 66

Rousseau, Jean-Jacques, 151, 152

Rowlandson, Mary: *Sovereignty and the Goodness of God*, 113

royalists, 12, 73, 75–76

sacrifice, 71, 83, 118, 153–55

Said, Edward: *Orientalism*, 84–85; *The World, the Text, and the Critic*, 183n8

Saturn (Roman god), 47

Schmitt, Carl, 14; *Political Theology*, 33–34

Scott, James, Duke of Monmouth, 48, 50

Scott, Walter: *Waverly*, 167

scriptural citations: Genesis 1:26, 83; Ecclesiastes 3:20, 67; Isaiah 1:4, 77; Isaiah 2:2, 13, 92; Isaiah 2:5, 77; Isaiah 4:2, 80; Isaiah 49:1–3, 77; Isaiah 49:8, 77–78; Isaiah 60:1, 77; Isaiah 60:21, 80; Jeremiah 22, 180; Galatians 2:19, 190n9; Revelation 20:12, 175; Revelation 21:2, 175, 176; Revelation 21:3, 175, 177; Revelation 21:4, 175; Revelation 21:8, 167, 175, 177

secularism: authority and, 20–21; capitalism and, 46; in Dryden's works, 28–29, 33, 42, 46, 63; in Edgeworth's works, 143, 169, 171; freedom and, 13; literature's role in, 3–4; Marx on, 6; modernity and, 4, 13–14, 112, 170; political theology and, 12; in Pope's works, 92, 100; in Richardson's works, 108, 110–11, 112, 120–21, 126, 135

self-constitution, 78, 96, 98, 100

self-governance: in Dryden's works, 30, 53; in Edgeworth's works, 25, 142, 144–45, 147, 160, 164, 172, 175–76; in Richardson's works, 109, 138

selfhood: in Dryden's works, 32, 46, 54, 65, 67; in Edgeworth's works, 142–43, 154–55, 165, 172, 177; modernity and, 25, 32, 66, 69, 128, 131; national identity and, 11; in Richardson's works, 112, 114, 135–36; Wahrman on, 32

self-possession, 24, 69, 100, 140, 147, 153–54

sexuality, 15, 17, 31, 144

Shakespeare, William, 90

sin, 25, 30, 40, 123–24, 126, 132–33

Skinner, Quentin, 181

slavery, 25, 140, 142, 146–48, 154–55, 177, 180, 192n5, 192n7. *See also* race and racism

Smith, Adam, 146; *The Wealth of Nations*, 148, 149

Smith, Nigel, 30

Smyth, Jim, 169, 171, 174

Societies for the Reformation of Manners (SRM), 29, 62–66

Soni, Vivasvan, 112
sovereignty: biopolitics and, 15–16; in Dryden's works, 10, 29–31, 33–35, 46, 49, 51, 53–54, 57–58, 61–63, 66–67; in Edgeworth's works, 175–77, 179, 181–82; freedom and, 30; justice and, 18; literature's role in, 23; political theology and, 14–21; in Pope's works, 73, 75, 82–89, 90; popular, 30; religion and, 17; in Richardson's works, 108, 124, 131, 134, 138; transcendence and, 181
Spillers, Hortense, 145
Starr, G. A., 3
Stoler, Ann, 85
Stone, Lawrence, 157
Strauss, Leo, 28
subjection: in Dryden's works, 39; in Edgeworth's works, 142, 154, 164, 171; Foucault on, 21; Marx on, 5; of modern individual, 8; in Pope's works, 71; as potential tool for liberation, 16; in Richardson's works, 109, 136
subjectivity: Bataille on, 17; in Dryden's works, 57, 65; in Edgeworth's works, 142, 144, 147, 155, 158, 177; Foucault on, 11; in Pope's works, 69, 103, 105; in Richardson's works, 138
Swedenburg, H. T., 36
Swift, Jonathan, 2, 10

Tate, Nahum: *The Loyal General*, 48
Taylor, Charles, 9
Tennenhouse, Leonard: *The Imaginary Puritan* (with Armstrong), 112–14, 116, 118
Thomson, James: "Rule Britannia," 141
Thorne, Susan, 85
Tone, Wolfe, 175
Tonson, Jacob, 189n13
Tory Augustan movement, 1–3, 10–11, 28, 68–69, 71, 100
transcendence: of authority, 20; in Dryden's works, 28, 67; in Pope's works, 92, 94, 96, 98, 102, 106; in Richardson's works, 110–12, 115, 120, 123, 132, 136–37; sovereignty and, 181
Treaty of Utrecht (1713), 70, 101
Trump, Donald, 1, 13
Turner, David, 190n6

United Kingdom: colonialism and, 104; political theology in, 19–20; secularism in, 13, 121; sovereign state of exception in, 67; sovereignty of individuals in, 16
United States: drone strikes by, 13, 184n16; political theology in, 20; racism in, 22–23; secularism in, 13, 121; sovereign state of exception in, 67; sovereignty of individuals in, 16

Van de Veire, Heidi Van, 166
Vatter, Miguel: *The Republic of the Living*, 145
Venn, John, 131
Virgil, 93, 102–3; *Aeneid*, 53, 101, 186n20; *Eclogues*, 35, 76, 101; *Georgics*, 54, 103–4; "Pollio," 76
Visconsi, Elliott, 28, 38, 185–86n11; *Lines of Equity*, 42
Voltaire, 100, 151

Wahrman, Dror, 45, 127; *The Making of the Modern Self*, 32
Walker, Kim: *The Absentee* introduction (Pickering edition), 166
Waller, Edmund, 187n32; "On St. James's Park," 95
War of Spanish Succession (1701–14), 78–79, 81, 89, 188n5
Wasserman, Earl: "Nature Moralized," 97–98
Watt, Ian, 2, 4; *The Rise of the Novel*, 119–20
Weber, Max, 126–30; *The Protestant Ethic and the Spirit of Capitalism*, 72, 75, 127, 129
Weheliye, Alexander: *Habeas Viscus*, 22–23, 144–45
Wesley, Charles, 122

Wesley, John, 121–25, 130, 133, 134, 138, 191n14; *Free Grace*, 190–91n13; *Justification by Faith*, 190n12; *On God's Vineyard*, 123
Whitefield, George, 121, 122, 124, 125, 130, 190n13
William I (William the Conqueror), 78, 87
William II (William of Orange), 51
William III, 27, 29
Williams, Aubrey, 87
Williams, Erik, 192n5
Wilmot, John, Earl of Rochester, 52, 187n25
Windsor Castle, 189n10
Winn, James, 38, 48, 185n10, 187nn28–29
Woodhouse, John, 64–65
Woodward, Josiah: *An Account of the Rise and Progress of the Religious Societies in the City of London*, 63, 65
World (newspaper), 126
Wynter, Sylvia: "Unsettling the Coloniality of Being/Power/Truth/Freedom," 144–45

Žižek, Slavoj, 191n18
Zwicker, Steven, 187n24; *Dryden's Political Poetry*, 34, 36, 61

www.ingramcontent.com/pod-product-compliance
Lightning Source LLC
Chambersburg PA
CBHW021706230426
43668CB00008B/738